TREASURED EARTH

Hattie Cosgrove's Mimbres Archaeology in the American Southwest

Hattie and Burt Jr. photographing Chettro Kettle ruins at Chaco Canyon. 1923.

Camp at Villareal Ranch, Gila Valley, Grant County, New Mexico. August 1929.

Digging on the Sapillo. September 1922. Irvin Goldstein, Stephen Boone, Burt Jr., and Hattie.

TREASURED EARTH

Hattie Cosgrove's Mimbres Archaeology
in the American Southwest

By Carolyn O'Bagy Davis

SANPETE PUBLICATIONS
and
OLD PUEBLO ARCHAEOLOGY CENTER
Tucson, Arizona

For C. Burton Cosgrove Jr.

Book layout and design by Lisa Pastore, Whaletale Productions.
Printed by Arizona Lithographers, Tucson, Arizona.

First Printing 1995.
Library of Congress Catalog Card Number 95-69564
ISBN: 0-9635092-1-7

Sanpete Publications
Post Office Box 85216
Tucson, Arizona 85754-5216

Old Pueblo Archaeology Center
Post Office Box 40577
Tucson, Arizona 85717-0577

Hattie and Burt Cosgrove at the Petrified Forest in northern Arizona. August 1920.

◀CONTENTS▶

◄ ACKNOWLEDGMENTS ►

So very many people have helped with the work of researching Hattie's life. So much information was shared and many people gave so generously of their time. I wish to extend my very deep gratitude and appreciation for their help. Laurie Webster spent precious hours of her own research time at the Peabody Museum to look up information about Awatovi. Beth Sandager, archivist at the Peabody Museum, came to work on a holiday and allowed me to work an extra day in the archives, in addition giving her invaluable help in locating research material. Mike Jacobs has been an advisor and general source of knowledge since the beginning of this project. He has generously loaned books from his personal library and has been an instant information resource for my many questions. John Mize, Hattie's charming and knowledgeable nephew, shared important family history as well as much of the background on the Blish, Mize, and Silliman hardware company. We spent a delightful and unforgettable day together, and as John drove about Atchison, pointing out various homes and buildings, I gained a sense of Hattie's life and surroundings as she grew up in that beautiful town.

I also wish to extend many thanks to Chuck and Jenny Adams, Judy Bennett, Susan Berry and the Silver City Museum, Evelyn Nimmo Brew, Alta and Vernon Brook, Doc Campbell at Gila Hot Springs, Lynda and Harlie Cox, Darrell Creel, Al Dart, E. Mott Davis, Hester Davis, Father Eugene Dehner of Benedictine College, Al Ferg, Helen Young Frost, Douglas Givens, Frank Hibben, Andy Hinton, Laura Holt, Steve Lekson, Florence Lister, Elizabeth Morris, Nancy Pariso, George "Laddie" Pendleton, Willow Powers, Barbara Alves Roberts, Hugo Rodeck, Bob Schiowitz, Harriet Patricia Snowden, Louise I. Stiver, Raymond and Mollie Thompson, Sharon Urban, Kim Walters, Joe Ben Wheat, Teresa Wilkins, and Gordon Willey.

Richard and Natalie Woodbury have been enthusiastic supporters of this project from its beginning. They helped with information and contacts, and I am indeed grateful for Woodbury's affectionate and thoughtful foreword. Only someone who knew Hattie could have written such fond words, and I am immensely grateful for his contribution. And finally, Dr. LaVerne Herrington spent many hours giving me background information about the Mimbres culture, loaning books and archaeological reports, and driving me about the Mimbres country, where she acted as a marvelous tour guide. On many occasions she eloquently discussed the Mimbres civilization as we drove along the Mimbres River or walked across a prehistoric site. Being with her on a summer day and standing in a pueblo ruin made the whole scene come alive, and I cherish the hours we spent out in the field. At Treasure Hill she talked of Hattie and showed where the Cosgroves had worked many decades earlier, and her great respect for the Mimbres country showed plainly in her words. To LaVerne I especially owe a great debt of thanks, and much of the respect and appreciation I have come to feel for the vanished people who once lived in this beautiful country comes directly from her generous efforts to share her impressive knowledge with me.

Hattie's Mimbres bowl drawings.

◀FOREWORD▶

From time to time—but too rarely—archaeology has been enriched by the contributions of "amateurs" (or avocationals as they are called now) whose work has achieved "professional" qualities even though they have had no formal academic training in archaeology. One immediately thinks of Watson Smith, Clarence Webb, Asa T. Hill, and Antonio Waring, to name only a few. They were attracted to archaeology, learned by doing, and achieved results that their contemporaries regarded highly.

Harriet (Hattie) S. Cosgrove and her husband C. Burton (Burt) Cosgrove are outstanding examples of how the self-trained could earn the respect and cooperation of their academically trained colleagues. For a period, 1915 onwards, when hardly any women became archaeologists, Hattie's accomplishments are the more impressive. She endured—enjoyed is a better word—the rigors of fieldwork in the 1920s, when the four-wheel-drive vehicle, the Coleman stove, and other conveniences later taken for granted were unknown. She and her husband were true partners in research, as were a few of her contemporaries, such as Ann and Earl Morris and Madeleine and A. V. Kidder. Recent essays by Dena Dincauze, Mary Ann Levine, Cheryl Claassen, Jonathan Reyman, and others, make clear the difficulties women have had in being admitted to archaeology on an equal footing with men, regardless of their talents and training.

Hattie was forty years old when she began her archaeological career and she continued it almost without interruption for some thirty years, in spite of the tragic death of Burt in 1936. Her substantial contributions to Mimbres and Hopi archaeology are well told in this biography. She is fortunate to have such an indefatigable researcher and enthusiastic writer to put her full career on record. For the history of archaeology, in which there is a growing interest today, the biographies and autobiographies of its practitioners are essential. Their archaeological reports can be important sources of historical information, but what they did, how they did it, how they felt about it are also essential if we are to understand how archaeology was done in the past. In this respect, Carolyn Davis has made a significant contribution to the history of archaeology in those very different days before World War II. But equally important is the success she has in bringing to life a wonderful person, whose enthusiasm, generosity, energy, patience, and varied skills made her a treasured friend for all who knew her.

I had the great good fortune to first meet Hattie when I was a student on the staff of the Awatovi excavations of Peabody Museum in 1938. She played, as Davis describes, a central role in not only the archaeological research but in the social interaction of the field staff in their isolated camp. It is hard to realize that she was in her sixties, as she was so young in spirit. At Awatovi her culinary skills, well described by Davis, were not needed, but I well remember how much her enchilada dinners in Cambridge were relished by students and friends. It is gratifying that she will live in these pages for the many who were not fortunate enough to know her personally. She might be astonished that she has merited a biography, but she would very much enjoy adding to her circle of friends through the printed page.

Richard B. Woodbury
Shutesbury, Massachusetts
April 1995

◀PREFACE▶

I first heard Hattie Cosgrove's name several years ago when a friend mentioned that Hattie would be an interesting person to research. Steve Lekson knew of my ties to Silver City, New Mexico, my avocational interest in archaeology and volunteer work with the Arizona Archaeological and Historical Society, and my work in writing biographies and women's history. Steve, a professional archaeologist, has done a great deal of work in the Mimbres country in southwestern New Mexico. I am extremely grateful for his stories that introduced me to Hattie. She has intrigued me from the first time I heard of her. Then Steve showed me a 1936 photograph of Hattie at Awatovi, wearing her expedition outfit of pants tucked into knee-high laced boots, her silver concho belt, and a straw hat, and I never did get that image out of my mind. There was something appealing and intriguing about that picture of Hattie, an older woman, standing in front of a tent at a remote archaeological site in northern Arizona. She was smiling at the world.

Hattie Cosgrove was born into wealth and very well could have enjoyed a comfortable life of teas and balls, church and society functions, a pampered life in an elegant home. Instead, Hattie followed her husband, Burton, out to a little town in southwestern New Mexico where they discovered the local archaeology and both of them devoted their lives to studying and preserving the traces of a long-vanished civilization. Instead of a comfortable home with servants to cook and clean for her, Hattie slept in a tent and cooked meals over a campfire. She spent long hours digging under the relentless New Mexico sun, struggling with ferocious winds that blew dirt into her eyes and skin and hair, and sleeping on a cot that was often covered with snow and frost in the morning. She rode and hiked into remote canyons in the vast Gila Wilderness, she climbed improvised pine tree ladders into cave shelters, and she swung from a rope held by a cowboy as she was lowered down over a sheer mountain wall to explore a cliff dwelling. She dug hundreds of burials; washed, sorted and catalogued hundreds of thousands of potsherds; and drew thousands of bowls, potsherds, petroglyphs, and pictographs. Hattie gave up a life of comfort, and endured the rough, dirty, and hard-working life of an archaeologist, and she loved every minute of her work.

Perhaps if Hattie and her husband, Burton, had gone to any other spot in the country, they might have been content leading conventional lives, with Hattie caring for their young son and attending women's club and Ladies' Aid Society meetings while Burt went off to work in the hardware store each day. But the Cosgroves went to Silver City, a small mining town tucked away in the southwest corner of New Mexico. Here was a land that enchanted them, and at the southern edge of the great Gila Wilderness there were miles and miles of unpopulated canyons and high mountains to explore. But there was also the

Hattie and Amanda Cosgrove digging at W. S. Ruin. 1914.

soon-discovered lure of the ancient Mimbres villages, occupied hundreds of years ago by a mysterious people. The prehistoric Mimbres civilization has fascinated people since traces of their existence were first discovered during the early years of the twentieth century. Local people noticed that if they dug in the mounds of rubble—that was all that was left of the early Mimbres sites—they would find wonderful artifacts. Indeed, the Mimbreños were rather unique in that they buried their dead under the floors of their homes. All a curious person had to do was locate a ruin, dig down to the floor level, go on through the floor, and there come upon a burial which held an almost magical treasure, a Mimbres painted black-on-white bowl.

For a very brief time in human history, from about A.D. 1000 to A.D. 1150, the Mimbres potters created breathtaking pictures on the interior surfaces of their bowls. There are scenes of people engaged in everyday activities such as hunting, fishing, planting crops, and dancing. There are images of stars, comets, animals, fish, birds, snakes, lizards, and bugs. The Mimbres paintings were magical and unique. They are found nowhere else in North America, and they were only created for a few generations before the people vanished from the area, leaving few clues about their existence, except for the beautiful bowls buried for centuries under the ground. The painted bowls were nearly always associated with a burial. After the body of the deceased was placed in a flexed position in a small cavity dug in the floor of a room, one of the painted bowls was placed over the head. Then a hole, often called a "kill hole," was made in the bowl. In addition to the wonderful bowls, there were other artifacts to be found in the burials such as arrowheads, beads, and turquoise pendants.

Like many local people, Hattie and Burt were fascinated with the ruins and traces of the vanished culture. When they went out on weekend picnics and camping trips, they delighted in digging in the popular sites. But it was not long before they realized that the real value of the ancient ruins was not the bowls and

Isleta Pueblo. Burton and Kitty Cosgrove are talking with the Indians. October 2, 1918. Note the strings of chilis hung from the edge of the roof to dry.

Petroglyphs near Rock House Ruin, Mimbres Valley, Grant County, New Mexico. 1920.

artifacts, lovely and enticing as they were, but in the knowledge that could be gained in scientific study of the sites. Gradually, the Cosgroves turned from digging in the ruins for treasure to a more scientific approach involving precise excavations and recording all information for future study by other archaeologists and researchers. They studied and visited professional archaeologists to observe their methods, and ultimately, their work in the Mimbres country made a great contribution to the study of one of the least known prehistoric southwestern cultures, but ironically, a culture whose art has had the greatest impact on twentieth-century southwestern regional art.

Today there are almost no Mimbres villages or sites left that have not been badly pothunted or even bulldozed into oblivion in an effort to find pots. But the work that Hattie and Burt did saved a great deal of vital information for scholars.

Camp at Ruidoso, New Mexico. October 1921. Hattie is standing in front of the car.

Although Burt died as a relatively young man, Hattie went on for many decades and did a great deal of important work in ceramics. In a great tribute to the work that the Cosgroves did in southwestern New Mexico, the famed archaeologist Alfred Vincent Kidder wrote that they should be known as Mr. and Mrs. Mimbres. From housewife and hardware salesman to respected Harvard archaeologists, Hattie and Burt followed their dreams and lived a life that was a bit unconventional and often demanded a lot of hard physical work, but their contributions to southwestern archaeology are many and enduring.

Today the profession of archaeology has become a mature, technical science, and the information gathered at an excavation goes far beyond the artifacts buried for centuries. But the lure of the unknown beneath the ground is at the heart of every archaeological expedition. The difference between a pothunter and an archaeologist, professional or avocational, is that one digs for himself or for financial gain, while the other searches for knowledge that will ultimately be shared and preserved for all time. Hattie and Burt were true archaeologists, motivated by a desire to preserve and study the fascinating ruins. They purchased their own Mimbres ruin, which they named Treasure Hill, and it remains a great treasure to this day. Through their efforts, it is one of the few Mimbres sites that has been preserved and protected from vandalism and thus offers great opportunities for future study by professional researchers. Hattie and Burt came to the field of archaeology at a time when the young discipline welcomed interested amateurs, and in spite of a lack of formal education in archaeology, they were encouraged and aided in their own work in the Mimbres country. They met and became close friends with some of the great archaeologists of the early years of American southwestern archaeology. They worked during a golden era, when the field was small and informal and friendly. Friends, family, and visitors were all welcomed at a site, and archaeologists visited each other at their field camps, sharing campfires and information. Children and spouses and casual visitors were put to work, and many of these people made important contributions to the early expeditions. It was a wonderful, friendly time and it will never come again, but because of that time, the Cosgroves were able to follow their hearts and ultimately undertake very important and lasting research in the Mimbres country.

My own research into Hattie's life and work has taken me across the country from the Peabody Museum at Harvard University to Swarts Ruin on the Mimbres River and remote caves in the Gila Wilderness to the enchanting Hopi country in northern Arizona. On a spring day in 1994, my husband, son, and I hiked several miles into a secluded canyon to visit a cave Hattie and Burt had excavated nearly seventy-five years earlier. I sensed her spirit nearby, and I knew that her dedication to the study and preservation of the marvelous sites was inextricably tied to her love of the wild and grand Mimbres country of southwestern New Mexico. When I later compared my photographs to the Cosgrove photos taken at the same cave in 1920, I felt the whisper of Hattie's presence when I saw my fourteen-year-old son, John, standing in a pose identical to one of Hattie's fourteen-year-old son, Burt Jr., at the mouth of the cave. I feel fortunate and blessed to share Hattie's love of the Gila Wilderness and the enchanting Mimbres culture. It is my hope that telling the story of Hattie's life will continue in the work that Hattie began many decades earlier to educate people about this wonderful culture that once existed in this corner of New Mexico and will help preserve for the future the few traces of those people and their unique art that still exists.

As an end note, I wish to thank Burton Cosgrove Jr. for the time and love he has put into this project. He has been an enthusiastic participant from the very beginning, sharing family letters and papers, photographs, and his mother's precise and breathtaking Mimbres bowl drawings. Unless otherwise noted, all of the photographs in this volume are from the Cosgrove family photo albums, and most of the captions are in Hattie's own words. Burt spent many hours reviewing early drafts of the manuscript, and his suggestions and corrections have added to the accuracy and flavor of the book. His amazing memory for names and details added a dimension to Hattie's story that would not have been possible through general research alone. I can only add that if I could not know Hattie, Burt's friendship has been more than compensation and a gift I will always treasure. This book is for you, Burt, with much love.

Hattie in camp at Swarts Ruin. 1924.

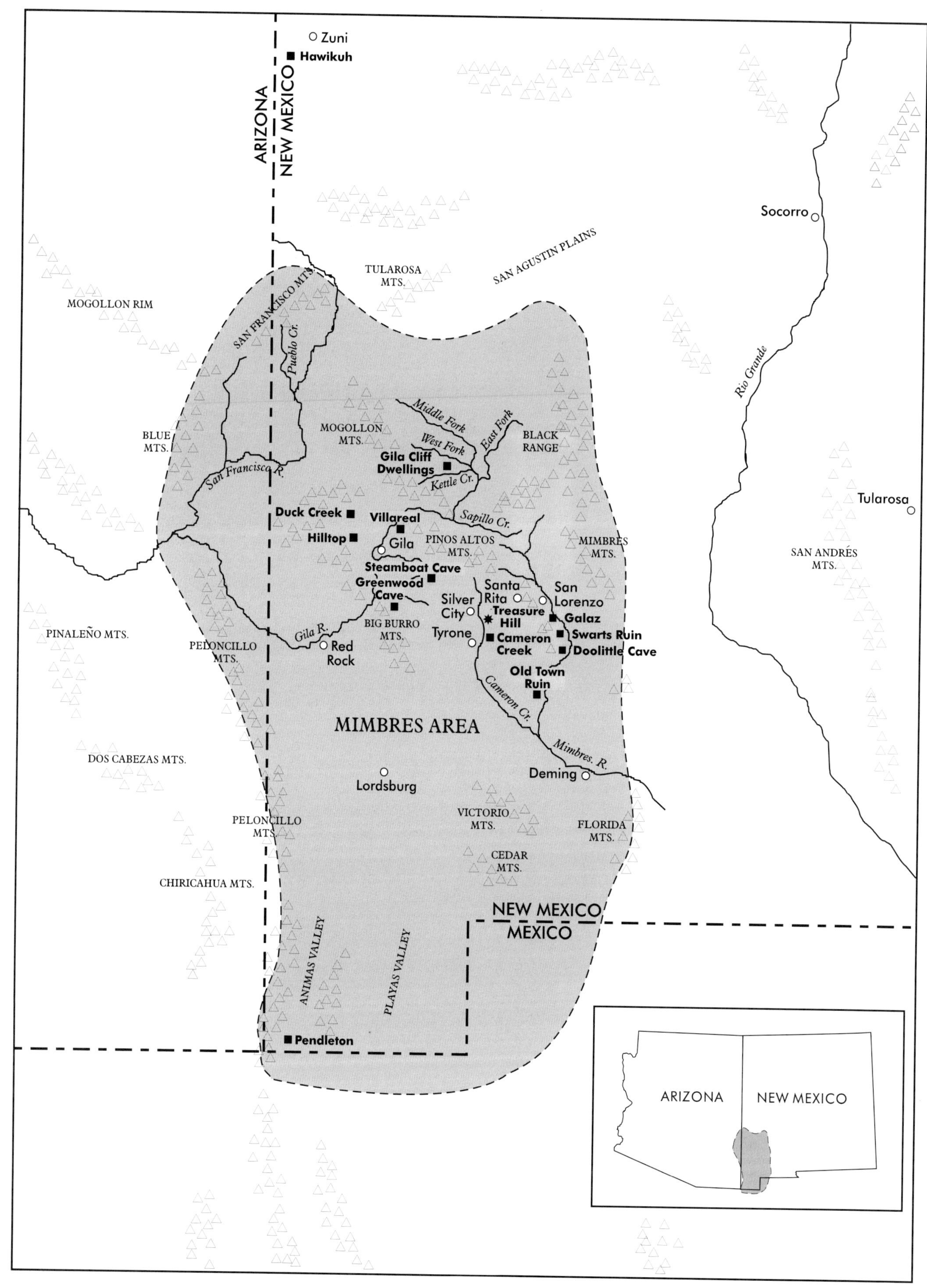

ARIZONA
NEW MEXICO
Zuni
Hawikuh
Socorro
MOGOLLON RIM
TULAROSA MTS.
SAN AGUSTIN PLAINS
SAN FRANCISCO MTS.
Pueblo Cr.
BLUE MTS.
MOGOLLON MTS.
Middle Fork
West Fork
East Fork
BLACK RANGE
San Francisco R.
Gila Cliff Dwellings
Kettle Cr.
Rio Grande
Duck Creek
Villareal
Sapillo Cr.
MIMBRES MTS.
Tularosa
Hilltop
Gila
PINOS ALTOS MTS.
SAN ANDRÉS MTS.
Steamboat Cave
Greenwood Cave
Silver City
Santa Rita
San Lorenzo
PINALEÑO MTS.
Gila R.
BIG BURRO MTS.
Treasure Hill
Galaz
PELONCILLO MTS.
Red Rock
Tyrone
Cameron Creek
Swarts Ruin
Doolittle Cave
Old Town Ruin
Cameron Cr.
MIMBRES AREA
DOS CABEZAS MTS.
Mimbres. R.
Lordsburg
Deming
PELONCILLO MTS.
VICTORIO MTS.
FLORIDA MTS.
CHIRICAHUA MTS.
CEDAR MTS.
NEW MEXICO
MEXICO
ANIMAS VALLEY
PLAYAS VALLEY
Pendleton
ARIZONA
NEW MEXICO

Hattie at sixteen, 1893.

◀TREASURE HILL SUNDAYS▶

When Harriet "Hattie" Silliman was born in 1877, she was the newest member of a family that had a history in the New World stretching back more than two centuries to the earliest days of the founding settlements of the American colonies. Through her father, John B. Silliman, Hattie could have claimed membership in the Mayflower Society, as his ancestors were the original Mayflower pilgrims John Alden and Priscilla Mullens, made famous by Henry Wadsworth Longfellow's narrative poem *The Courtship of Miles Standish*. Other Silliman ancestors fought in the Revolutionary War. An early American ancestor on her mother's side was Baron Resolved Waldron, who came to New York, then known as New Amsterdam, in 1647. He worked with Governor Peter Stuyvesant and received a huge land grant that comprised a generous portion of Manhattan Island. Hattie's mother, Harriet Lovejoy Silliman, also had a great grandfather who was a soldier in the Revolutionary War. By the time of Hattie's birth in the last quarter of the nineteenth century, her paternal line of the family had progressed westward to Atchison, Kansas, where her father was part owner in a large and prosperous hardware and freighting business.

Equally as dynamic as her illustrious early American ancestors, Hattie's mother, Harriet Lovejoy Silliman, was also energetic and adventurous. Orphaned in 1848 at two months of age, she was taken in and raised by her aunt, Harriet Leavenworth, for whom she had been named and who was also the widow of Colonel Henry Leavenworth, who established Fort Leavenworth, Kansas, in 1827. Harriet Lovejoy Silliman's aunt took her to Pennsylvania, and she later attended

Blish, Mize, and Silliman families at the Silliman home, 1897. J. B. Silliman is standing second from left. Mrs. Silliman is seated second from right. Hattie is fourth from the right. Photo courtesy of John Mize Sr.

school in Albany, New York, before moving to Chicago, where she met and married J. B. Silliman in 1869.

J. B. was a salesman for Field and Leiter, now Marshall Field and Company, of Chicago. On a sales trip to Fort Scott, Kansas, in 1870, he learned that J. E. Wagner Hardware in Atchison was for sale. After visiting the store in Atchison, he returned to Chicago, determined to purchase the business and relocate to this booming young town in northeastern Kansas. Located on a western bend of the Missouri River, Atchison promised to become an important freighting center, as boats traveling up the river could unload merchandise, which was then routed on western freighting trails to Indian reservations, army posts, and mining camps. There seemed to be unlimited opportunities in the booming, sixteen-year-old

town of Atchison, the "doorstep to the western frontier," and just as their ancestors dared to risk their lives and futures in a new country, J. B. and his bride were not afraid to journey to what at the time was one of the western edges of civilization, anxious to build new lives and raise a family in what promised to be a land of opportunity.

Money to purchase J. E. Wagner Hardware came from Harriet Lovejoy Silliman, who gave her husband $4,500 for the downpayment on the business. J. B. convinced his brothers-in-law, married to his sisters, Caroline and Lucinda, to join him in the venture, and the three young families all traveled together to begin a new life and business in Atchison. On January 1, 1871, D. P. Blish, E. A. Mize, and J. B. Silliman formally began business at the former Wagner

Silliman home in Atchison, Kansas, c. 1900.

Hardware as Blish, Mize, and Silliman, a venture that not only flourished under the direction of the three brothers-in-law, but also entwined the three families through the next century as they lived and worked together in a happy and thriving alliance.

The original site of the hardware store was at Fourth and Commercial in a building measuring only 22 1/2 feet wide. The wholesale business concentrated on agricultural implements and supplies for the overland wagon trains heading west; the family sold wagon bows, ox shoes and yokes, plows, harrows, the Buckeye Reaper and Mower, rope, nails, and axle-grease. The Mohawk Indian trademark of the company stood for a guarantee of "superior quality." J. B. became the firm's first traveling salesman. Well over a century after its founding, Blish, Mize, and Silliman still thrives as one of the largest wholesale suppliers of hardware and plumbing supplies in the midwest. The offices and warehouses now spread out

Hattie at twenty, Atchison, Kansas, 1897.

over a several-acre complex, and the business enjoys multimillion-dollar annual sales throughout the midwestern and eastern states.

Hattie was born in Atchison, six years after the Sillimans settled in Kansas and started into the hardware business. Growing up among this close and enterprising family, Hattie enjoyed a comfortable and happy childhood. One sister, Anna, died as a young woman, but another sister, Jessie, was always a companion, as were all the Blish and Mize cousins. The Silliman home on Fourth Street, where the family moved in 1887, is a large and elegant Victorian edifice, high on the banks above the Missouri River. A popular family story is that Mrs. Silliman had complete control over the design and furnishings of the lovely home, while the only opinion that J. B. expressed was that it could be any color, so long as it was yellow. Of course, Mrs. Silliman had the house painted a cheerful yellow, and it remained that color for many years. A tower over the front porch with a high, pointed roof rises above the four bedrooms on the second story. The bluff where J. B. and Harriet built their home was known as Silliman Hill, and the road in front was a favorite sledding run for local children. From the back of the house there was a grand view of the Missouri River and the broad valley winding to the south. A carriage house at the back of the lot had an apartment above it for the cook and other domestic help.

Hattie attended the Atchison Latin High School with her cousins, Grace Blish and Caroline Mize. Hattie's family were staunch members and supporters of the Trinity Episcopal Church, and several gifts to the church, including a lovely stained glass window, still display the Silliman name. Several blocks to the north of the Silliman home lived Judge and Mrs. A. Otis, close friends of Mr. and Mrs. Silliman. The Otis's granddaughter was the well-known Amelia Earhart and, coincidentally, aviation would later play a major role in the lives of Hattie's family. In great contrast to many of Hattie's later years when she slept on a cot and lived in a tent and bathed in a bucket at various

archaeological sites for months on end, her early life was comfortable and privileged. She was surrounded by elegance and a house full of beautiful furnishings.

Hattie was a slender young woman with dark brown hair and sparkling eyes. In spite of her affluent and pampered beginnings, she had a core of strength and endurance, qualities that were necessary to work and survive in the remote and rugged country of the American Southwest, where she lived in the middle years of her life. An energetic and outgoing person, Hattie loved people, and her innate kindness and caring created friends throughout her life. Wherever she went, from the scholarly, traditional Harvard campus to the Hopi and Zuni reservations and New Mexico ranches of the Southwest, Hattie made friends. She fit in anywhere and found lifelong friendships that cut across barriers of race or status. A likely benefit of her privileged upbringing was the ability to mix with wealthy eastern benefactors and the imposing scholars at Harvard, and her own graciousness and interest in people enabled her to fit in equally as well with the people of widely varying races and ethnic backgrounds with whom she shared many campfires in her later years.

Although her education concluded with high school, Hattie had easily mastered the skills expected at that time of an affluent young lady growing up in the Victorian years of the late nineteenth century. She was taught sewing and stitchery skills, and although sewing her own wardrobe was never a necessity, she could stitch and mend any garment. She especially enjoyed crochet and embroidery and even designed original patterns for embroidered linens and clothing embellishments. She became an excellent cook and always took great pleasure in her aptitude for cooking for her family and the many friends she entertained. Hattie was trained in all the appropriate social skills and graces, and she had a natural courtesy and gracious manner, but in spite of the relentless pressure to be a proper lady, she did have a love of adventure and the outdoors that could never be contained. One talent for which she became known was her exceptional

Silver City, New Mexico, 1906. Negative no. 07167. Courtesy of the Silver City Museum.

drawing and painting ability. Most young women of Hattie's time were expected to become somewhat competent in drawing and watercoloring, but Hattie's early artistic training was only a beginning. As an adult, she developed her drawing and painting skills, and those talents became a vital asset in her later work.

While attending the Atchison Latin High School, Hattie met Cornelius Burton Cosgrove, who was two years her senior. A scholarly young man, Burton left Atchison after graduation to attend school at the University of Nebraska, where he earned a degree in law in 1899. He returned to Atchison, where his mother and sister lived, but also because of Hattie, who returned the affection of the handsome young lawyer. Two years later, Hattie and Burt were married at the Trinity Episcopal Church. Burton was a slender man, just under six feet tall, with a mild and quiet manner, and in spite of having spent his younger years out in the rough and untamed New Mexico territo-

ry, he was never known to have uttered a curse or use rough language. But under his calm and scholarly demeanor, there was a remarkable core of physical strength and a great capacity for endurance.

If Hattie's family was energetic and enterprising in business, Burton's family contributed a zest for exploring new places and a deep love for the harsh beauty of the American Southwest. Burton's grandparents were immigrants who left Ireland and came to New Orleans in 1836. From there they traveled on a riverboat up the Mississippi and Missouri Rivers to Independence, Missouri, where they bought property for a home and a blacksmith shop. After settling they returned to Ireland to get their four children, who had been left behind in boarding schools. Anthony and Bridget Cosgrove returned to Missouri and eventually had five more children. Independence, Missouri, was the eastern terminus of the Santa Fe Trail, an ideal location for a blacksmith in the 1830s. In the late 1840s, Anthony participated in the boom of western exploration when he became a member of the Fremont Expedition to California.

In 1859 the seventh son, Cornelius, "Con," went to New Mexico and was soon followed by three more of the Cosgrove brothers, Eugene, William, and Mike. Another brother, Frank, went to Arizona, where he settled and married Isabel Urias. Frank worked as a blacksmith at Fort McDowell near Phoenix. Con went to Santa Fe and started a stagecoach-and-freighting business, an endeavor that he continued for the next three decades. He earned the grand wage of $100 per month running the stage line from Santa Fe to Albuquerque in 1869. One year later he gave up his contract when he went into business with Colonel Joseph F. Bennett, a well-established freighter who lived in Mesilla, New Mexico. Con further cemented that partnership when he married the colonel's widowed sister and became a devoted father to her four-year-old daughter Caroline, better known as Kitty. Amanda Bennett and Con Cosgrove were married on Christmas Eve in 1870 in the colonel's house on the southeast corner of the historic plaza in old Mesilla. Through the Bennett Freight Company they secured the mail contract from Santa Fe to El Paso. This stage line ran seven days a week. Later they also acquired the mail contract to Tucson, Arizona. This three-hundred-mile run was made three times a week. The route went through the dangerous Apache Indian country of southeastern Arizona and over Apache Pass. The Apache wanted the mules, horses, and the leather harness equipment from the wagons and would attack travelers. Drivers often traveled at night and hid in an arroyo during the day. Many times an unlucky driver suffered a horrible death when he was caught by Apaches who tied him to the wagon, piled the mail bags around him, and then set it all on fire.

Amanda Cosgrove left a handwritten account of Indian encounters during her years in New Mexico, including a horrifying description of a fatal attack on a group of travelers just a day after she and

her daughter had journeyed over a road on their way to Mesilla. One family treasure is a delightfully tender 1871 letter from Con to Amanda after he had safely made the dangerous trip to Tucson, just a day after one of their drivers had been killed by Indians. His simple words plainly illustrate the dangers of travel in the southwestern territories; he noted that "the poor fellow lies there in his lonely grave thousands of miles from his home and relatives who in all probability will never know what became of him." Con wrote to Amanda that he would make the five-day return trip as soon as possible and would "clasp you my darling to my breast." He added that he would try to bring some oranges from Tucson as a special treat for Kitty.

It was a harsh country that attracted the four Cosgrove brothers, but it was also a land full of opportunity for hardworking and strong young men. William Cosgrove went to Silver City but later moved to Roswell, New Mexico, and established a hardware and general merchandise store. Later he became a postmaster and eventually went into banking. Eugene worked for his older brother, Con, driving a stage for J. F. Bennett and Company between Santa Fe, Mesilla, Tucson, and Silver City. When the company opened a store in Silver City in 1873, Eugene moved to that city to take a job as a salesman. He bought shares in local mining interests in nearby Georgetown and acquired the Studebaker wagon dealership. Several years later he established Cosgrove's Hardware, which, in addition to the usual hardware and domestic items, carried dynamite and mining supplies for the numerous mines in southwestern New Mexico. The youngest brother, Mike, worked at a mining venture in Hillsboro with Con, and later he drove the mail wagons.

An interesting story about Mike concerns the notorious Billy the Kid. Mike had often run into William Bonney and his friends while working on the mail routes and in Billy's childhood home of Silver City. In 1880 Billy the Kid and three others were captured and taken to Las Vegas, New Mexico, where they were tried for murder and sentenced to hang.

W. S. Cox Hardware and Furniture Store, 202 West Bullard Street, 1910. The horse-drawn float in what is possibly a Fourth of July celebration features Sherwin Williams paints sold by Cox Hardware. Cornelius Burton Cosgrove (wearing a hat) is standing in the doorway of the store. The young boy on the sidewalk is Burt Cosgrove Jr. Original photo courtesy of Sid Curtis, 1968. Negative no. 707. Courtesy of the Silver City Museum.

Mike took four new suits of clothes to the jail and passed them out to the prisoners. He remarked that he wanted "to see the boys go away in style." Mike Cosgrove's kindness in wanting to give them a decent suit of clothes to be hanged in was all for naught. Billy the Kid and the three other prisoners escaped before they could make use of their new "hanging" clothes.[1]

Over the years the four Cosgrove brothers often joined together in business ventures, and while none of them ever became rich, none of them ever left the Southwest. They grew to love the grand southwestern country, and in spite of the dangers and hardships of the thriving young towns, the brothers stayed to

Burt Cosgrove Jr. in front of the Cosgrove home at 711 Black Street, Silver City, New Mexico. Photo taken October 1910. The pottery olla hanging from the porch roof cooled drinking water on hot summer days.

In a field of prickly poppies Burt practices shooting with his handmade bow and arrows. 1909.

build their homes and businesses. In an 1864 letter to a friend back east, Con wrote, "This country has a charm about it that a man cant see while here but I suppose when a man leaves it and is gone a month or 2 he thinks it is a hell of a country the best in the world." Four years later he wrote in another letter, "I will live in this country the balance of my days."

Con did remain in the Southwest. He and Amanda and Kitty settled in Santa Fe, where they lived in an adobe house on Palace Street just one block east of the plaza and the Palace of the Governors. One of their neighbors in the Palace was New Mexico's territorial governor W. F. M. Arney, who had a great fondness for the young Miss Cosgrove. While visiting Fort Wingate on the Navajo reservation in 1874, Arney purchased a fringed saddle blanket and horsehair saddle whip for young Kitty and a beautiful, green-striped blanket for Amanda. These rare and exceptional Navajo blankets were ultimately sold to the Museum of New Mexico. Another resident of the Palace of the Governors, and a close family friend of the Cosgrove's (known as "Uncle Lew" to Kitty), was Lew Wallace, governor of New Mexico from 1878 through 1881. Wallace was perhaps better know as the author of the best-selling novel *Ben Hur*, published in 1880. In the course of completing his monumental book, Wallace wrote seven drafts of the story, and one of these handwritten versions was given to Con and Amanda. In later years the manuscript was in Kitty's possession, and she often showed it off proudly to friends.

Con and Amanda's only child, a son named Cornelius Burton after his father, was born in 1875 in the Palace of the Governors, located on the historic Santa Fe Plaza and across the street from the Cosgrove's adobe house. Like his father who was 6'2", Burton was also tall and very slender. He was a quiet, intelligent young man who learned to survive in the wild and arid country and loved exploring the mesas and canyons of the Southwest. Burton's early years were spent in the frontier town of Santa Fe, a main stop on the trails from the East, Mexico, and the route to southern

California. He often traveled with his father on various mail and stage routes. He saw a lot of country in the Southwest and met people everywhere they stopped.

Con's untimely death in 1889 at the age of forty-nine from tuberculosis left Amanda alone in a country that was still very much a rough frontier. Consequently, she moved to Atchison, Kansas, where her brother, Tom Murphy, operated the Massassoit House, a hotel established in 1859. Twenty-five-year-old Kitty loved the Kansas town, and she and her mother never left Atchison except for short vacation trips. Amanda's fourteen-year-old son Burton started high school and settled into life in a bustling mid-western town, but he never forgot the beauty nor escaped the lure of the grand southwestern country of his birthplace.

Burton was always curious about the traces of habitation left by Indians and early settlers in New Mexico and later in the Atchison area. After moving to Kansas he explored the country around his home, picking up arrowheads and digging about in the ruins of abandoned homesteads and Indian campsites. One ruin that particularly fascinated him was the site of the old Pensoneau Trading Post on Stranger Creek near Atchison. Burt returned to this place many times during his youth, as well as to a nearby Woodland culture site and a Kickapoo cemetery that he discovered nearby. He saved a blue porcelain mug and strings of trade beads that he had collected there until the end of his days. He followed a different path in his university studies and career, but ultimately the enchantment of his early experiences with archaeology drew him back into that field in the later years of his life.

Although he had earned a degree in law in 1899, Burton never practiced that profession. When he returned to Atchison from the University of Nebraska, he took a job in the hardware business with Blish, Mize, and Silliman. Burt and Hattie had known each other all through their school days, but they had more contact with each other after Burt began working for the large hardware company. They were married two years

Camp above Alma, New Mexico, W. S. Ranch. October 1914.

Hattie digging at W. S. Ranch Pueblo. October 1914.

Hattie at Sycamore Canyon Cave. July 5, 1915.

Mimbres trip, C. B. Cosgrove. July 1916.

Hattie at Craig Ranch, Cameron Creek Ruin. July 1916.

after Burt's graduation from the University of Nebraska, and their only child, Cornelius Burton Jr., was born five years later in 1906. During the early years of their marriage, Hattie and Burt often went out exploring the country around Atchison. The Stranger Creek area had many traces of earlier Indian habitation, and the young couple loved to spend their free Sundays walking across the hills, exploring and searching for arrowheads and other Indian relics.

Within a year after they became parents, Burt and Hattie decided to relocate to New Mexico, where Burton had spent most of his youth. Burton's Uncle Eugene offered him a job in the Cosgrove Hardware store in Silver City. There were also Bennett relatives on his mother's side of the family who lived in Silver City. His uncle, Cornelius Bennett, was a judge and prominent citizen of the town. Bennett owned several mines in the area, served on the school board, and was a member of the town's first city council. The Cosgroves moved to the small town in southwestern New Mexico in 1907, traveling by train from Atchison to Albuquerque and then transferring to a southbound train for Rincon and Deming and another that took them northwest to Hurley and Silver City. It seemed to be understood that Burton would eventually manage the store, a practical idea considering Eugene's age. This move would offer Burton opportunities for advancement that were not as accessible to him at Blish, Mize, and Silliman. However, circumstances were to change. Eugene had several children, some of whom expressed an interest in going into their father's business. Meanwhile, Eugene's health was failing quickly. He died in February 1910, and Cosgrove's Hardware was sold a few months later to a group of Silver City businessmen. The company remained in business on Bullard Street for many more years, but after its sale there was no further association with the Cosgrove family. Before Eugene's death Burton took a job with W. S. Cox Hardware, a larger company located directly across Bullard Street from Cosgrove's. Cox's also had a specialty in sheet metal and an affiliated business,

W. S. Cox Undertaking. Burt worked for Cox Hardware until his retirement from retailing in 1924.

There was never any discussion of the young Cosgroves leaving New Mexico and returning to Kansas after Eugene's death. They had both fallen in love with the wild and awesome beauty of the Gila River country. Located in southwestern New Mexico at the southern edge of the Gila Wilderness, Silver City is the gateway to a rugged country encompassing a thousand square miles of dark forests, deep canyons, enchanting streams and rivers, and, everywhere, cliff dwellings, ruins, caves, petroglyphs, and all the traces of a vanished people that centuries ago roamed this breathtaking land. In 1924 the Gila was designated the nation's, and the world's, first wilderness area. Along with the adjacent Aldo Leopold Wilderness Area and the Gila National Forest, it comprises one of the largest wilderness areas in the United States, spreading across 3.3 million acres.

Silver City is a charming old town set in the foothills of the Piños Altos Range, an extension of the Mogollon Mountains. At an elevation of 5,900 feet, the town straddles the Continental Divide. Visitors in its early years were trappers and explorers; the prospectors and miners came next. In prehistoric times the Mogollon (Mimbres) Indians roamed this land and eventually constructed the pueblos where they farmed and hunted and created the famous black-on-white pottery with its vivid, naturalistic portrayals of insects, animals, and people involved in everyday activities such as hunting, fishing, planting, gambling, and giving birth.

Silver City began in 1870 as a small Spanish settlement called San Vicente de la Cienega (St. Vincent of the Marsh). Miners soon came to exploit the rich veins of silver ore, hence the town's name of Silver City, although gold and other minerals were also present in abundance. Ore and bullion was hauled to Silver City with twelve- and fourteen-horse teams from mining camps in the Mogollon Mountains. By 1881 the railroad was built to carry ore out of the area for processing. When the silver gave out miners turned

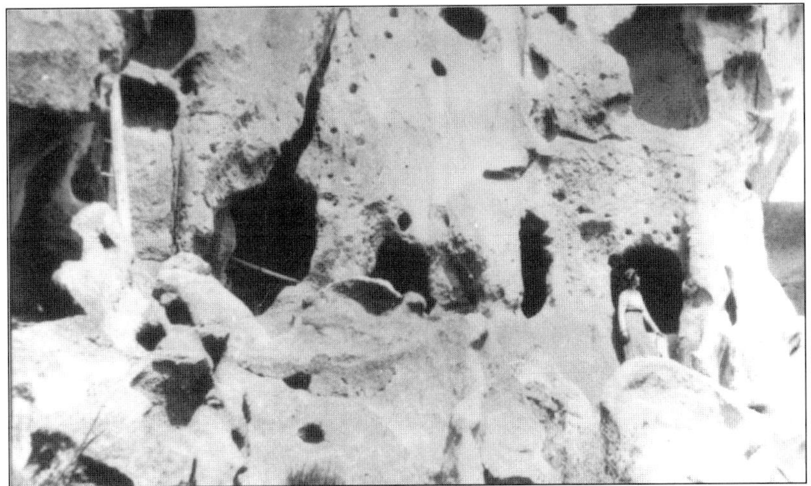

Burt Jr. at his father's birthplace on Palace Avenue, Santa Fe, New Mexico. August 1917. The Palace of the Governors is just visible behind the trees at the left.

Hattie at the cave dwellings in Frijoles Canyon, New Mexico. August 27, 1917.

Hattie, Burt Jr., and Burton in camp at top of Frijoles Canyon, New Mexico. August 27–28, 1917.

Animas Canyon, Sierra County, New Mexico. September 30, 1918. Hattie and Burt Jr., Amanda and Kitty Cosgrove.

to the copper that occurs throughout the area, and large open-pit mines eventually replaced the numerous small and independent mining ventures. Nineteenth-century settlers were continually menaced by the Apaches, and travel in any direction out of the city was at great risk. Tales of Apache raids are still told in Silver City. William Bonney, "Billy the Kid," grew up in Silver City, where his mother took in washing to support her family. Very likely it was in those early years that he first met the Cosgrove brothers.

Silver City, the seat of Grant County, is a lovely town tucked away from the major trails and popular traveling routes, and because of its location at the southern edge of the Gila Wilderness, it remains even today a little-known area and an ideal location for people interested in the solitude of undeveloped and little-explored backcountry. It is a town in a country that has always attracted independent people. When a huge flood in 1885 sent a twelve-foot-high wall of water down Main Street, leaving a thirty-five-foot-deep ravine, the townspeople simply named the hole Big Ditch Park and moved Main Street businesses one block west to Bullard Street. The saloons and houses of ill repute had always existed on Hudson Street, a block east of Main. Mountain men, ranchers and entrepreneurs, saloons, gambling and

"Shady Lanes," all the colorful aspects of Old West lore, existed well into the twentieth century. Elizabeth Farnsworth, a founding member of the Silver City Women's Club, would have disputed the existence of any bawdy houses when she wrote in a piece for the New Mexico Federation of Women's Clubs that "there is nothing of the atmosphere of the typical western mining town as celebrated in cheap fiction. Silver City is lawabiding, the morale of the town is high." In fact, the town's last madam, Millie Clark, retired in the early 1960s, but she continued to be a benefactor to the town, and until her death in 1993, Millie rode in the Fourth of July parade, just behind the mayor and the state senators' cars. The independent and nonconforming people who are attracted to Silver City find a place that is big enough to accept individuals and to offer challenges that they would not perhaps have encountered in another place. Silver City was made for Hattie and Burt Cosgrove, and it always remained the home of their hearts.

Silver City was a progressive town. The first incorporated city in the state, Silver also opened the first public school in the territory. Surrounded by the rich mineral district, it was one of the most substantially built towns in New Mexico; most of its homes and businesses were constructed of brick and stone. It also gained a national reputation as a health resort. Popular flyers boasted of its fine climate and noted that with a latitude the same as Savannah, Georgia, and Cairo, Egypt, the mild winters and "delightful summers" placed it "in the heart of the 'Land-of-the-Well' country." Several sanatoriums were constructed, and Fort Bayard, located just nine miles east of Silver, was given a million and a half dollars to develop a United States Army hospital for treating tuberculosis. A popular slogan for the town, in its quest to attract health seekers, was "A Silver City with a Golden Climate."

Here in this beautiful Mimbres country where the land ranges from brown, scorching desert to willow and flower-lined streams in pine-shaded canyons and high, snow-covered peaks, Burt and Hattie found a place that always called to them. From the time they first arrived in Silver City, when Burt Jr. was a small boy, they were intrigued by this vast corner of New Mexico, and they spent all their free time exploring the country, camping and hiking and picnicking. It was not long before they began to notice the evidence of the area's early inhabitants. Everywhere they went they saw the rounded depressions of pithouse villages, the rubble of cobble-walled pueblo ruins, and the occasional panel of petroglyphs on a hilltop or along a stream. And of course, almost anyone in town could have told them about the Gila Cliff Dwellings located forty-four miles in a straight line north of Silver City and accessible for most of the early twentieth century only by foot or horseback. Increasingly, Burt and Hattie's interest and curiosity about the people of this vanished civilization began to weave a hold on them that would lead to remarkable directions in their lives.

For all that they would love to spend their days tramping about the Gila, Burt and Hattie did have a young son and responsibilities. Burt spent long hours at W. S. Cox Hardware while Hattie cared for Burt Jr. and kept house at their small, single-storied brick home at 711 North Black Street. When they decided to enclose the back porch to make a screened sleeping area, it was typical of their relationship that Hattie joined in with the new room's construction. Hattie sawed boards and pounded nails right alongside Burt. With Burt Jr. the three made a close family unit and spent most of their time together. Burt belonged to the Elks Club, but he was never one to spend his evenings out with friends; he always came home after work to be with his family. And Hattie was not one to be left behind while her husband went off into the mountains. She loved exploring the wild backcountry and didn't mind the hardships of cooking over a campfire and sleeping on the ground, even though camping in a forest was a completely new experience for the privileged young woman raised in the Midwest. Together they bundled up young Burt and rode off every weekend to new adventures.

The young couple was never rich,

Hattie and Burt Jr. fishing in Mogollon Creek. June 1, 1919. Hattie's long skirts are tucked up to her waist for wading in the cold water.

Fried chicken at Treasure Hill. H. S. the cook while C. B. C. Jr. and A. M. Cosgrove wait patiently to say nothing of Pero. October 26, 1919 Note the bundle of wood, which has been brought from town, because by the early 1900s the country surrounding Silver City was stripped of trees for firewood by the soldiers and settlers.

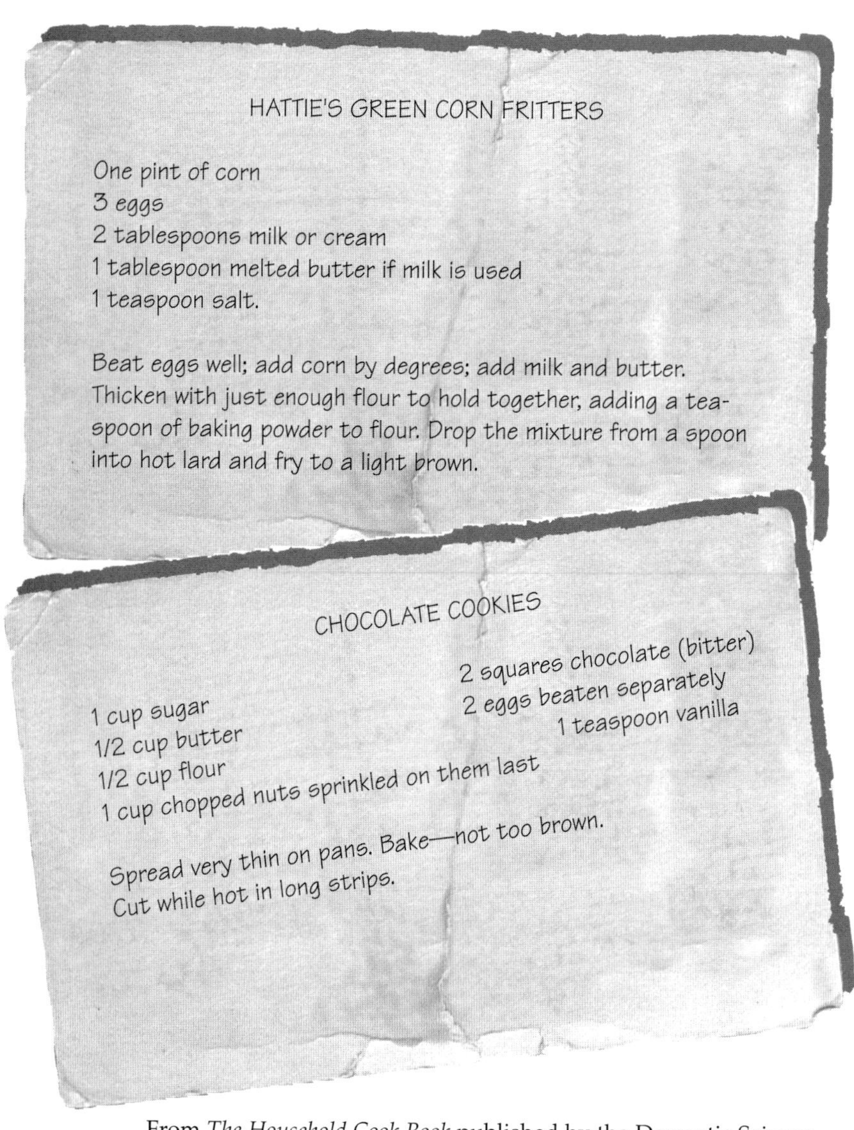

From *The Household Cook Book* published by the Domestic Science Department of the Silver City Women's Club, 1913.

but Hattie did have some lovely furnishings, many of which were from her Silliman childhood home. She was always a proper lady when friends came calling and she enjoyed serving tea and coffee in her lovely old china and beautifully polished silver, accented by her hand-embroidered and decorated table linens. She was a faithful attendant of the Episcopal Church, and for many years her embroidered altar cloths were used in the church services. Hattie was also an early member of the Silver City Women's Club, which was founded in 1909 as the Mother's Club. The women voted in 1911 to change their name to the Silver City Women's Club and to allow all women, even those who were not mothers, into their group. Their stated goals were "sewing for the needy, finding employment for the idle and distributing Christmas baskets." Meetings were held the second Friday of each month, and presentations were given on cooking, parenting, arts, and women's issues, such as voting and property rights. In 1912 and 1913 Hattie chaired the Domestic Department and later served on the Advisory Board. Ten years after its founding, the club had more than one hundred members, and in 1923 the women built a clubhouse that is still in use by the Silver City Women's Club.

Hattie only had a wood cookstove for many years, but she enjoyed a reputation as a fine cook, and she was especially well known for her spicy Mexican and Indian dishes, which she learned to cook after she came to New Mexico. In 1913 when the Women's Club published *The Household Cook Book*, Hattie contributed several entries, and it is likely that as head of the Domestic Department of the Silver City Women's Club, she would have held a major role in organizing the cookbook and overseeing its publication. Among the recipes she contributed were Graham Nut Bread ("makes 25 sandwiches"), Chocolate Cookies, Green Corn Fritters, and Creamed Venison (another speciality that she learned to cook after her arrival in New Mexico). Her Blue Corn Enchiladas and Texas Hash later became a favorite with archaeologists across the country, and just as she was known as a fine cook, she also had a reputation as a gracious hostess. Out in camp she was just as competent as in her kitchen, and she could fry up tasty chicken over an open campfire to feed a hungry group. In 1927 the Women of the Church of the Good Shepherd and Their Friends published *A Cookbook of Choice and Tested Recipes*. Hattie had always been a member of the church's Women's Guild, and her contribution to the cookbook was a recipe for vanilla wafers.

In 1907 in their first year of residence in Silver City, Burt and Hattie made the long trek into the wilderness to the Gila Cliff Dwellings. Hattie rode a pack horse from Sapillo Creek to the ruins in what

Ceremonial Cave, Greenwood Canyon, Grant County, New Mexico. C. B. Cosgrove Jr. at the entrance of the cave. May 9, 1920.

was her first experience with a long trip on horseback. Sore and aching from the long trek, she planned to soak in the nearby hot springs across the river as soon as the camp was set up, but a flash flood came down the Gila River and she and Burt were stranded until the water receded. As the years went by, Hattie became a very competent horsewoman, and when the Cosgroves went on long horse packing trips Burt Jr. often rode behind her, holding on tight as they crossed rivers and climbed steep hillsides.[2]

Some Sundays the family hitched up a buggy and rode to Faywood Hot Springs Resort, southeast of Silver City, for a Sunday dinner. They rented a horse and buggy from Old Man Corral located a few blocks away at Bullard and Yankie Streets. Proprietor Bob Boulware offered "Day and Night Service," and when the Cosgroves wished to use a rig they just had to pick up the telephone and dial 9. When they returned to town late in the day, Burt tied the reins to the buggy and sent the horse on alone to the stables. With increasing frequency, their trips took them to caves where they discovered painted walls or pictographs, and to

ruins where they dug in the rubble of abandoned Mimbres villages. They did a bit of excavating at the WS Ruin near Alma, New Mexico, and at Craig Ranch (Cameron Creek Ruin). They explored Animas Canyon and caves in Sycamore Canyon, but their favorite place was a Mimbres village ruin just east of Silver City near Whiskey Creek. Early on the site was locally known as Whiskey Creek Ruin, named for the nearby creek and the freighting route. Whiskey was a very popular commodity with the miners who came down from the hills to meet the mule trains, and huge quantities of the liquor were consumed on the spot; hence the name Whiskey Creek. The Cosgroves called the nearby ruin Treasure Hill, and the three of them spent many Sundays here digging in the pueblo rooms. They brought a picnic lunch or a bundle of wood and supplies for cooking an outdoor Sunday dinner on the windswept, treeless hill. But it wasn't long before they realized that digging only for treasures was destroying all the clues about these wonderful, silent villages and the people who left ceremonial offerings in the caves and painted the beautiful designs on the pottery. They began to seek out people who could help them to understand the prehistoric cultures and show them ways to become more scientific in their excavations.

Hattie and Burt became members of the the Santa Fe Society of the Archaeological Institute, which was affiliated with the Archaeological Institute of America. The society was formally organized in February 1916, and the Cosgroves had joined by that summer.[3] As a result of their membership in the society, they met through correspondence several archaeologists working out of Santa Fe. To further aid in their explorations, Burt and Hattie bought a Dodge touring car, which they outfitted with extra gear, such as water and gasoline cans, shovels, and a waterproofed tarp that rolled up alongside the length of the roof and could be unrolled and staked out to create a lean-to shelter. With the additional purchase of folding chairs, a table, and cots for sleeping, the family would go off into the backcountry for days and weeks. Shortly after they joined the archaeology society, they decided to travel to northern New Mexico to visit museums and ruins and perhaps meet some of the archaeologists who were working for the School of American Research in Santa Fe. The school advertised in local newspapers, offering opportunities to learn more about archaeology.

In 1917 the three Cosgroves, along with Burt's older sister, Kitty, who was visiting from Atchison, spent several weeks camping near Santa Fe and Taos and visiting museums, pueblos, and ruins in the area. In Frijoles Canyon at Bandelier National Monument, they climbed up into the Great Ceremonial Cave. They climbed the stone stairway and toured Acoma Pueblo, made camp on Tesuque Creek, and explored Cuyumungue Pueblo Ruin. In Santa Fe Burt and Kitty visited their childhood home on Palace Avenue and strolled across the ancient plaza that had been their front yard when they were young. Hattie and Burt also met a few of the archaeologists with whom they had corresponded in Santa Fe. Their growing interest in archaeology led them to seek

out professionals who could give them direction in their amateur excavations and help them acquire the skills necessary to retrieve information from the fascinating sites rather than just make a collection of the interesting relics.

In the fall of 1918 they took another trip to northern New Mexico to visit ruins and archaeologist friends. They camped for some time at Pecos Ruin, a large Indian pueblo and grand mission church occupied during early Spanish days, but burned and abandoned during the Pueblo Revolt. The Cosgroves made a surface collection of worked shell, stone, and bone. Young Burt explored side canyons and on one walk up a sandy wash discovered a sheltered area under a rock overhang where the prehistoric Indians had sat about in the warm sunny area and made stone arrow and spear points. More than a hundred points were gathered at this shelter area and in the large ruin, along with many other artifacts they picked up as they explored the ancient site. Unfortunately, when the Cosgroves went on to the cliff dwellings at Pajarito Park, their trip was abruptly and sadly ended when Hattie received a telegram informing her of her father's death in Atchison. They returned to Santa Fe, and Hattie made plans to go to Kansas to be with her family and attend J. B. Silliman's funeral. It is interesting to note that even in 1918, when their work in archaeology was just beginning and their attempts at excavation were still very amateur, the Cosgroves were so respected and well thought of that Hattie's father's death was reported in *El Palacio*, a monthly review of arts and sciences in the Southwest. This journal was published jointly at that time by the Archaeological Society of New Mexico, the School of American Research, the Museum of New Mexico, and the Laboratory of Anthropology.

In the years after she was widowed, Hattie's mother, Harriet Silliman, began to travel and she enjoyed spending her winters in the Southwest visiting Burt and Hattie in Silver City. Burt's mother also traveled often to New Mexico to visit with her family and join in some of their backcountry excursions. Many charming

black-and-white photos in the Cosgrove family albums show Mrs. Silliman or Mrs. Cosgrove or both exploring ruins or enjoying a picnic lunch under a shady tree.

The following year brought the first serious attempts by Hattie and Burt to do scientific excavations. Mimbres sites in southwestern New Mexico were being pothunted and vandalized at an alarming rate. Local people organized "skeleton picnics" to the prehistoric villages, where they dug in the ruins for turquoise and shell pendants or beads and other treasures, but most especially for the beautiful black-and-white bowls and pots that they found in the burials under the floors of the rooms. Mimbres scholar J. J. Brody noted that as early as 1902 when Walter Hough, chief ethnologist of the United States National Museum, made his first archaeological survey of the area, many Mimbres sites had been heavily pothunted and it "was obvious that many of the local people considered archaeology to be a pleasurable avocation."[4]

Looting of the ruins and destruction of valuable information about the architecture and cultural material of the Mimbres Indians was escalating, and although it was the lure of the spectacular Mimbres bowls that first piqued their interest in archaeology, the Cosgroves soon began to apply scientific methods to their studies. Rather than dig for a collection of relics, Hattie and Burt hoped to learn more about the lives and culture of the vanished civilization, which up until that time was virtually unknown and unstudied. Initially, with only their own intelligence and logic to guide them, they began to map and excavate, recording their work with notes, drawings, and photos. An archaeologist friend noted that Burt and Hattie "certainly had no specialized instruction in archaeology or anthropological method, but they were very careful, methodical people and they recorded, and photographed, and made notes and measurements. I've seen them do it, and you'd be amazed at the care which they took in their excavations."[5]

In 1919 Burt and Hattie purchased their own Mimbres pueblo located on a terrace above Whiskey Creek between

Camp Harmon, Hawikuh. Zuni, New Mexico. August 5, 1920. Note the American flag at the left of the photo and the garden glider under a piñon-roofed ramada.

Camp Harmon, Hawikuh, New Mexico. Museum of the American Indian. F. W. Hodge in charge of expedition. Zuni Dick carved a post for each Zuni Clan. August 5, 1920.

Silver City N. Mex
6/30/20

Mr. F.W. Hodge
Zuni. N. Mex

Dear Mr. Hodge

A short time ago I wrote Mr. Nusbaum at Zuni, but am now afraid he may not be back there soon, as I understand he has gone east.

My wife, boy and I are planning a trip to northern N. Mex in our car, and we very much wish to meet you, and watch the scientific excavation work for a few days at Hawikuh. Would appreciate it if you would let me know how long you will be there and the best way of getting down from the Gallup road to Zuni. I have a leanto tent for the car, so we can be comfortable most any place.

Mr. Walter of Santa Fe kindly gave me your post office address.

I assure you we will not be in the way of the work, and will be an interested audience, as we are enthusiastic amateur archaeologists.

Sincerely
C.B. Cosgrove
711 Black St.

Letter from C.B. Cosgrove to F. W. Hodge, June 30, 1920.
Letter courtesy of the Southwest Museum, Los Angeles, California.

Silver City and Fort Bayard, a site they had first begun exploring more than a decade earlier. They fenced the two-acre property, posted it against trespassers, and renamed it Treasure Hill. Here they began to spend all their free time digging in the ruin, but now they were proceeding as methodically and as scientifically as they were able. Both Hattie and Burt loved digging, and as their expertise grew, they learned to measure and map the rooms. Although their Treasure Hill records have all been lost over the years, they kept notebooks and records of their work at the site for the next several years. They meticulously cleaned and saved each artifact along with a record of its location in the ruin. Hattie also began making full-sized pen-and-ink drawings of each bowl that was uncovered during their excavations. An undated newspaper clipping from this time proclaimed: "EVIDENCE OF PREHISTORIC PEOPLE NEAR SILVER CITY." The article said, "In business Mr. Cosgrove is a hardware merchant—on holidays and Sundays he is a keen and intelligent archaeologist . . . Savants who visit Silver City invariably go direct to the Cosgrove menage—except in event of arriving on a Sunday or a holiday in which case they go direct to Treasure Hill with a certain conviction that in the midst of their ancient pueblo the Cosgroves will be found busily delving into the ruins and adding little by little to their remarkable store of knowledge and relics of a long departed race . . . I would be unfair to exclude from the story the personality of Mrs. Cosgrove whose enthusiasm fully equals that of her husband."

Hattie and Burt dug in their ruin for the next three or four years and eventually uncovered several rooms and hundreds of artifacts. One of the artifacts that was found in Treasure Hill Ruin was a bowl with the painted image of two masked figures. Sometimes referred to as the "twin war gods," this image has been reproduced countless times and is perhaps the most famous of all Mimbres motifs. In addition to the famous bowl, some contemporary archaeologists feel that Treasure Hill has produced more ceramics with astronomical images, such as stars, than any other Mimbres site. One little-known bowl features two comet motifs, and as Halley's Comet did make an appearance in A.D. 1068 during the Classic Mimbres era, it is very likely that an early Mimbes potter wished to commemorate this event in her art.

The original two acres that the Cosgroves purchased comprises about one-half of the total site. It is estimated that the pueblo contains about one hundred rooms grouped in six one-story roomblocks, two plazas, two unexcavated kivas, and an unknown number of pit-houses. It has since been determined that Treasure Hill is the largest Classic Mimbres site in the middle Arenas drainage, an area extending over seventeen linear miles. Hattie and Burt always felt that Treasure Hill was a very important village site in prehistoric times, and contemporary research supports their convictions. Treasure Hill commanded a large agricultural area with sophisticated water and canal systems, prehistoric fields, and widely dispersed field huts. Burt and Hattie excavated the first recorded rectangular kivas found in that area and wrote a small article titled "Two Kivas at Treasure Hill," which was published in *El Palacio* in 1923.

By 1920, however, after one summer of intense excavating at Treasure Hill, the Cosgroves realized that they were very much in need of professional training and guidance if they hoped to make any lasting discoveries that would contribute to the knowledge of the Mimbres culture. Consequently, Burt wrote to a prominent archaeologist who was planning to do summer fieldwork in the Southwest, asking if he and Hattie and their boy could visit his camp. The man Burt wrote to was Frederick W. Hodge, who worked at Hawikuh near Zuni, New Mexico, from 1918 to 1923, and later became director of the Southwest Museum in Los Angeles, California. In Burt's June 1920 letter he wrote: "we very much wish to meet you and watch the scientific excavation work for a few days at Hawikuh." Then he added: "I have a leanto tent for the car, so we can be comfortable most any place . . . I assure you we will not be in the way of the work, and will be an interested

Zuni, New Mexico. Hattie and Ed Coffin are seated on corner of roof in center of photo. August 8, 1920.

Zuni Rain Dance. August 8, 1920.

Zuni Rain Dance. Old priest scattering sacred meal on ground. August 8, 1920.

Wesley Bradfield (Brad), Hattie, C. B. C.,
Kenneth Chapman. February 1922.

Lansing Bloom, Kenneth Chapman, C. B. C.,
Hattie. Mimbres River. February 1922.

Wesley Bradfield. 1921.

audience, as we are enthusiastic amateur archaeologists."[6]

Hodge issued an invitation to the Cosgroves to visit his camp, and in their July and August camping trip through northern Arizona and New Mexico, they spent some time in Camp Harmon at Hawikuh. Their family photo album contains several pages of pictures of the camp and the ruins, and surviving letters in the Southwest Museum archives indicate that Hodge and the Cosgroves corresponded for many years. A 1932 letter congratulates Hodge on his appointment as director of the Southwest Museum, and the last letter in the file is a 1954 card from Hattie on the occasion of his ninetieth birthday. The work Hodge was conducting at Hawikuh was the most extensive and some of the most systematic work being done in the Southwest at the time. He was an excellent teacher to introduce the Cosgroves to the newest scientific techniques for digging, recording, and classifying that were being developed then.

At Hawikuh Hattie formed a fast friendship with Zuni Dick and his wife, who was a potter. Zuni Dick was a medicine man who was in charge of the native workers at the dig, and he also became rather well known for his work with ethnologists in recording Zuni culture. One of Hattie's cherished possessions throughout her life was a necklace that he made and presented to her at the end of her visit. The three-strand necklace consists of hand-drilled shell heshi, orange coral, and turquoise nuggets. Zuni Dick shaped the turquoise and shell pieces by rubbing them on sandstone and then smoothing them with pieces of soft deerskin. Holes for stringing the beads and nuggets were made with a hand-operated pump drill.

At the end of their stay at Hawikuh, the Cosgroves visited the nearby town of Zuni, where they attended a Rain Dance. They climbed ladders to sit on the rooftops with other spectators to watch the ceremony as the long line of dancers filed into the plaza wearing their colorful costumes and headdresses. The rain ritual apparently worked very well, because the last photo in the Zuni series in the

Cosgrove family photo album shows their car stuck on the road from Zuni with Burt shoveling mud from under the wheels.

After their stay at Zuni, Hattie and Burt went on to Pecos Mission, just a short distance southeast of Santa Fe. Alfred "Ted" Kidder had begun excavating at Pecos in 1915 for Phillips Academy in Andover, Massachusetts. Even though the Cosgroves had visited the site earlier, it is unlikely that they would have met Kidder before 1920, because he had served in the army during World War I and didn't return to Pecos until that summer. Ted Kidder's wife, Madeleine, worked with him each season at Pecos, where she was in charge of sorting and cataloguing the mounds of pottery sherds and vessels that were excavated each day. Their five children were also in attendence each summer if they were not off at camp or traveling. The meeting between the Kidders and the Cosgroves instantly marked the beginning of a long and intimate friendship between the two couples.

When the Cosgroves traveled to northern New Mexico in 1920 on their quest to learn more about archaeology, they were among a very small group of people interested in applying scientific techniques to their excavations. American archaeology was then a fairly young discipline, and when Ted Kidder received his Ph.D. from Harvard in 1914, he was one of only half a dozen archaeologists to have earned that degree in the United States.[7] When he began to study anthropology, there was not a formal department at the university. The field was mostly a side interest of several professors in various fields, although William C. Farabee and Alfred M. Tozzer were anthropology instructors. Most support for archaeology came from the Peabody Museum at Harvard, and those funds for archaeological expeditions generally consisted of public endowments and private donations. Up to the time when Kidder began his professional career, the emphasis in Southwestern archaeology was in excavating sites to gather specimens for museum collections, because at that time most Southwestern archaeology was

Old house at Mesilla, New Mexico, where Burt's folks lived in early days about 1870. Amanda and Kitty Cosgrove. September 28, 1921.

Broken axle 40 miles north of Roswell, New Mexico. September 5, 1921.

financed by museums, and most archaeologists were museum employees.[8] More attention was focused on the artifact or pot itself than on the clues or information it could provide. Kidder is credited with "almost single-handedly" changing the direction of Southwestern archaeology from assembling a museum collection with some descriptive overview to examining artifacts themselves in their context to "yield a historical record of their makers' activities." Kidder also collected potsherds, making "sherd surveys," which could be catagorized by site to define "regions and eras."[9] He often referred to "sherding" a site, which indicated that he had gathered a descriptive collection of sherds that could be referred to at some later time for comparison and study. He believed, as did many archaeologists of his time, that scientific analysis of ceramics could be a key in determining prehistoric chronology, and he was also one of the first to use stratigraphy to unlock the mysteries of cultural sequences for the prehistoric Southwest. Archaeologist and biographer Richard Woodbury's high respect for Kidder's contributions is plain when he notes that in addition to the obvious influence Kidder had on leading American archaeology into scientific and analytic methods in the early twentieth century, he was also a teacher, friend, and advisor to untold numbers of younger archaeologists for more than five decades. And it may be his advice and generous counsel that had the deepest and most lasting affect on the profession. Certainly Kidder's patronage and friendship profoundly affected the direction of Burt and Hattie's lives.

In Dr. Kidder, Hattie and Burt happily chanced upon not only a leading scientist, but a man who would generously share his time and expertise with the eager couple from a small town in the corner of the state. And perhaps in Burt and Hattie, Kidder recognized not only curiosity and intelligence, but also a genuine commitment to study and preserve the traces of the prehistoric inhabitants of the Mimbres culture. Years later he wrote of the Cosgroves that "long before they had the slightest idea of going into the work professionally, they acted as archae-

ologists rather than as pot-hunters."[10] The Cosgroves observed intently and returned to Grant County to apply their knowledge to their ongoing excavations at Treasure Hill, where Kidder also noted that they "kept notes, made plans, took photographs, saved every sherd and bone and broken tool."

The next fall Burt Jr. entered the New Mexico Military Institute in Roswell, New Mexico. The Cosgroves drove their son to the school, located about three hundred miles east and slightly north of Silver City. On their way to Roswell they visited Mesilla to see the old house where Burt's parents had lived and Colonel Bennett's house, where Con and Amanda Cosgrove were married in 1870. They also stopped at White Sands northeast of Las Cruces and walked over the crystal white sand dunes. Burt Jr. attended the New Mexico Military Institute all through his high school years, and Burt and Hattie commuted between Silver City and Roswell several times each semester throughout the four years until his graduation.

Back in Silver City, Hattie and Burt continued to spend their free time excavating at Treasure Hill or exploring the surrounding countryside locating other Mimbres sites. Nels C. Nelson from the American Museum of Natural History in New York City heard of the Cosgroves' work in the Mimbres country and paid them a visit in the late summer of 1920. Hattie and Burt showed him several sites in the area, and the three of them spent some time at Treasure Hill. Nelson was very interested in the ruin, and his hand-drawn map and several photos of the pueblo are now in the New York museum.

Aware of the tremendous amount of vandalism that was going on in their area, the Cosgroves began a campaign to try to interest professional archaeologists in working in the Mimbres area and to further protect prehistoric sites. Because most of the major village sites were on private land, they were not protected by the Federal Antiquities Act, a bill passed in 1906 to protect archaeological sites and material. Motivated by their deep concern for the fragile sites, Burt and Hattie

Cave dwelling, Cureton Ranch. Irvin Goldstein, Burton Jr., Mrs. Nunn, Hattie, Mr. Nunn. December 1921.

persuaded many ranchers and land owners to post their properties and not allow any digging at their ruins. And as a result of their having met Hattie and Burt through the Santa Fe Archaeological Society, Kenneth Chapman and Lansing Bloom from the Museum of New Mexico came to visit the Cosgroves in Silver City in February 1922. Burt and Hattie took them on a tour of the Mimbres River country, where they picnicked and walked over sites in the area.

Another visitor who became a family friend was Wesley Bradfield, also from the Museum of New Mexico and the School of American Research. Bradfield was intrigued by the area, and after several visits by other members of the staff of the museum, arrangements were made with John Sully of the Chino Copper Company for Bradfield to begin excavations at a site on Cameron Creek at the old Craig Ranch during the summer of 1923. Burt Jr. was recruited to work with Bradfield for two seasons while he was in Silver City on summer vacation. Burt Jr. and Bradfield boarded at the mine's company housing in Hurley, New Mexico, and by 7 A.M. each morning they picked up their five local workers in Bradfield's truck and made the half hour drive to the site.

Bradfield wrote a delightful account for *El Palacio* of a typical day at the site. One morning, shortly after work on the pueblo rooms had begun, "over the hills came a group of autos—visitors from Fort Bayard." Later other visitors came, but after counting forty-seven people, the crew lost track of the rest. Fortunately, the Bayard group brought enough food to share with everyone, and when the group had finished the fried chicken and lemon pie, they all marched over to the ruin to see the work going on. Under the floor of a very early room, the archaeologists uncovered a burial that took three hours of painstaking work to expose. All during this time the banks above the room and "every available bit of floor space" was occupied with the interested onlookers. In the burial the workers discovered several bowls, a number of tiny beads, four shell bracelets about the left arm above the elbow, and two large shell bracelets

C. B. Cosgrove family. September 5, 1922.

Golf at Treasure Hill. Edward Hesser, Irvin Goldstein, and Burton Cosgrove. December 1921.

Burton Jr. home for Christmas. December 1921.

Walpi (The place of the gap). August 1923.

Walpi Pueblo, Hattie in doorway.

carved with a design of intertwined serpents. With the burial excavated and the day's work over, the guests began packing up to leave with many hearty thank-yous. They had all thoroughly enjoyed their interesting time. And Bradfield, Burt Jr., and the crew, the gracious hosts, "trucked back to town" to rest up for another long day of working in the field.[11]

Wesley Bradfield worked at Cameron Creek Ruin for five seasons, but he was not the only archaeologist Hattie and Burt introduced to the Mimbres region or assisted in locating sites and in helping secure excavation rights. The Cosgroves were instrumental in obtaining excavation rights for Paul H. Nesbitt at the Mattocks Ruin and for Earl Morris from the University of Colorado, who worked briefly at a number of sites along the

Mimbres River. This early contact resulted in a long friendship between Morris and the Cosgroves. And in his introduction to *The Ancient Mimbreños*, Nesbitt thanks the Cosgroves for helping to secure "an ideal site" in the Mimbres valley. He goes on to comment that the Cosgroves, "ardent workers in the field," have "contributed immensely to our knowledge of the Mimbres culture."[12] In later years Burt and Hattie befriended and assisted many other archaeologists who worked in the Mimbres region, such as Ned Danson, Emil Haury, and Frank Hibben. Others who worked in the area in the following decades always called on Hattie at some point in their research to ask her advice and share new discoveries with the woman who was later labeled "Mrs. Mimbres." The Mimbres culture was always closest to the Cosgroves' hearts. They cared passionately about unlocking the secrets of the vanished civilization through scientific archaeological research, and they deplored the increasing vandalism and destruction of the magical sites.

Burt and Hattie continued working at Treasure Hill, and over the years they unearthed a large and valuable collection of Mimbres artifacts. A 1922 issue of *El Palacio* commended their meticulous excavations and careful recording, noting that "Mr. and Mrs. Cosgrove are making careful record of the locations and exact conditions under which the artifacts in their collection are found, as well as making a careful study of the ruins themselves."[13] During the summer of 1922, Burt and Hattie again visited their archaeologist friends who were working at sites in northern New Mexico, and Ted Kidder took time away from his work at Pecos to travel to the southwestern corner of the state to tour the Mimbres country with the Cosgroves. After a trip along the Mimbres River to view the Mimbres village sites, the party also ventured north and west into the Gila National Forest to explore cliff dwellings, rock shelters, and several caves, including Greenwood Ceremonial Cave, which the Cosgroves excavated four years later as part of their survey of caves of the Gila country.

In the summer of 1923 Hattie and Burt planned another trip to northern New Mexico with stops at major sites where they could observe professional archaeologists at work. They returned to Pecos to visit with their friend and mentor, Ted Kidder, and his wife, Madeleine, who worked at Pecos along with her husband. Under Madeleine's direction, thousands and thousands of potsherds were washed and sorted and catalogued, but she also shouldered the responsibility of running the camp and acting as hostess for the many guests, tourists, and scholars who visited the site. From the time of their earliest meeting, Madeleine and Hattie formed a fast and enduring friendship that lasted for the rest of their lives. Madeleine's daughter Faith remarked that "Hattie was my mother's dearest friend." In addition to their compatibility, the two women shared a strong interest in ceramics and over the years had an occasional opportunity to work together at various sites.

Just as Hattie and Burt took their son on all their trips and involved him in their archaeological expeditions, the Kidders also brought their five children with them each summer to Pecos, where Ted worked for nearly fifteen years between 1915 and 1929. Along with the children came their mother and their nurse, their grandfather, Alfred Kidder, their father's secretary at the Peabody Museum, and various friends and college students. Much serious archaeology was conducted each summer at Pecos, but like many expeditions of the time, there was a welcoming and hospitable aura about the camp that extended to friends and relatives, scholars and students, locals and tourists. To the Kidder children, Pecos was a marvelous summer camp complete with picnics and field trips, shopping excursions to Santa Fe and evenings with talk and stories around the campfire.[14]

After leaving Pecos during that 1923 summer, the Cosgroves camped at the Puye Ruins with several other archaeologists and their families. The group included Kenneth Chapman from the Museum of New Mexico, Wesley Bradfield, who had just completed his

Hattie at San Bernadino Mission church ruin at Awatovi. Built about 1629 by Fra Parras. Destroyed 1700. Known to the Navajos as Tally-hogan (Singing house). August 1923.

season at Cameron Creek, and Odd Halseth who became resident curator of Puye Ruins for a short time in the mid 1920s but moved on to the Arizona Museum in Phoenix in 1927. The Cosgroves spent some time at the Hopi Villages of Walpi and Hotevilla. They saw the Antelope and Snake Dances. Hattie was enchanted with the Hopi culture and visited with people at the villages. A touching note to her enthusiasm about the Hopi life is obvious from photographs from that summer of Hattie, who began wearing her hair in a modified "butterfly whorl," the style of young Hopi women, with her hair pulled into a bun over each ear.

Also evident in the photos of their summer trip through northern Arizona and New Mexico is what eventually became Hattie's trademark outfit of jodhpur-style pants tucked into knee-high laced boots and cinched at the waist with a Navajo silver concho belt. Topping off this ensemble was a light-colored, long-sleeved men's shirt and generally a straw hat for protection from the sun. This outfit was practical for camping or digging in ruins, but it was still decades before pants would become common and acceptable attire for women, and as daring or practical as Hattie was in camp, she always changed into a dress if visitors showed up or when she went out in public.

Cosgrove camp at Pueblo Bonito. Chaco Canyon, New Mexico.
August 1923.

Chaco Canyon,
New Mexico.

The Cosgroves also visited the "San Bernadino Mission ruin at Awatobi" (as Hattie recorded it in her photo album) in the Hopi country, a prophetic visit, as Awatovi would later play a major role in the lives of both Hattie and Burton. But the highlight of their summer's trip was the visit they made to Chaco Canyon in northwest New Mexico. Neil M. Judd spent seven field seasons at Chaco from 1921 to 1927, working for the United States National Museum. A lifelong friend of Ted Kidder, Judd was also an eminent archaeologist and an authority on the prehistory of the Southwest. Burt and Hattie spent time at the majestic ruins observing Judd's methods and educating themselves on the current scientific thought and techniques. It is interesting to note that even though they were amateurs, hardware store merchants, they seemed to have been accepted and befriended by prominent scientists and scholars who generously gave their precious time during the busy working days of a typical, too-short field season to patiently educate and explain their "scientific methods" to the Cosgroves. This speaks well of their generosity, but it is also an indicator of the exceptional nature and intelligence of both Burt and Hattie that they could have so easily fit in with these trained professionals and that they could have learned enough through such casual instruction that they eventually would become respected colleagues.

Not only were the Cosgroves well respected but during that summer of 1923, while they visited with Dr. Kidder, he invited them on behalf of the Peabody Museum at Harvard University, and through his position as Curator of Southwestern Archaeology for the Peabody Museum, to direct the Peabody Museum Expedition to the Mimbres Valley, New Mexico. Burt and Hattie's son would graduate from the New Mexico Military Institute in the spring and planned to attend the University of Arizona in Tucson in the fall. This passage in his life allowed his parents to make a major change at a time when they would have to choose between continuing on as before, with Burt working at the hardware store and fitting archaeology in during weekends and vacations, or giving up that position to work in the profession that they had both come to love. This was their last opportunity to change directions in their lives. Burton was forty-nine and Hattie was forty-seven, and even though long-term employment was not a guarantee, the salary was minuscule, and funds for excavations constantly had to be begged and solicited, Burt quit his job and the Cosgroves went to work for the Peabody Museum.

Fortunately, there was some family support for this move. A surviving 1923 letter from Harriet Silliman to her daughter, Hattie, in Silver City, New Mexico, clearly shows the pride and approval she felt at hearing the news of the rather startling changes about to take place in her daughter and son-in-laws' lives. Mrs. Silliman wrote from Atchison, Kansas, that everyone was delighted with the news and knew how much they would enjoy the adventure and travel that would likely be a part of this new work. Perhaps she also felt that archaeology was a step up in the world from the hardware business, especially since they would be in the "companionship of such a profound scholar and cultured gentleman as Dr. Kidder." Mrs. Silliman ended with a comment that things did seem to come full circle in life because her father was a distant cousin to the Peabody family, and she noted that "it seems rather peculiar when I think of you trailing along on the tag end of the Peabody endowment fund." Indeed, Hattie's association with the Peabody Museum changed the direction of her life forever.

It appears that for the first several years Burt was the only official Peabody employee in the Cosgrove family, but as was not uncommon for the time, the museum got Hattie's full labor as well. She had always worked alongside Burt, shoveling dirt from a ruin or hiking up a mountainside to investigate a cave. Along the way she had acquired considerable expertise in ceramics and was often sought after to supervise the sorting, cleaning, and cataloguing of all the pottery and sherds during an excavation. Hattie also developed a remarkable

Hattie and Burt Jr. on the stairway behind Pueblo Bonito, Chaco Canyon.

Hattie and Burt Jr. at Pueblo Alto, Chaco Canyon.

Hattie at Pueblo Bonito. August 1923.

Camp at Puye. September 11, 1923. Mr. and Mrs. Kenneth Chapman, Mr. and Mrs. Odd S. Halseth and son Edwin, Mr. W. T. Grant, Mrs. Wesley Bradfield, Mr. Albin Polasek, Mr. and Mrs. C. B. Cosgrove.

talent for drawing pottery and transferring a rounded, concave image of a pot or bowl to the flat plane of paper. Her hundreds of drawings of Mimbres bowls are nothing short of fine art, and it wasn't long before the value of her contributions to the Mimbres research was recognized and she also became a legitimate employee of the Peabody Museum.

Hattie's employment at Harvard University beginning in the 1920s is especially remarkable because it came at a time when very few women were able to obtain positions in that profession, although many women developed considerable skills and assisted their husbands in their archaeological projects. Not only was it very difficult to work in that field, but it was often necessary for women of that time to overcome many obstacles in order to receive the education and training necessary to do the work. H. Marie Wormington, the first woman to earn a doctorate in anthropology at Harvard University in the late 1930s, more than a decade after Hattie's association with the Peabody Museum commenced, had a very difficult time acquiring the knowledge and training she needed for her later work. Many anthropology professors preferred not to have females in their classrooms, although when Wormington and another Radcliffe student wished to attend Professor Earnest A. Hooton's physical anthropology class, and there was some question about whether their Radcliffe registration allowed them to attend classes at Harvard University, Hooten stretched the rules and told them that if they sat outside in the hallway near the door by the podium, he would speak loudly so they could hear all of the lectures. Professor Hooten's kindnesses aside, it was still many decades after Hattie began her work in the Mimbres before women in archaeology enjoyed full access to education and fieldwork training.

Camp at Swarts Ruin, Mimbres River, New Mexico. 1924.

◄ON THE MIMBRES►

Up until the 1920s very little was known about the Mogollon Mimbres. Indeed, few people outside of southwestern New Mexico even knew of the existence of such a prehistoric culture. In 1902 Walter Hough, chief ethnologist of the United States National Museum, made an archaeological survey of the area, and although he did not do any excavating, his 1907 report discusses the Mimbres sites and contains two photographs of painted Mimbres pottery with naturalistic designs. In 1913 an amateur archaeologist from Deming, New Mexico, wrote to the Bureau of American Ethnology of the Smithsonian Institution in Washington, D.C., describing his collection of Mimbres pots. E. D. Osborn included photographs of some of the pottery and bowls. The pots that he showed were so remarkable that the following year J. Walter Fewkes, an eminent south-western archaeologist, went to Deming to see the collection for himself. He purchased a number of pieces for the museum, did a bit of excavating at Old Town Ruin, and soon afterward wrote about the exceptional Mimbres art he had discovered. Fewkes's 1914 article is credited with being the vehicle that introduced the Mimbres to our century.[1] Before that year only a few people knew about the beautiful "Mimbres paintings" that had lain buried under the ground for nearly eight centuries. Now the recognition, and the realization of a market for the pots, ignited an interest that fueled study of the Mimbres, but perhaps also led to the near obliteration of sites and other traces of their existence as pothunting increased.

Although Fewkes did very little excavating in the Mimbres country, he was clearly fascinated with the unique images

Camp at Senator Albert Bacon Fall's Ranch. Three Rivers, New Mexico. April 1924.

Mrs. D. B. Smith and Lola Villegas standing. Burt Cosgrove, Eileen Alves, Hattie Cosgrove, and Frank Smith. Three Rivers, New Mexico. April 1924.

on the Mimbres bowls. He made a second trip to southwestern New Mexico to excavate a bit, collect more Mimbres ceramics on behalf of the Smithsonian, and study bowls in private collections. A 1921 trip resulted in a booklet titled "Designs on Prehistoric Pottery from the Mimbres Valley, New Mexico," and a second trip in 1923 produced a follow-up pamphlet, "Additional Designs on Prehistoric Mimbres Pottery." During Fewkes's 1923 trip he met with Burt and Hattie and examined their collection of Treasure Hill pottery, and the three of them went out to the Mimbres site east of Silver City for a brief tour.

The Mimbres civilization centered in the Mimbres River Valley but also took in the upper Gila River country and parts of the San Francisco River drainage to the west. The word Mimbres, which was ascribed to the culture that constructed the pueblos and villages along the Mimbres River, is the Spanish word for willow, a tree that grows abundantly along the streams and rivers of that region. In the early years of the twentieth century, it was thought that the Mimbres were a distant relation of the Anasazi to the north, a prehistoric culture that also created black-and-white painted ceramics. Later work by archaeologist Emil W. Haury determined that there were three distinct prehistoric cultures in the Southwest, the Anasazi to the north, the Hohokam to the west in central and southern Arizona, and the Mogollon culture, which centered in the areas along the Arizona–New Mexico border and east into New Mexico. The Mimbres are now considered to be distinct from the Anasazi but a part of the Mogollon tradition, although only in this narrowly defined geographic region in southwestern New Mexico where the extraordinary Mimbres black-on-white pottery was created, and even then for only a very brief moment in time before the entire civilization vanished.

The Mimbres region has been inhabited since 10,000 B.C. by nomadic hunting and gathering people. Then around A.D. 200, during a phase known to archaeologists as the Early Pithouse Period, these people began to settle in small, permanent pithouse villages located on high knolls and ridges. The floors were excavated three or four feet deep, and posts to support the roof were set in the center and around the edge of the room. Supports were laid across the posts to hold the roof of branches, and walls were constructed of reeds and sticks. The interior walls and ceiling were plastered with a thick layer of mud, creating a snug dwelling. Entrances were through a hole in the roof, which also allowed smoke from a fire to escape, or through a ramped entryway on one of the side walls. Wild plants became less important in the Mimbres diet as they started to grow corn and began to make pottery. The population of the settlements grew, and around A.D. 550, during the Late Pithouse Period, the Mimbreños moved into village sites away from the ridges and down onto terraces near the rivers. They still lived in pithouses dug into the ground, although the shape changed from round to rectangular, but now they also constructed large, below ground, kiva-like communal or ceremonial structures. Burials were initially made in the fill of abandoned dwellings, but during this period the people began to place the burials of children and adults under the floors of pithouses still in use. It is in these subfloor burials in the pithouses and in the later pueblo rooms that the majority of painted Mimbres bowls have been discovered. Generally, a bowl was placed painted side down over the face of the deceased, who was laid on the side in a flexed position in a pit dug into the floor of a dwelling. The bowl was then struck or "killed," breaking it completely or sometimes just knocking a hole in the bottom. A few Mimbres burial chambers also contained large grinding stones, metates, which had also been ritually broken or killed. Other ceramics, jewelry, tools, and artifacts were also placed in the grave.

By A.D. 1000, the Classic Mimbres Period, the Mimbres population had grown and villages were located about every three miles along the Mimbres River. The pithouse type of dwelling was abandoned for single-story, pueblo-style construction, with contiguous rooms of

Mimbres Valley looking southeast. Swarts ranch house is on the left side of photo.

Camp at Swarts. 1924. The canvas tents were for sleeping and eating. The large building on the right was the work area. It had a roof and wooden walls halfway up the sides. The top half was screened and had canvas covers that could be let down to keep out rain. Hattie nailed a sign to a tree in front of the work shack naming the walk Riverside Drive. The path behind the tents was Park Avenue.

Finds at Swarts Pueblo. 1924.
Hattie is sitting in an excavated room at Swarts Ruin sifting dirt through a sieve to find beads and other small artifacts. Scattered about her on the floor are a painted Mimbres bowl, seashell "tinklers" (trade goods from the Gulf of California), potsherds, her field notebooks, a large metate, and several stone grinding tools.

Glycymeris shell bracelets, trade goods from the Gulf of California.

stone masonry walls built over the earlier pithouses. Rooms were generally entered from the roof by climbing down a ladder. These roomblocks were arranged about a plaza, and subterranean kivas were constructed for ceremonial use. Continuing in the earlier tradition, burials were placed in the floors of the pueblo rooms.

Agriculture provided the bulk of the diet, and the Mimbres developed wide trade relations throughout the Southwest.[2] Copper bells and parrots came from Mexico, and beads, pendants, and bracelets crafted from shell came from the Hohokam in Arizona. There were some local sources for turquoise in the Burro Mountains and in other nearby areas, but the Mimbres also traded for turquoise and other minerals from northern New Mexico. Naturally, with the rich mineral deposits in the area, the Mimbreños were able to use many of those resources. Quartz crystals and other mineral specimens were often placed in burials. One mineral found in the region that occurs nowhere else in North America is meerschaum. There are two deposits in Grant County that were heavily mined during the late 1800s by the American Meerschaum Company and the Dorsey Meerschaum Company. This white, porous mineral is easily carved and polished and in modern times was used for pipes and smoking articles. Examples of shaped meerschaum objects have been discovered in Mimbres ruins.

It was during the next century and a half of the Classic Mimbres Period (A.D. 1000–A.D. 1150) that the Mimbreños created the spectacular painted bowls that feature images of animals, fish, flowers, insects, and people. And it was in a Classic Mimbres site that Burt and Hattie began their professional work for the Peabody Museum. They later wrote that there was always a moment of excitement when they uncovered a burial, and in that instant before a bowl was turned over they sometimes speculated on the scene or image that would be revealed; each new find never failed to enchant them. Although thoughts of a burial excavation may conjure grisly images, these graves were centuries old, and time and the elements left only a few fragile bones in the pits.

Interestingly, most Mimbres bowls were painted only on the concave interior. Very little attention seemed to be given to the outer surface of the bowls, which were most often left plain, although the exteriors were sometimes polished or had a fine clay slip applied. In addition to the many intricate, geometric designs there were naturalistic renderings of a great variety of insects, animals, snakes and lizards, several species of fish, including some marine species, antelope, frogs, birds, bears, and flowers. Scenes of daily life were portrayed, including hunting, fishing, trapping, planting, and gambling. There were curing ceremonies, images of copulation and childbirth, and scenes of rituals and other mythological and astronomical phenomena (including the appearance of Halley's Comet). In their earlier work at Treasure Hill, the Cosgroves had unearthed a geometrically painted bowl that they and Ted Kidder believed to be a depiction of the comet. In addition, modern astronomers who have studied the images on Mimbres pots theorize that some paintings relate to lunar eclipses and even the A.D. 1054 supernova. One star image on a Mimbres bowl has twenty-three rays, the same number of days the supernova was visible during the day.[3] As the Cosgroves and other archaeologists began working in the Mimbres country, and as pothunting increased, more attention was focused on the art of the Mimbres, and remarkably, for a culture that was virtually unknown until the 1920s, it is generally agreed today that Mimbres art has had a great impact on southwestern art, greater than any other prehistoric culture.

These remarkable paintings had lain undiscovered under the ground for nearly eight centuries, and the Cosgroves were the first to begin scientific excavations to attempt to unravel the mysteries of Mimbres civilization, for after A.D. 1150, the Mimbres region was abandoned. There is speculation that after the population grew to about two thousand or three thousand, the area was depleted of timber, wild food, and animals, and after a few years of undependable rainfall

Burt standing on the floor of an excavated room at Swarts Pueblo. 1924.

Room 20, Swarts Pueblo. 1924.

Swarts Pueblo. 1924.

Sub-floor ventilator. Swarts Pueblo.

and meager crops, the people began moving away from the large villages. Some may have stayed in southwest New Mexico, and some archaeologists now believe that Mimbres turned into a sequence known as Black Mountain/El Paso, but it is likely that many of the people journeyed south to Casas Grandes, located in the northern part of the Mexican state of Chihuahua and a cultural center that was achieving a major flowering shortly after the Mimbres civilization went into decline. This cultural center became the largest community and trading center in the prehistoric Southwest, with thousands of rooms, ball courts, temple platforms, and irrigation systems.[4]

Perhaps the greater population at Casas Grandes simply overwhelmed the immigrating Mimbres people. Perhaps the severe drought that devastated the entire Southwest in the last quarter of the thirteenth century spurred the final abandonment of the Mimbres region and ended the cultural and artistic tradition of the Mimbreños, but it is remarkable to note that after A.D. 1150, there are no further traces of the beautiful Mimbres paintings. The Mimbreños seem to have not taken their unique tradition of decorating their pottery bowls with naturalistic designs out of the Mimbres region. Some authors have speculated that the Mimbres artistic tradition was instigated by a single gifted artist and her followers, and after their lifetimes the Mimbres artists simply went on to create their own art, abandoning the traditional style of naturalistic painting. Perhaps further investigations will eventually unlock the mystery of the disappearance of the Mimbres art and culture, but for now there can be only speculation on the causes of the rather abrupt end to that remarkable era. At the time that the Cosgroves began their work in the Mimbres valley, none of the preceding history of the Mimbres civilization had been discovered through modern archaeological methods. Origins of the Mimbres culture, reasons for its demise, and explanations for the apparent lack of any continuing Mimbres traditions in the Southwest were simply unknown at the time.

The painted Mimbres bowls were almost always found with burials, usually located in pits dug below the surface of a once inhabited room, and archaeologists have long noted that in spite of centuries of trade relations between prehistoric communities throughout the Southwest, the naturalistic Mimbres pottery is almost never discovered in other areas, though Mimbres pots with strictly geometric designs were distributed well beyond the Mimbres Valley, as far as eastern Arizona and northern Mexico.[5] Obviously, these painted bowls had a greater value to the Mimbres than just serving as utility vessels. Artist Tony Berlant wrote: "To a people who lived directly above their ancestors, the bowls are a direct link between the living and the dead. Today, these extraordinary bowls have become a "spirit line" between the Mimbres and ourselves. Like love notes from a distant culture, they reassure us that the human spirit is immortal. Through them, immortality is granted to the vanished Mimbres themselves."[6] And in a report to Peabody Museum supporters of the Cosgroves' Mimbres Expedition, Ted Kidder eloquently summed up the lure and the mystery of the Mimbres: "But of the history of the ancient people who lived along the Mimbres we as yet know almost nothing. We have no hint of their origin, no clue to the cause or manner of their disappearance. And yet, when one works for a time with the relics of these vanished folk, one feels that one knows them better than many another tribe whose history is far clearer. For they, to a degree most unusual among primitive races, have impressed their individuality upon the things they made, and when we see depicted on their pottery the animals they hunted, the birds they snared, the fishes they caught, even the mosquitoes that bit them and the locusts that devoured their crops . . . we get a feeling of almost friendly intimacy that makes them stand out sharply among the misty peoples of the prehistoric Southwest."[7] Without a doubt it was the unique and exceptional quality of the prehistoric Mimbres artwork that lured Hattie and

Lifting bowl. Burial at Swarts Ruin. 1924. For Hattie and Burt the moment when a bowl was lifted was always filled with excitement. They would often speculate whether the image would be an intricate geometric, a scene of daily Mimbres life, or a group of insects or animals captured forever by an ancient Mimbres artist. No matter what the image, the scene on the amazing painted bowls never failed to enchant them.

Burt into a lifelong love of digging for clues to unravel the mysteries of vanished peoples. In 1924 the Cosgroves began full-time work in the field of archaeology and remained active and enthusiastic participants until the last days of their lives.

In the early months of 1924 the Cosgroves made a survey of village sites in the Mimbres River Valley in order to select an appropriate, "typical" site for study. The place they chose was the Swarts Ruin, a Classic Mimbres site located about fifteen miles south of the present-day town of Mimbres. Perhaps this site was chosen because it is generally in the middle of the Mimbres region, but it was also a logical choice because there had been relatively little pothunting conducted on the ruin. Further to the north the river runs year round, but the land is rugged and has less tillable acreage. To the south the land flattens out and becomes more arid and barren. Although the larger Mimbres villages are located at the southern end of the Mimbres Valley, the water supply is less reliable; the river flow becomes intermittent and often nonexistent as it sinks underground for most of the year. Timber, wild plants, and animal resources would have been scarcer in the arid lower country. Of course, the larger Mimbres villages located at the southern fringes of the Mogollon country did have nearby springs for local water sources, and in stark contrast to the normally dry, sandy riverbed of today, the Mimbres River flowed a greater part of the year in prehistoric times according to some archaeologists.

With its central location, Swarts was not the largest of the villages, but perhaps it was a more stable community because of its greater number of dependable food and agricultural resources. Interestingly, Swarts village is located on a low mound in the river floodplain, just one hundred yards west of the river, rather than on a terrace above the river as were most of the Mimbres villages. Because it was situated further downstream where the valley becomes broader and is a good distance from the mountains, there was lesser chance of flooding, although there certainly have been floods over the centuries that have come up over the ruin. In fact, the Cosgroves noted that a flood around the turn of the century would have accounted for the scarcity of surface sherds, and in the second year of excavations a flood nearly covered the ruin and came within inches of carrying away their camp and all the artifacts and evidence of their season's work. But it was

also thought that flooding was a more recent occurrence caused by heavy cattle grazing and excessive harvesting of timber. Hattie and Burt believed that with more trees and vegetation to hold back the water, flooding would have been less severe in earlier times.

Swarts pueblo is located on a slight rise above the surrounding land, which had historically been plowed into fields for alfalfa on the north and west. The pueblo itself had never been plowed for planting because of the great quantities of river rocks that had been carried in for construction of the pueblo walls. Over the centuries the rock walls have tumbled down and Mimbres ruins today have almost no tall standing walls. There are now only mounds where a village existed at one time, although excavations do uncover the bottom three or four feet of wall remnants. There was an earlier extension of the pueblo to the south of the main ruin, but that area was destroyed years earlier when an orchard was put in. As was the local custom, the ruin was named for the owners of the Swarts Ranch, which was situated a short distance to the southwest. One of the expenses of the excavation was a twenty-five-dollar fee paid to Mrs. E. J. Swarts Sr. for rent of the pueblo for the season. The village consisted of a large, central plaza area and two single-story pueblo structures with rooms three to four deep, each containing about sixty rooms, including living and work areas, storage rooms, and communal ceremonial areas. The roomblocks were laid out in a U-shaped configuration about the plaza. Later work and modern dating techniques have determined that the village was first occupied about A.D. 950. The dwelling structures of this earlier period were rectangular pithouses, and the later multiple-room, stone-walled residential complexes were built over the earlier houses.

According to their 1924 Field Notes, now archived at the Peabody Museum at Harvard University in Cambridge, Massachusetts, Burt and Hattie began their season at Swarts on May 5, and continued for four months.[8] Their first work was at the room complex they named

South House, where they excavated forty-five rooms, eight of which were earlier pithouses located beneath the floors of the pueblo rooms. They typically worked down to the floor level of a room, which averaged a depth of five feet, then after photographing, measuring, and recording each feature of the room, they broke through the floor and excavated down until clean river gravel was reached. Each day Hattie typed the notes for the work that was done, meticulously describing each room, its location, dimensions, and features. Very little material was found on the floor surfaces, which led the Cosgroves to speculate that the village had experienced an orderly abandonment. Burt recorded that they had moved, with the help of workers, 1,143 yards of dirt in their first season's work.

The Cosgroves uncovered 350 burials and 307 whole or nearly complete bowls. After centuries of burial, the skeletons at Swarts were in extremely bad condition because of moisture from rains and occasional floods from the nearby river. The bones were fragile and brittle and sometimes crumbled to powder upon exposure to air. Each burial had to be meticulously excavated with a small knife or trowel and soft brush. Sometimes only the teeth survived the exhumation, and occasionally only grave goods, including the painted Mimbres bowls, indicated the site of a burial. If a skeleton was discovered in good condition, it was kept shaded from the sun, thoroughly cleaned and treated with melted paraffin in preparation for removal to a laboratory for further study. Mimbres historian J. J. Brody has noted that more painted Mimbres bowls have been excavated at Swarts than from any other Mimbres site, and the Cosgroves recorded that while some rooms had only one or two graves, others had as many as ten to thirty-two burials below the floors. Unfortunately, because of the extreme deterioration and fragile condition of the skeletons, and to the lament of later archaeologists, only sixty-two complete or partial skeletons (skulls) of the more than one thousand burials were sent back to Peabody Museum for further study.

Burt Jr., Hattie, Burt, Madeleine Kidder, and Dr. Ted Kidder. The Kidders took a break from their excavations at Pecos to visit Hattie and Burt and tour Swarts Ruin. Even though they lunched under the cottonwood trees along the river, it appears to be a rather formal visit. Hattie and Madeleine are both wearing dresses and Burt and Ted are wearing ties rather than their usual excavation work clothes.

Hattie with the Peabody Museum flag she stitched for the flagpole at Swarts.

Burt constructed a practical but somewhat precarious framework to photograph aerial views of the excavations.

Swarts Pueblo, Plaza 13, to northeast. 1924.

But in spite of the small number of skeletons that were preserved, the Cosgroves did record and save all burial information, artifacts, and pottery, and their detailed notes have allowed present-day archaeologists to study and incorporate the Swarts data in their research.

Burt devised a workable, but slightly precarious, three-point photography scaffold consisting of a ladder lashed to two juniper poles. By holding very still at the top of the pyramid created by the ladder and poles, he could shoot down into a room. He had a better than average talent for photography, and even now after many decades, his photographs are still sharp and clean, with details easily discernable. Burt was a remarkable excavator. He loved the physical work of the digging and had a great talent for locating features and analyzing data. Hattie was in charge of cleaning, sorting, and cataloguing the tens of thousands of sherds and bowls recovered from the ruin. She reconstructed many of the broken pots that came from the burials because they were seldom whole. Great numbers of them had either been broken deliberately or by the weight of the many feet of soil that had accumulated on top of them in the ruin.

Popular belief contends that the kill hole in burial bowls allowed the spirit of the deceased to pass on to the afterworld, and another theory is that "killing" the bowl allowed its spirit to accompany the soul of its dead owner. Among some modern-day pueblo cultures there is also the belief that the sky covers the earth like a huge, solid, inverted bowl, and in order to travel upward to a higher spiritual place, a being or spirit had to find a break to pass through the domed sky. Similarly, there was a domed sky covering the underworld that had to be penetrated so that people could pass through to come into this world. In her extensive study of Mimbres ceramic art, *Within the Underworld Sky*, art historian Barbara L. Moulard postulates that the painted Mimbres bowls can be fully understood only in their final mythical context as the domed covering of the underworld sky. Moulard examines the rich heritage of contemporary pueblo mythology to correlate Mimbres imagery to the timeless themes of birth and death, life, existence and fertility, and the use of mythology and ritual to give meaning to the human drama.

Moulard is not alone in looking beyond the obvious utility of the vessels to unravel the mythical and ritualistic symbolism of the paintings. And even though the painted bowls do depict many mundane images and were thought to have been used in ordinary daily work, many scholars feel they have too many ritual clues to have been casual decorative ware. Other scholars and historians have commented on the shape of the hemispheric bowls and have noted that when a painted bowl is held up over one's head there is a likeness to a richly symbolic domed sky. Thus, the "kill hole" does more than allow the spirit of the deceased to escape from the place of internment; it allows the spirit a passageway to travel beyond the underworld sky to a metaphysical upperworld, or heaven. And perhaps the richly embellished interiors of the painted hemispheric bowls are a ritual metaphor for the deceased soul's journey, a sort of personalized tomb painting.

Interestingly, although Burt was an excellent photographer, the Cosgroves did not rely on his camera to record the hundreds of beautiful bowls recovered from the site. Instead, Hattie made drawings on heavy sheets of acid-free paper about thirteen by thirteen inches square, with a pen and a brush, using India ink to record the hundreds of pots they excavated at Swarts. Kidder referred to these lovely paintings as "field drawings," because Hattie did make them out on the site, hanging them to dry outside in the sun with clothespins on line strung between the trees. She also drew pots from many museum and private collections. Because many bowls were being taken out of the Mimbres country, and many were in private collections, Hattie and Burt hoped to make a record of every Mimbres bowl they saw. They often approached local people and asked permission for Hattie to draw the pots in their collections.

One logical reason for drawing the

Lunch at Swarts. C. B. C., Burt Jr., and Hattie. 1924.

The two Cornelius Cosgroves cooling off.

bowls rather than photographing them is that distortion would occur in trying to take a photograph of a concave object. Another problem is that in many Mimbres bowls the focal center of an image is not the center of the bowl but is up on the curving periphery of the bowl's interior. This is often the area that would suffer the greatest distortion in a straight-on photograph, so Hattie's drawings became a valuable record of the bowls discovered at Swarts and other sites throughout the Mimbres region. Over the years she drew thousands of pottery bowls and broken sherds, and her surviving pottery drawings comprise an amazing, and largely overlooked, collection of original art.

Because it would have been about a thirty-mile daily drive each way from

Leaving camp at Swarts Ranch. 1924.

Silver City to the Swarts Ruin, the Cosgroves set up a nearly permanent camp at the site and set about making it as comfortable as possible. They could return to their home in Silver City on weekends to visit their friends and family in town and to pick up supplies, but they generally spent most of their time at camp, taking advantage of the summer work season. Hattie stitched a flag for the camp at Swarts (material was purchased at J.C. Penney in Silver City for sixty-nine cents), letting all visitors and passersby know that this was the Mimbres Expedition of the Peabody Museum. She also nailed up a sign designating the shady path from the camp to the river edge as "Riverside Drive." The trail between the work and sleeping tents was "Park Avenue."

Burt Jr. graduated from the New Mexico Military Institute and spent part of the summer working at Cameron Creek Ruin with Wesley Bradfield, and visiting and helping his parents at Swarts when he had time off. At the field camp at Swarts there were two sleeping tents, a third one for cooking and dining, and a fourth tent for the work area. The canvas tents were lashed to ridgepoles for support, and the work tent was a semipermanent structure with a wood floor, door, and wood halfway up the sides. The top portion was screened for ventilation and protection from mosquitoes and biting black flies, and the roof was of waterproofed canvas. Mosquitoes and bugs were a constant problem, and one of the expenses that Hattie recorded was for thirty-two yards of mosquito netting at a cost of $4.80. "Ant dope" from Howell Drug Company in Silver City cost a dollar. A wash bench was crafted of poles lashed together supporting a board to hold a towel, washbowl, and water pitcher. All water for drinking and cooking had to be boiled, and canvas-covered canteens of purified drinking water were hung in the trees to provide cooled water. For four months the Cosgroves slept on cots in walled tents, worked long, hot hours in the New Mexico sun, and wrote up their notes in the lingering summer twilights or by lantern light. It would have been a lovely setting for a summer camp, with the ancient cottonwood trees along the river providing pleasant shade for an occasional break from the constant sun out in the ruins. But there was no electricity, no modern conveniences, and only the river for water. At nearly fifty years of age, Hattie and Burt took to the rugged life as though they had always done it. Truly, they loved their work.

Hattie kept methodical records of every expense, including such supplies as twenty-nine cents for five whisk brooms, thirty-five cents for drawing ink, and eighty cents for two pair of gloves.[9] In June their expense for labor for two hired workers totalled $114.00 for seventy-six days at $1.50 per day. Isabel Lara, a young woman who lived on a nearby ranch, was hired for each season at Swarts as the camp cook. She was paid $24.00 per month, and each day she walked the mile and a half up to the camp, where she prepared meals for the Cosgroves, their workers, and any guests. Hattie and Burt did receive a small salary from the museum, but money for the expedition had to be raised each year, generally through Dr. Kidder's untiring efforts. In the foreword to the report that the Cosgroves later wrote on their Swarts investigations, nearly seventy people were thanked for their generous support in funding the Mimbres Valley Expedition.

At the end of the season all of the artifacts were packed for shipping by railroad back to Cambridge, Massachusetts. The bowls were wrapped round and round with string and placed in barrels (20 Packing Barrels for $10.00) that were packed with straw (4 Bales Straw for Packing Pottery-$4.00). The top of the barrel was mounded to a dome shape and covered with burlap, which was tacked down around the sides so that the barrels could not be stacked. This could present a risk of smashing the pottery inside.

One interesting expense is for twenty pounds of salt for bleaching pottery (70 cents). Because the bowls were underground for so many years, the moisture from rainfall left iron deposits on the surface of the pots. Sometimes these brownish-black stains were so heavy that the painted design could not be seen. Housewives of that era had traditionally used salt, lemon juice, and sun to remove rust stains from linens, and Hattie borrowed that idea and developed a method of using a paste of salt and lemon juice spread on the surface of the pot, which was then left out in the sun to dissolve the deposits and reveal the painting on the bowl. It was a slow process, but it worked well to restore the bowls to their original whiteness and expose the paintings underneath.

At the end of their first season at Swarts, Hattie and Burt returned to their home in Silver City and rented a small building to store all of their excavating equipment. In November they visited Burt Jr., who was attending his first year of school at the University of Arizona. They toured the old missions in southern Arizona and attended an Indian festival at San Xavier Mission. On the way back east they stopped off in Atchison, Kansas, to visit "the mothers," Harriet Silliman and Amanda Cosgrove. Then they went on to Cambridge, where they rented rooms and spent several weeks working with the Swarts material.

Early in the spring of 1925 they returned to the Southwest, where they worked on a short project by invitation and with funding from the El Paso Archaeological Society. In April of the previous year Hattie and Burt had camped at Senator Albert Bacon Fall's ranch near Three Rivers, New Mexico,

Papago [Tohono O'odham] and Yaqui Indians dancing in front of San Xavier mission church. Tucson, Arizona. December 1924.

Festival and Dance at San Xavier. Tucson, Arizona. December 1924.

with Mr. and Mrs. R. Burrow Alves, Mr. and Mrs. D. B. Smith, and Colonel M. L. Crimmins, president of the El Paso Archaeological Society. Eileen Alves and her sister, Gertrude Smith, had a strong interest in archaeology, and Eileen was one of the organizers of the El Paso Archaeological Society, which is still thriving many decades after its founding. In 1924 the society invited the Cosgroves to tour the numerous ruins and petroglyph sites in the Three Rivers area, and in the spring of the following year, Crimmins, the Smiths, Alveses, and Cosgroves returned to do several weeks of excavation. Burt and Hattie wrote a detailed report of the excavations, but it was not published until many years later.

Eileen Alves remained a close friend of the Cosgroves until her death in 1935.

East wall, room 2, Three Rivers, New Mexico. 1925.

Colonel M. L. Crimmins, president of the El Paso Archaeological Society, recording petroglyphs at Three Rivers, New Mexico. In April 1925, Hattie and Burt directed excavations and surveys of the El Paso Pueblo District, sponsored and financed by the El Paso Archaeological Society. A report of their work in the area was published four decades later.

She was an avid amateur archaeologist, not only a founding member of the El Paso organization, but also an officer of the Southwest Archaeological Section of the American Association for the Advancement of Science. She presented papers on her work at their annual meetings, as well as for the Texas Archaeological and Paleontological Society. Over the years Eileen corresponded with the Cosgroves when they were working at Harvard during the winter months, and she and her husband visited them at their camps when they returned to the Southwest during the summers.

By early May Hattie and Burt had finished the excavations at Three Rivers and returned to Silver City to make preparations for the second season at Swarts. On May 25 they set up their tents and gear at Swarts and began their work. Burt Jr., who had spent the previous two summers just a few miles away at Cameron Creek with Wesley Bradfield, arrived from Tucson in his roadster, "Desdemona." He spent the summer working at Swarts with his parents. In addition to Burt Jr., there were five men employed full time as excavators. The season officially began on June first and work continued until October third. The Cosgroves finished excavations on South House and began working on the plaza. There were unrewarded hopes of locating a kiva beneath the plaza, but the discovery of early pithouses and the wealth of information they contained compensated for that disappointment. Ted and Madeleine Kidder visited Swarts, as they had the previous summer, and upon their return to Pecos, Ted wrote another of his friendly and informative reports on the expedition to be sent to the subscribers. The Cosgroves also enjoyed an overnight visit from Eileen Alves, who drove her husband, Burrow, up from El Paso in mid-July.

It had been a very dry spring and summer in southwestern New Mexico, some areas not seeing rain for over a year, and because the river was so low and muddy the Cosgroves had to strain as well as boil all of their drinking and cooking water. The second season at Swarts was miserably hot and dry without the summer rains to cool the land. For nearly three months Hattie and Burt dug under the full sun, contending every day with the heat and the dust that billowed up with every touch of the shovel or trowel. Then in late August it began to rain, and for several days Burt and Hattie watched the river rise. On a Monday in late August they were preparing for the arrival of Dr. and Mrs. Henry W. Gillett, major sponsors of the expedition. Dr. Gillett was a member of the wealthy family that had established the Gillette razor blade and shaving products company. They were arriving on a small train that ran between Deming and the mines in Central and Hurley, and they would get off at Faywood, which was nothing but a boxcar with no attendant, miles from any houses. Burt decided that he would try to get through to the train line so the Gilletts would not be stranded, and he packed his car with a shovel, picks, and ropes in case he got stuck in any of the flooded washes, and food and camping gear in the event that he had to spend the night on the road. Burt set off in the early afternoon, and within just a few hours the river had risen to an alarming level. Hattie packed all of their field notes, records, maps, and photographs and took them up to the Swarts ranch house. She made a second trip and was returning for the pottery when the river jumped the banks and rushed down the field toward her. She managed to run back to higher ground, but when she turned to look behind her she saw that the camp and the low mound of the ruins was now a small island, completely surrounded by the raging waters. In a letter to Ted, Hattie wrote that she felt despair at what she thought would surely be the total loss of the camp and their whole summer's work. It was especially difficult for her because with Burt away, responsibility for the camp fell on her.[10]

Burt returned that evening. He did make it all the way to Faywood, but he had learned that many bridges had been washed out because of flooding and it would be some time before any trains were able to get through. Burt and Hattie went back to the camp and Burt was able to wade through the waist-high water to get to the tents. He piled the boxes of pottery on the cots and tables and weighted them down. Then he waded back through the water to the higher ground to the west of camp. During the night the rain continued and the water rose to the floor of the tents, but there it stopped, sparing the loss and destruction of all the artifacts and hundreds of beautiful bowls that had been recovered that season. In the morning Hattie and Burt got a team and wagon and crossed the water to their camp. They loaded the boxes of artifacts, their tents and cots, and other gear and moved the entire camp higher to the west

Camp at Swarts Ranch. 1925.

Cosgrove Camp is in lower left of photo. Swarts Ruin is in the alfalfa field in the center of the picture. After a late summer flood nearly carried away the camp which had been located along the river, the tents were moved to higher ground west of the ruin.

side of the alfalfa field. The Swarts work continued a few days after the river receded and the ruins had a chance to dry out a bit. The only losses were some of the ancient cottonwoods that had grown along the river.

By the end of the season, work on the plaza and the west wing of the pueblo was completed and about two-thirds of the site had been excavated. Dr. and Mrs. Gillett eventually came to Swarts, where they visited and worked with the Cosgroves for a month. One of Burt Jr.'s favorite stories is about Mrs. Gillett, who was afraid of not being recognized when she got off the Deming-to-Hurley train at the Spaulding stop at Faywood Springs. In correspondence with the Cosgroves

Dr. and Mrs. H. W. Gillett, subscribers to the Peabody Museum's Mimbres Expedition, visited Swarts Ruin in September 1925.

Mrs. H. W. Gillett.

she meticulously described her traveling suit and hat of gray tweed. When they stepped off the train at Spaulding Station, which consisted of only an old boxcar, she and Mr. Gillett were the only people for miles about, except for Burt and Hattie, who had driven down from Swarts to meet them.

Subscribers and benefactors to the Mimbres Expedition were always "most heartily" invited to visit the site, but most were wealthy easterners who never made it all the way west to the fairly remote Mimbres valley. The Gilletts, however, had a great interest in southwestern archaeology, and Dr. Gillett, a dentist, wrote an article about the importance of studying ancient peoples as a method of improving the health of modern-day societies. Some of the material for his report was gathered during the time he spent with the Cosgroves at Swarts Ruin. Gillett's "Contacts Between Archaeological and Dental Research" was published in 1927 in the *American Anthropologist*. As was not uncommon for the time, it also appears that a gift of fourteen Mimbres bowls and other artifacts was made to the Gilletts for their financial support of the Mimbres excavations. Fortunately, these were later returned to the Peabody Museum's Swarts collection, but the importance of the subscribers to the Southwest expeditions cannot be overlooked. The university and the museum contributed a small portion of the money to fund archaeological expeditions to the Southwest, but the greater portion of the expenses had to be raised each season through donations from interested and generous subscribers who sent in checks ranging from $25 to $500 and more. The Peabody Museum archives contain files of letters to the subscribers and potential backers of the various museum expeditions and many thank-you letters from the Cosgroves to their benefactors. Kidder especially seemed to have a talent for raising money to fund archaeology. His long letters to subscribers are friendly and chatty, even when there was no money forthcoming, and in addition to the annual reports with photographs of sites and artifacts, he sent out almost monthly short reports on the progress of the work during that season and information about interesting or unusual finds. One Swarts burial that he described at length that season contained a bowl inverted over the skull, ten shell bracelets circling one forearm and fifteen bracelets about the other, and an additional bracelet consisting of 104 turquoise beads.

In their 1925 field notes the Cosgroves discussed the 605 burials found during their second season of fieldwork for the Peabody Museum. Most burials were located around the edges of a room, most likely to avoid disturbing the firepits, which were generally more centrally located on the floor. Bodies were often buried in a flexed position with the knees drawn up to the chin. Most lay on their backs, but there were a few on their sides and a few in a semi-seated position. Three females were buried with manos and metates, the milling or grinding stones used to crush plant foods and herbs, such as corn, mesquite beans, and seeds. With so many burials, many older graves were naturally disturbed, and that may have accounted for some burials represented by an incomplete skeleton. But the painted bowl inverted over the deceased's head was never disturbed or removed when a new burial was made in the same room.

Toward the end of September the Cosgroves began winding down their work at Swarts. Madeleine and Ted Kidder had finished their season at Pecos and after a night in Albuquerque they drove to the Mimbres where they spent a day or two àt Swarts Ruin, visiting with the Cosgroves and going over the season's work. When the Kidders left for Gallup, New Mexico, Hattie and Burt hauled their gear back to Silver City where it would be stored for the winter, and the pottery and other artifacts were packed into barrels to be shipped by railroad back to Cambridge. They closed up their house on Black Street with the intent of spending several months at Harvard working on the Swarts material and writing a formal report on their Mimbres work. Their last day at Swarts was October 3 and by the end of the month they were on a train to Cambridge.

At the Peabody Museum Hattie and Burt had an office in the basement, where they wrote and catalogued the Swarts artifacts. Hattie was now a legitimate employee of the museum, receiving a small salary each month independent of Burt's wages. Dozens of copies of their 1925 season's report, along with Burt's photographs and Hattie's Mimbres bowl drawings, were printed and bound to be sent off to subscribers. Hattie catalogued and mended pottery all through the long winter and on into late spring, but she soon discovered that her old formula of lemon juice, salt, and sun to bleach out the iron stains on the Mimbres bowls was ineffective in the gray and overcast winter skies of Massachusetts. A call on Harvard's Department of Chemistry resulted in a preparation of oxalic acid, which dissolved the stains and worked much more quickly than the old sun-bleaching method. Another technique that the Cosgroves used in preparing the pots for exhibition was a glue that had been developed during the war for cementing together thin layers of wood for airplane propellers. Known as Ambroid, this permanent, waterproof glue worked very well in the reconstruction of bowls, some of which were broken into nearly a hundred pieces.[11]

The 1926 season was delayed until midsummer, and taking advantage of the later start in the field, Burt Jr. joined his parents in Cambridge in May. They went on to visit New York and Washington, D.C., where they toured museums and other popular attractions. But by late June they were back in Silver City preparing their gear for another Mimbres expedition. One difficulty the Cosgroves had discovered in their Swarts excavations was the absence of any soft materials such as bone, wood, fiber, or feathers, objects that would have given them important information about the Mimbres people. Exposure to the elements had long ago obliterated traces of these objects, but it was very likely that a great deal of material probably still existed in the many dry, sheltered caves in the area. Accordingly, the Cosgroves planned a "reconnaissance" of caves in the Mimbres region, although this survey

Burt Jr. and Desdemona. Swarts Camp. 1925.

Burton assembling a broken bowl at Swarts Ruin. 1925.

was later extended past the Mimbres borders and included most of southwestern New Mexico, western Texas, and Oklahoma.

Fieldwork began at Swarts on July 1 and lasted until October 31. In their 1926 field notes, Burt noted that the labor force consisted of four men, himself, and two assistants, Burt Jr. and Hattie. Two of the workers were returning for their third season and had become extremely skilled at uncovering walls, floors, and the exceedingly delicate burials. Work began on the north roomblock and, as usual for Swarts, yielded a wealth of information and material. Near the end of the season Burt wrote a brief report for *Teocentli*, an informal archaeology newsletter, where he noted that "at times burials appear so rapidly below the floors of the rooms that it is strenuous work getting them record-

ed. This is forgotten when we can take breath for a moment and make guesses as to what the design will be in the bowl inverted over the skull. The guess may be wild but we are never disappointed in the beauty of design that is revealed when the bowl is lifted."[12] Two hundred thirty-one burials were recorded in the Cosgroves' third summer at Swarts. Kidder captured the sentiment precisely when he wrote in the Peabody's 1926 report to subscribers that work in the Mimbres "is without question the richest digging to be had in the Southwest."[13]

A brief note about *Teocentli* is warranted because of the role it played in facilitating informal communication among archaeologists beginning in the 1920s and continuing through today. *Teocentli* is a casual newsletter instigated in 1926 by Carl E. Guthe of the University of Michigan. The name came from the "native Mexican grass from which maize [corn] is supposed to have developed."[14] It was intended to provide information among archaeologists "who are working in various phases of those Indian cultures which came to owe their development to a knowledge of maize cultivation." Naturally, this group was comprised heavily of archaeologists working in the American Southwest, and because Burt's contribution was included in the first issue, it can be assumed that the Cosgroves were among the initial group of forty-five people invited to send contributions to the early issues. It is likely that Guthe knew the Cosgroves because he had worked with Kidder at Pecos and had earned his Ph.D. at Harvard, and both were places where he would have encountered Hattie and Burt. *Teocentli* was issued each June and December with contributors sending brief, nontechnical reports of their field and laboratory work, along with news of their travels, families, and other events in their lives. Guthe produced the newsletter for several decades, and his son, Alfred Guthe, gradually took over the responsibilities as the years went by. Burt sent brief reports to *Teocentli* regularly, commenting on the work that he and Hattie were doing on the Mimbres and adding notes about their travels, including their annual visits to Atchison to visit "the mothers."

In July Hattie and Burt investigated several caves just east of their camp. One was called Picture Cave because of the pictographs painted in red on the cave walls. Hattie made drawings of these images. Toward the end of the month Ted Kidder paid a visit to the camp and he and Burt, Burt Jr., and Harold Gladwin from the Gila Pueblo in Arizona made a brief trip to Greenwood Ceremonial Cave northwest of Silver City. The Cosgrove family had visited the shrine cave on several occasions, and even though it was well known among local people who had dug and collected at the site, the group of archaeologists was able to excavate a good deal of rare and perishable material, including pahos (prayer sticks or medicine sticks), painted wood tablitas, a complete bow and fragments of bows and arrows, cotton and yucca cord, reed cigarettes, and a cache of grass, buckskin, and yucca and cotton cord.

In August Burt and two workers spent ten days at the NAN Ranch Ruin with the permission of its owner, J. C. McElroy. The site is on the east side of the Mimbres River and three miles below Swarts. Burt excavated seven pueblo rooms similar to those at Swarts, as well as one exceptionally large room that yielded forty-seven subfloor burials. Plaster had been applied to the stone masonry walls, and there were no doorways, indicating that the rooms were entered by means of a ladder extended down through a hole in the roof. Two pithouse rooms were found under the floors of the later rooms. Altogether fifty-four burials were excavated at the NAN Ranch Ruin along with fifty bowls. In a child's burial that contained an unusually rich collection of artifacts, they discovered two large turquoise beads, two wing-shaped shell pendants, two small human figures about three inches high and carved of shell, and a pair of carved shell birds with turquoise inlay on the side.

Burt learned of another ruin just a mile south of the NAN Ranch site that had been heavily pothunted and was in danger of being destroyed. The McSherry Ranch Ruin was known to be an extreme-ly rich site, but it had been badly vandalized. Part of the ruin was fairly undisturbed as it was under a large pigpen, but the ruins mound was proving to be such a nuisance to the owner that he had plans to level the whole site. Hattie and Burt had all the work they could handle at Swarts, and there was not enough money to extend the excavations to McSherry, so with permission from the ranch owner, the Cosgroves contacted southwestern archaeologist Earl Morris, who had access to funding from the University of Colorado. Morris and his wife, Ann, arrived quickly with a team of workers and set up camp with the Cosgroves at Swarts. He excavated McSherry and several other small sites, including a small ruin just across the river from Swarts, and in the process recovered two hundred fine Mimbres bowls. In the Morris biography, *Digging in the Southwest*, Ann noted that Earl was so anxious to see the images on the bowls that had been excavated each day that they pieced them together every evening at the camp,

Burt and Hattie at the National Museum, Washington, D. C. 1925.

Hattie and Burt at Harvard University. May 1926.

rather than wait until they were back in the laboratory in Colorado. One of the remarkable bowls Morris found had a scene of a decapitation. Hattie made a drawing of this bowl, along with the rest of the bowls that Morris excavated before he took them back to the University of Colorado. Another interesting and important find was a string of little copper bells, which proved a trade contact with Mexico. The bells were strung with a cord made of milkweed fiber.[15]

In mid-August Burt left Hattie in charge at Swarts and took two men with him to investigate a cave with the hope of finding evidence of perishable Mimbres material. Doolittle Cave is located about four miles directly south of Swarts, eight miles by road, near Dwyer, New Mexico. The cave is forty-two feet long and thirty feet deep and had suffered greatly from years of casual digging. Large pieces of rock had fallen from the cave ceiling, and when these were removed a wealth of material was located in the area beneath them. The floor of the cave was dug to a depth of about five feet, and Burt and his workers unearthed thirty-nine sandals, basket fragments, bits of cotton cord and netting, three hundred pointed arrow foreshafts and ten large bow fragments, gourd rattles, pahos, stone and turquoise beads, and a painted wooden bird. Doolittle Cave showed very little evidence of occupancy, and Burt surmised that like many of the caves he and Hattie later explored in the Gila, it was a shrine or ceremonial cave. It is interesting to note that of the sandals recovered, all but

five or six were children's sandals. The greatest quantity of material found in the cave was traceable to the Mimbres culture, but there were a few items that indicated earlier Basketmaker occupation, including part of an atlatl, a piece of twined-woven cloth, and fragments of toe sandals.[16] In addition to certain caves that were thought to be shrines or ceremonial sites, springs in the Mimbres region were also recipients of ceremonial offerings such as beads, pipes, arrowheads, and miniature votive vessels.[17] While the role of the springs in the Mimbres society is not precisely known, it is rather obvious that in the arid Southwest, a permanent water source would be of great importance to any people living in the region whether they were prehistoric or contemporary.

In early September Eileen and Burrow Alves again drove up from El Paso to spend a night with Hattie and Burt in their camp at Swarts. Burrow never drove a car, but Eileen drove and maintained the Alves family automobile for all of her adult life. She was the one who drove them about on their camping and business trips throughout the Southwest. In her unpublished journals she notes the weather and road conditions on these frequent trips, as well as the mileage and often the amount of gasoline used. Frequent entries refer to tire punctures, broken shocks and belts, and long delays because of mud or washed-out roads. In her September 1926 entries, Eileen recorded that she and Burrow "visited Silver City, Central, Hurley and Santa Rita then drove via San Lorenzo to Cosgrove Camp-where we stayed. Rain in San Lorenzo & had a little trouble in mud." (Eileen also noted that on the way she was caught by a "speed cop" and fined $8.50.) The following day, Friday, September 10, they "spent day with Cosgroves digging in pueblo. They gave us piece of Mimbres pottery & other fine stones. Found some shard pieces in pueblo across river on hill." The following morning they left Swarts "at 20 to 7" and reached El Paso five hours later. On another occasion Eileen and Burrow Alves visited Hattie and Burt's camp and Eileen noted that they "Left Silver at 10 with load of Mimbres stone things." Although by today's standards it would be completely unheard of for an archaeologist to casually give away artifacts, in earlier times it was a fairly common practice, especially if the recipient was a major donor to a museum or archaeological expedition.

At the close of the season at Swarts in late October, Hattie and Burt had all their gear again hauled to Silver City for winter storage. For their own equipment they used their Buick, which had been pressed into service as an expedition vehicle. Behind it they towed a two-wheeled trailer piled with belongings. Once again they closed up their house in preparation for their return to Cambridge to work on the Mimbres material. In the closing lines of his 1926 report to subscribers, Ted Kidder gave very high praise when he wrote: "It is safe to say that no archaeological project of the Museum has ever been more efficiently or more economically conducted than the Mimbres excavations under the Cosgroves." He went on to note that "the expedition has produced really remarkable results, both in scientific data and in collections." His comments would be flattering to any archaeologist, but they are all the more noteworthy because they refer to two largely self-trained amateurs.[18]

In the early spring of 1927, Burton Jr. was working in Arizona at Casa Grande National Monument. Frank Pinkley was in charge of the monument, but Burt Jr., Ted Amsden, and Bill Felts worked under the direction of Harold Gladwin, who later founded Gila Pueblo but at that time worked for the Southwest Museum in Los Angeles. At the close of the work in Arizona, Burt Jr., Felts, and Bruce Bryan moved to Grant County to do some Mimbres work. In Silver City, Burt and Hattie met with a rancher who owned the Galaz Ruin on the Mimbres River near San Lorenzo. Through their influence they obtained permission for Burt Jr. to excavate the large Mimbres village near the Galaz ranch house. Burt Jr. worked there for one season, and although his parents had assisted in getting permission to rent the site for the Southwest Museum, it was probably also

Burt Jr. at Swarts Ruin. August 1926.

Swarts Ruin. Center of South House looking north. 1927.

Ted Amsden and Burt Jr. after a storm had blown down their tent.

Ted Amsden and Bill Felts. Breakfast. Burton's camp. Casa Grande, Arizona. March 1927.

helpful that Burt Jr. had formed a friendship earlier in school with the two Galaz sons, Alfredo and Gustavo. Burt Jr. began work at Galaz on May 1 and excavations continued through August 1, but he did not return for a second season. In 1928 the Cosgroves met with Mr. Galaz to discuss leasing the ruin for excavation by Peabody Museum, but the University of Minnesota had already contracted to continue the Galaz work under the direction of Albert Jenks.

The Peabody Museum's Mimbres Expedition began the fourth and last season at Swarts in June 1927 and continued for four months. Burt and Hattie had their usual summer crew, but they also had the assistance for part of the season of Karl Ruppert, a friend and associate of Kidder's through the Carnegie Institution of Washington. Ruppert was working on a long-term excavation project at Chichen Itza in Yucatan. He became a close friend of the Cosgroves after assisting them for part of the 1927 season in the Mimbres. When the Cosgroves began their digging at Swarts the only indication of the ruin was a low mound of dirt and stones from the pueblo wall foundations. Potsherds littered the site, and a few bleached bones from pothunter's holes gave clues to the abundant remains of the vanished culture just beneath the surface of the ground. Hattie and Burt's friend Ted Kidder had not been impressed with their choice of a site to begin excavations for the Peabody Museum, but in the end their judgment was rewarded through the wealth of finds and information that the Cosgroves produced in their four seasons of work at Swarts. In 1927 there were still forty rooms to excavate, and that work uncovered 176 of the beautiful Mimbres bowls and pots, in addition to hundreds of other artifacts. Because it was the only Mimbres village to be entirely excavated under scientific and professional guidance, Swarts has yielded the largest quantity of Mimbres bowls of any Mimbres site. Perhaps other Mimbres villages would have produced equally rich assemblages and archaeological information, but Swarts remains the only Mimbres village excavated "end to end" by professionals, and Ted Kidder's judgment in hiring the Cosgroves proved a wise choice.

On July 31, Hattie celebrated her fiftieth birthday at Swarts. Most likely, the Shadels Bakery purchase listed in their expense account sheets was for her birthday cake. Burt had celebrated his fiftysecond birthday two weeks earlier. And as they ate birthday cake at a folding camp table under one of the towering cottonwood trees that lined the Mimbres River (and as they had done for their past three birthdays) it must have seemed a most unlikely spot for a celebration for the lawyer and the hardware store heiress. But after a century of years between them, both the Cosgroves were reveling in their circumstances and loving every minute of their archaeological careers.

In August Burt and Hattie were invited by Ted Kidder to attend an informal gathering of southwestern archaeologists at Pecos, New Mexico. This historic and noteworthy meeting was the first of an annual series of conferences traditionally held at a site in the Southwest at the end of the summer field season. These Pecos Conferences have continued into the present day and have become valuable sessions where archaeologists can present the results of their current field work, meet other researchers, and informally share information, discuss problems, and generally disseminate knowledge of southwestern archaeology. In that first summer meeting in 1927 the archaeologists spent the first day touring Pecos and the nearby Forked Lightning Ruin, and the next two days were spent discussing archaeology of the Southwest and the work that was being conducted by the various participants. In the evening the group gathered around the campfire with their spouses and children to visit, gossip, and share stories of their adventures over the summer.

In his history of the Pecos Conference, Richard Woodbury commented that the most notable achievement of the 1927 Conference was the development of the Pecos Classification, a sort of time line of southwestern prehistory. This classification stood for many years, with modifications, as a framework for categorizing southwestern cultural developments. But the ongoing and enduring legacy of the Pecos Conference, "an archaeological force that changed the course of Southwestern archaeology," was in providing an opportunity for professionals and students to gather, share information, and generally to promote their profession.[19] Burt Cosgrove took a classic photograph of the participants of the 1927 conference that Hattie carefully saved and sent to her archaeologist friend Emil Haury many years later. This photograph is now in the photography archives of the Arizona State Museum, and a copy is displayed in the museum at the Pecos National Monument. There is also a second photo in which Burt and Emil changed places, and Emil took a picture with Burt standing in the picture at the far left. These photographs became

"Old Blue" and Alfred Kidder (Ted Kidder's oldest son). Pecos, New Mexico. 1927.

valuable not only because they recorded the participants of that first memorable Pecos Conference, but also because it was the first gathering of nearly every archaeologist working at that time in the Southwest, as well as of students who would continue to do very important work in archaeology.

Hattie and Burt returned to Swarts for another four weeks of fieldwork, but when they packed their Buick with their tents and gear, notebooks and artifacts at the end of September, they could not have known that their four years of laboratory and fieldwork would stand for decades, and perhaps forever, as the most complete study of a typical Mimbres site ever made. Other sites were partially excavated, but Swarts Ruin was the first, and only, Mimbres village to be completely excavated by trained archaeologists. They did plan to return to the Mimbres country to work on other village sites as soon as they finished their cave reconnaissance, but circumstances, most notably the Great Depression, intervened, and Hattie and Burt were never able to work again in the Mimbres villages that they so loved.

After the Cosgroves did their work at Swarts, time ran out on the Mimbres, and even though archaeologists today still study the field notes, collections, and reports of earlier excavations, and some go out into the field to conduct their own work, the years of vandalism and pothunting took their sad toll. From the

Ted Kidder at Pecos. 1927.

Conference at Pecos, New Mexico. August 28–30, 1927. The 1927 Pecos Conference was the first of an annual gathering of southwestern archaeologists that has continued into the present. Burt took this photo. Hattie is sitting at the far right side of the group.

local families who enjoyed the "skeleton picnics," to the professional pothunters who came with bulldozers, the lure of the beautiful Mimbres painted pottery was too great, and today there does not exist a single Mimbres site that has not suffered from the heedless digging. Entire sites have been completely bulldozed by pothunters, and others are pockmarked by dozens of holes left by illegal digging. It is a tragedy that the culture that created some of the greatest artistic expressions on the North American continent, may forever be one of the least understood. Sadly, the great beauty and artistry of the Mimbres people contributed to the unprecedented looting of their silent villages, and many secrets of their lives will remain an eternal mystery. But the extraordinary work of Hattie and Burt Cosgrove will always stand as one of the major attempts to explore and uncover the secrets of the ceremonial and daily life of the Mimbres. The treasures they dug for were not the painted bowls or other artifacts; they were searching for the information that would allow people today to understand the stories the long-dead Mimbres potters painted into the bowls, as well as the mysteries of the people who created and valued those unique stories in their works of art.

Burt and Hattie worked on their notes and collections for four years. *The Swarts Ruin: A Typical Mimbres Site in Southwestern New Mexico* was published in 1932 by the Peabody Museum of American Archaeology and Ethnology, Harvard University. Dr. Alfred Kidder wrote the introduction and William White Howells wrote an analysis of the skeletal remains. In the course of their four seasons of field work, the Cosgroves had excavated 172 rooms, 2 inner courtyards, a walled plaza, and the large dance plaza. They uncovered 1,009 burials, stone palettes and bowls, pestles, hundreds of metates and manos, axes, scrapers, flake knives, and projectile points. There were bone tools, thousands of bone, stone, and shell beads and pendants, turquoise beads and pendants, and, of course, nearly 1,000 of the treasured Mimbres bowls, jugs, ollas, pipes, and ladles. Hattie classified and catalogued many thousands of potsherds, and she drew detailed reproductions of hundreds of the painted bowls and sherds. Burt and Hattie were somewhat hampered at that time by a lack of historical information. A scientific chronology of the prehistoric Southwest was just in the process of being developed, and they chose to publish their information without delay to make it quickly available to other researchers, rather than attempt a premature classification. Another drawback was a lack of the modern advances in archaeological techniques and tools that have been discovered in the last few decades. Even tree-ring dating, a valuable and often used technique for dating archaeological sites in the Southwest, was just being developed and implemented at the close of the Cosgroves' work at Swarts. But in spite of these weaknesses, created essentially by the times in which they were laboring, the work of Hattie and Burt Cosgrove has stood well through the decades. Another publication that came out at the same time as their report was a folio of reproductions of the Mimbres bowls from the Swarts book. Each sheet in the folio had one pot with the artwork taken from the drawings that Hattie had made. The set of more than 100 images was a brisk seller for the Peabody Museum. In addition to being an important archaeological document, the set of Hattie's Mimbres bowl drawings was an important collection of art and an enduring testimony to Hattie's talent and her almost spiritual connection to the long-vanished Mimbres artists.

At the close of their work at Swarts, and after the camp had been dismantled, the equipment was put in storage, and the artifacts shipped East, Burt and Hattie spent just over a week excavating a cave near Las Cruces, New Mexico. For the Cosgroves, this short expedition was the start of a new chapter of digging in the Southwest. In the spring they had been told of a cave just a few miles northwest of Las Cruces. Jacobo Chavez had hired eight workers to spend a month digging for artifacts in the floor of a cave that was known locally as Chavez Cave. When Chavez met Burt he showed him a broken wooden object that he mistakenly

Peabody Museum, Harvard University, Cambridge, Massachusetts.

thought was a bow for a fiddle. Cosgrove was very excited when he recognized the spear-thrower, or atlatl, and several other Basketmaker objects.

When Hattie and Burt returned to Chavez Cave in early October, they located an undisturbed area of the floor and there they excavated a quantity of Basketmaker artifacts. After a week in the Las Cruces area, they went to the Hueco Mountains near El Paso, Texas, to search for caves in that district. Their old El Paso friend Eileen Alves had recently purchased a collection of objects taken from a cave by a local hunter, and she urged the Cosgroves to do cave surveys in the Hueco Mountains. Here they found three mummified burials, each body wrapped in a "fur-cloth blanket." In contrast to the later burials such as those found at Swarts Ruin, there was no pottery associated with these sites, but there were baskets, some containing grains. An October 18 entry in Eileen Alves's journal indicated that the group dug in the cave until midafternoon, and they found "rabbit sticks, sandals, apron & beads. Very successful."

These and other Basketmaker artifacts were startling finds for the Cosgroves. Most of the fragile and perishable cave material represented a much earlier people, and although the Basketmaker culture had been studied in southern Utah and northern Arizona, the cave material from the Gila country and the Hueco Mountains was the first

Burt Jr. and the Martin Bomber. Tucson, Arizona.

Hattie and Burt Jr., Tucson, Arizona. 1927.

Municipal Airport. Tucson, Arizona. Dedicated November 1, 1925. In 1928 Burt Jr. became the first director of the Tucson Airport.

evidence of the Basketmaker culture this far south. The Basketmaker people were first named by Richard Wetherill, who discovered many of the ruins and cliff dwellings at Mesa Verde in Colorado. It is a term that was used in the 1920s and 1930s but is not used today, as new data has changed dating sequences and their appropriate names. Wetherill noticed that much of the cultural remains below the pueblo material was of an earlier people. He called them "basketmakers" because of the finely woven baskets found in their caves; pottery making was unknown to them. The bow and arrow was not introduced to this area until later, and the people subsisted on the wild foods they were able to gather, as well as the game which they hunted with spears and atlatls.

With this new material the Cosgroves would be able to extend by many centuries the history of the early inhabitants of the Southwest, most notably in the Gila country. Except for writing a complete report, their work at Swarts was finished, but after their brief time at Chavez Cave and Hueco Tanks, they recognized that further work in the dry, sheltered caves of southwestern New Mexico and nearby areas would perhaps fill in the earliest parts of the mystery of the origins of the Mimbres peoples. When Burt and Hattie returned to Cambridge late that fall, they were already making plans to return in the spring to begin an extensive survey of caves and cliff shelters.

Cave #1, Middle Fork, Gila River. October 1928.

◄CLIMBING INTO CAVES►

After a winter of working at the Peabody Museum in Cambridge, Hattie and Burt planned to return to the Southwest to embark on their reconnaissance of caves. They would spend at least four months in the field, in what would be the most physically challenging work of their careers. In the June 1928 issue of *Teocentli*, Burt wrote from Cambridge, "I am leaving here within a day or so and am anxious to continue our investigations of caves in southern New Mexico, where last year we were so fortunate in discovering Basket Maker remains near Las Cruces. Our present plans are to browse around in the Gila National Forest and do some more work in the El Paso district where we also ran across our friends the Basket Makers." On the way west they stopped off in Atchison to visit their mothers and other relatives and old friends. Before going into the field, they

gave a stereopticon lecture to the members of the Southern New Mexico Historical and Archaeological Society in Las Cruces. The Cosgrove family albums contain many newspaper clippings reporting talks and slide shows Burt and Hattie gave from Silver City to Cambridge. People across the country were fascinated, as they are today, with their stories of digging up the fabulous Mimbres bowls.

Another stop they made on June 22, before they went into the Gila, was in San Lorenzo in the Mimbres River valley. Burt and Hattie had a meeting with Mr. Galaz to talk about leasing the Galaz Ruin for excavation by the Peabody Museum. Unfortunately, this project was never begun, most likely because the Great Depression put an end to most archaeological expeditions for several years, and although some work was done

Camp at Hueco Mountains, northeast of El Paso, Texas. July 1928.

Hattie at cave in Hueco Mountains. July 1928.

by other archaeologists, only a portion of this extremely large Classic Mimbres village was ever studied. The entire site was later plowed over, and today it is only a flattened terrace above the river. Passersby on the highway that runs alongside the ruin now see a herd of cattle quietly grazing in the field, and there is no trace of the grand Mimbres village that once existed there.

In their first season devoted entirely to cave exploration, the Cosgroves surveyed 104 caves and cliff house ruins. They began their season in the El Paso area, where many of the 42 caves they mapped and excavated had been located by Eileen Alves, who also helped with local introductions and practical arrangements for camping and hauling water and supplies. Two of the notable caves

they mapped were Picture Cave, named for the many red pictographs of figures, birds, and snakes painted on the walls, and Ceremonial Cave, which seemed to have been used as a shrine, as there was virtually no evidence of habitation. Most of the material excavated from the fill in the cave floor was ceremonial, including nearly one thousand worn yucca sandals. In his notes for the season's report, reprinted in the 1929 *Harvard Alumni Bulletin*, Burt remarked, "It makes one wonder what quirk of the Indian mind caused him to stop and say a prayer, set up a paho or two and with these offerings leave his worn out shoes."

In their field notes for the 1928 season, Burt and Hattie left a fairly complete daily journal of their work.[1] Burt made the working notes and Hattie typed them up in a report at the end of each day or when they returned to their main camp. Together they went over the notes and reports to clarify and write in details, and Hattie drew in pictures of artifacts, pictographs, or weaving details, as she did for the final published reports. These journals contain archaeological information as well as occasional informal entries about people and events. A July 7 entry reads, "While Mrs. Cosgrove made drawings of the pictographs the workman and myself looked into two caves near by but found no evidence of occupation in them." And later that day, "Mrs. Cosgrove and I investigated 5 caves above and east of camp."

The Cosgroves spent four weeks camping out in the hot, barren country of the Hueco Mountains and other cave areas northeast of El Paso. These low mountains are dry and rugged. *Hueco* is the Spanish word for "tanks," and the only natural water available in the area is that which has run off the rocks and collected in the natural basins in the rocks and crevices. Even with their experience with the arid conditions further north at Swarts, the Cosgroves found this summer work exceptionally difficult. The El Paso country is lower in elevation than the Mimbres, and the summer days were extremely hot and dry. It was exhausting, dirty work. The dry, powdery soil of the cave floor billowed up at the slightest disturbance. Mixed in the soil is bat guano, rat droppings, and masses of cactus carried into the cave by pack rats to protect their nests. In some places the rat droppings had cemented together the huge pack rat nests constructed of cactus, sticks, and debris. In addition, one always had to be on the lookout for rattlesnakes, which are plentiful in the Southwest and often enjoy the cool, dark shade of a cave on a scorching summer day. The Cosgroves found that a respirator, protective clothing, and heavy gloves were a necessity for cave work. After a long day in a cave or shelter, they dragged themselves back to camp looking as dirty and grimy as hard rock miners. Vernon Brook, a friend and member of the El Paso Archaeological Society, recalled that Hattie insisted on cleaning up every night. Water was scarce and had to be hauled in barrels from local wells to the camp, but Hattie would scrub and get herself clean with just a "teacup" of water.

On August 6 Hattie and Burt broke camp and packed to leave for Silver City. Fifteen miles east of Deming they had an accident and smashed their trailer and had to arrange to have all their gear hauled into town. Breakdowns and flat tires were not uncommon occurrences for the intrepid archaeologists as they traveled the backcountry. Car trouble and washed out or impassable roads are often mentioned in field notebooks or recorded in photos, and if Burt couldn't fix a problem they traveled with enough emergency gear to wait for help. Some family pictures show Burt changing a tire or digging the car out of mud or sand; others show Hattie setting up a shade awning from the side of the car as she prepared to wait for help to come along. The mishaps and adventures of traveling in the Southwest in the 1920s and 1930s were a not uncommon theme in archaeological notebooks, and in her classic book, *Digging in the Southwest*, Ann Axtell Morris devotes an entire chapter to that topic. In the section titled "Southwestern Road Song," she wrote: "When one is off the beaten track, just the sheer feat of going somewhere and triumphantly arriving there becomes of such cosmic significance that the mere reasons for

Jacinto Compos, Hattie, and Burt. Ceremonial Cave northeast of El Paso, Texas. July 1928. Face masks were a necessary protection from the fine dust that filled the air when a cave was excavated.

Ceremonial Cave, Hueco Mountains.

Hattie in Copperas Canyon, Grant County, New Mexico. September 25, 1928.

Cliff ruin in S. A. Canyon. September 1928.

doing it fade into an inconsequential background."[2] The Cosgroves certainly knew firsthand the problems she described, such as washed out bridges, sandy roads, "gluey 'dobe," and such impossibly long distances between towns that even spare cans of gasoline often proved inadequate.

Back in Silver City Burt and Hattie rented horses and pack mules to carry them into the Gila to do more cave explorations. Their expense accounts list the rent of a saddle at $1.00, three horses for six days at $18.00, and mules at $2.00 per day. Jacinto Campos was a local man who had worked with the Cosgroves at Swarts, and because of his growing expertise and appreciation for the ancient sites, he was also hired each season to assist in the cave work. They had already received a permit from the Department of Agriculture to carry out their work in the Gila National Forest, and they traveled to Cliff, New Mexico, northwest of Silver City, where they stayed a night or two at the Hooker Ranch. They then began exploring for more caves and shelters, which were plentiful in the remote canyons.

It was not easy work. In addition to the fact that there were long hikes and scrambles up steep, slippery talus slopes, the caves were often nearly inaccessible, and ladders had to be built on the spot to climb up into a cave. On one occasion Burt told of climbing up a tree and swinging across from a branch into the cave. Many caves would not have been accessible at all to the faint-of-heart. In September Burt wrote in their field book, "Mrs. Cosgrove, Jacinto and myself piloted by Mr. Fleming managed to get down into S.A. Canyon, using rope as an aid." This brief description does not mention that the canyon is hundreds of feet deep, narrow, and sheer-sided. Today's archaeologists often use technical rock-climbing equipment and even helicoptors to gain access to a cave. Hattie and Burt's adventures swinging from a rope belayed by a cowboy must have been thrilling and a little terrifying, and when they had finally gained access to the cave there were always the disagreeable aspects of cave work, the dust and bat and rodent droppings. In one cave the bat guano was more than five feet deep. It was strenuous and challenging work for any archaeologist, and the Cosgroves were not energetic young students—they were both in their fifties at the time. Cave explorations also involved many more weeks of packing and camping in the backcountry. In mid-August they noted, "Rained half the night. Makes camping cold and very disagreeable in this narrow canyon." But if the prehistoric Indians had used the caves for shrines or shelters, the early settlers and ranchers had also found them, no matter how remote, and dug for relics. On August 23 they recorded a lament common in all their work in the Mimbres area: "It is discouraging to see how things have been destroyed and trampled to pieces by ignorant relic hunters." Hattie and Burt cared deeply about the prehistoric cultures that they were investigating. Knowing that they were in a race against the elements and relic hunters, the hard physical work of exploring the caves, and the hardships of camping out for weeks at a time in all kinds of weather were the price they willingly paid to save the artifacts and information before it would all be lost forever.

After a trip back to Silver City to replenish supplies, Burt and Hattie spent two days exploring a canyon off Mogollon Creek and then headed for the San Francisco River country northwest of Silver City. Burt noted that it was all "volcanic and rough to travel over." They collected a great deal of cave material and mapped and surveyed several large caves. This was the furthest west they went in a secondary goal of their explorations, which was to establish the boundaries of the Mimbres country. They returned to Silver City a week later to restock their supplies once again before traveling up to the headwaters of the Gila River. They drove to the GOS Ranch on Sapillo Creek, where they left their car, paid $20.00 to have a truck haul their camp equipment to the trail head, and then went by horseback to Gila Hot Springs, deep in the wilderness at the confluence of the three forks of the Gila River. After establishing a main camp at the hot springs, they spent the next three

Gila Hot Springs. Starting for the Middle Fork of the Gila River. October 1, 1928. Juan, Jacinto Compos, Mrs. Leslie Fleming, Hattie, and Delbert George.

Hattie, Bobbie Fleming, and Jacinto Compos. TJ Ruin. Pueblo village ruin across Gila River from Heart Bar Ranch and below mouth of Middle Fork of Gila River. October 4, 1928.

Middle Fork of Gila River, cliff ruin #3 and #4. October 1928.

On inside west wall, cliff ruin #2. Inner wall plastered, animal figure painted in black. Middle Fork, Gila River.

Cliff dwelling #2, West Fork of Gila River.

weeks mapping ruins, exploring canyons, and excavating caves and shelters.

One of the major sites they explored and roughly mapped during the first week of October was TJ Ruin, across the river from the Heart Bar Ranch. The site is located on a terrace overlooking the Gila River near the confluence of the Middle and West Forks, and above the present-day Gila Cliff Dwellings National Monument Visitors Center. This huge Mimbres village at one time had buildings that were two stories high and would have contained about two hundred rooms, according to contemporary estimates. After making a collection of surface sherds, which represented pottery from all the surrounding districts, the Cosgroves noted in their field notebook that TJ Ruin should be completely excavated as "it appears to be the key and the finest example so far discovered in definitely determining the cultural relationship in this section." They again made a formal recommendation to study the site to the National Resources Board in 1934, but that course was never acted upon. Today TJ Ruin exists as nearly the only large unexcavated and almost pristine Mimbres site in southwestern New Mexico.

After some time spent at TJ Ruin, Hattie and Burt returned to their camp at Gila Hot Springs for one night before continuing their cave explorations in the West Fork of the Gila River. They excavated a cliff ruin just north of the caves that contain the impressive cliff houses of the Gila Cliff Dwellings National Monument but, strangely, did not conduct any explorations in the large dwellings themselves. In his history of the monument, Peter Russell surmises that because a major goal of their cave work was to gather archaeological information before it was lost through vandalism, perhaps they believed that the cliff dwellings were already receiving sufficient protection, and further work on their part could be redundant. But the excavation work that they did in Cave 6, a small shelter to the side of the Gila Cliff Dwellings was significant, because they established the presence of two occupations. Russell noted that, using the 1927

Pecos Conference Classification, "the Cosgroves were the first to record for Gila Cliff Dwellings two components, or distinct occupations, one of which was very early. This observation was only recognized in the adjoining caves years later and independently of their work."[3]

Burt and Hattie continued mapping caves and shelters in the West Fork and down along the Gila River to the mouth of the Sapillo, which is not accessible from the east because of an impassable box canyon, and several sites in Water Canyon. On October 15 they made the thirty-mile ride out of the Gila back to the GOS Ranch, concluding a grueling three-and-a-half-month-long season of field work in the dry and scorching deserts of southeast New Mexico and western Texas, and the remote canyons of the Gila. After packing up the quantities of cave artifacts and shipping them back to the Peabody Museum, Hattie and Burt took a few days of vacation to visit Burt Jr. in Tucson. Also in Arizona was Hattie's mother, Mrs. Harriet Silliman, who spent her winters at the Desert Sanatorium, located just a few miles east of Tucson. During the late 1920s, the Desert Sanatorium was advertised in newspapers nationally and internationally as a facility offering treatments for a wide range of medical problems and simply as a winter refuge for rest and relaxation. Most visitors came from the east coast and the clientele included wealthy and well-known people such as Gary Cooper, Ring Lardner, and General John J. Pershing. Another visitor was Mrs. Coats of the Coats and Clark Thread Company, who came from London with an entourage that included three of her own nurses. Today the facility still exists as the Tucson Medical Center, one of Tucson's largest hospitals, but the town has expanded and now surrounds the grounds of the former Desert Sanatorium.

Mrs. Silliman spent her winters at "the San" for many years, returning to her Atchison home each spring. Hattie and Burt were able to visit her there because Tucson is only a two-hundred-mile drive west from Silver City. Burt Jr. was still attending school at the University of Arizona, and it was through Mrs. Silliman that Burt Jr.'s passion for aviation was awakened. In spite of the influence of his parents and the seasons spent digging in the Southwest, he gave up a blossoming career in archaeology to pursue his love of flying. Mrs. Silliman indulged her grandson with the wildly extravagant gift of a fifteen-hundred-dollar airplane. The ninety-horsepower Curtiss "Jenny" was a World War I training biplane, purchased from a government surplus mail-order catalog and shipped to Tucson in the original military crates. It came with an instruction booklet for building and flying the machine, and Burt Jr. constructed the airplane and took off from a barren patch of desert southeast of town. He recalled a few frantic moments in those first flights, as he hurriedly flipped through the instruction book, searching for a bit of help. Burt Jr. went on to become the first manager of

Desert Sanatorium, Tucson, Arizona. Santa Catalina Mountains in background. October 1928.

Crossing the Savannah River to Stallings Island in bateaus. January 1929.

Workmen at Stallings Island. January and February 1929.

Starting trench across Stallings Island Mound.

the Tucson Airport and later flew for the air force; he had a distinguished career and retired as a colonel. Burt Jr.'s parents supported him in his career choice, but Hattie did confess to an occasional regret that he had not followed them into the field of work that they had so grown to love. Burt Jr. did work on one last project for the Laboratory of Anthropology in Santa Fe in 1934. Under the supervision of Harry P. Mera, he directed the excavation and stabilization of several sites at the Petrified Forest National Park in northeastern Arizona, including the Puerco Ruin and the Flattop Site. Burt also was responsible for the reconstruction of the Agate House in the Petrified Forest. This was an eight-room pueblo style building in which all of the walls were made of petrified wood (agate). But in spite of Burt Jr.'s obvious expertise and experience in the field of southwestern archaeology and years of working under the ground, the pull of the skies overhead proved a stronger attraction, and he never worked in archaeology again except for the occasional bit of work if he happened to be visiting his parents at one of their sites.

Perhaps through her grandson, Harriet Silliman was able to enjoy her own fascination with flying. She took her first airplane ride from Tucson to Phoenix and back to Tucson when she was in her early eighties, and an undated Tucson newspaper clipping from the early 1930s notes that Miss Amelia Earhart spent a day and a night with Mrs. Silliman at the Desert Sanatorium. The clipping reads: "Mrs. Silliman is an old friend of Miss Amelia Earhart's grandparents, the late Judge and Mrs. A. Otis, and of her mother, Mrs. Amy Otis Earhart. Miss Earhart who spent a day and night at the sanitarium spent much of her time with Mrs. Silliman asking about Atchison people she knows. Mrs. Silliman says the distinguished woman aviator is distinctly feminine and womanly with charming manners." Burt and Hattie also felt the lure of flying, and in the fall of 1928 they both took short flights over the Tucson skies in an airplane piloted by their twenty-two-year-old son. Before their visit was over, Burt Jr. flew them to San Diego for a few days at the ocean.

After the Cosgroves' return to Harvard, the Boston *Globe* reported on their summer work in a December 5 story: "SKELETONS THOUSANDS OF YEARS OLD DISCOVERED: Mr. and Mrs. Cosgrove of Peabody Museum Find Relics of Ancient People in New Mexico." The article covered the travels of the Cosgroves in the Gila National Forest and described "one of the most important discoveries" made during their season's work: "The discovery was made one afternoon by Mrs. Cosgrove as she sat, wearily, digging into the dust of a cave with the long trowel of the archeologist, waiting for her husband and his helper to complete their work. As she stirred the soil casually, little expecting to find anything, she dug up bits of fur cloth. She called her husband, and slowly they removed the dust of thousands of years. The man lay a dried skeleton in the debris of the cave, at his head the little skeleton of the child." The article goes on to describe the artifacts discovered in the caves, again lamenting the work of vandals who had dug in the caves and carried off the irreplaceable relics, and ends: "In the cellars of the Peabody Museum in trays, boxed and numbered, rest the traces of the past. Mr. and Mrs. Cosgrove plan to return next summer to the scenes of their labors."

The first months of 1929 brought an opportunity for archaeology of a very different sort for Hattie and Burt. William H. Claflin, treasurer of Harvard University and also an amateur archaeologist who later privately funded several archaeological expeditions, had long been interested in the shell mounds found in the Southeast. As a boy, he made several visits to the mound on Stallings Island in the Savannah River in Columbia County, Georgia, the first in 1906. In 1921 and again in 1924 he spent a week at the island, sinking test pits and trenches and doing a bit of general digging. The site had held a fascination for him for many years, but when an opportunity came to send an expedition to do a complete excavation, he invited the Cosgroves to conduct the investigations. They went to Augusta on December 28, 1928, and worked until March 1, 1929. With a crew of fourteen workers, they cut a sixty-foot-long trench across the face of the mound. Composed almost entirely of mussel shell deposits, the mound averaged a depth of four feet, but in some parts it reached nearly eight feet.

Digging in the damp Southeast was a great departure from the sort of climate and archaeology that Hattie and Burt were accustomed to. In great contrast to the arid Southwest, rain was an almost daily problem, and much time was lost because the wet conditions generally prohibited work on the site. They had a large crew, and each day they crossed the river in small, nearly flat rowboats called *bateaus*. The artifacts they uncovered were also of a very different sort and included burials, storage pits, hearths,

Sixty foot cut. Stallings Island Mound. View to east. 1929.

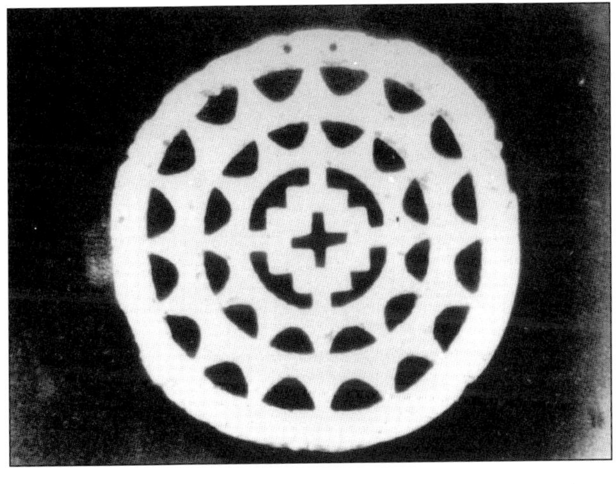

Shell gorget with skeleton #69. Stallings Island Mound.

Camp at Duck Creek, Grant County, New Mexico.
September 1929.

Painted ceremonial pahos from cave in canyon tributary
to Mule Creek Canyon.

shell beads and pendants, and a great quantity of unpainted, incised pottery. Claflin wrote a report of the excavations that was published in 1931 as one of a series of the papers of the Peabody Museum. Burt also wrote a brief report on a fragment of a trephined skull that was uncovered during the excavations at Stallings Island. Very few examples of this type of prehistoric surgery (in which a hole is drilled or cut into the skull) have been discovered in North America, but it is believed that this operation was sometimes performed to relieve head pain or to lessen the effects of epileptic siezures. In the case of the fragment of the Stallings Island skull, a section of bone aproximately thirty-eight milimeters in diameter was removed. The marks of the flint knife can be seen around the incision, as can signs of healing or cicatrization, although the adult patient obviously did not live for a very long time after the drastic primitive surgery.

There was also another crew member on the Stalling's Island expedition who eventually turned his interest to southeastern U.S. archaeology, perhaps in part because of his experience as a young man working with Hattie and Burt on the Stalling's Island project. Robert Wauchope had completed his first year of college when he was invited to spend a summer working for Ted Kidder at Pecos. He also attended the Pecos Conference in the summer of 1927, and although the Kidder children were the youngest people at the conference, Wachope was the youngest person with an interest in archaeology, according to Richard Woodbury, who wrote a history of the Pecos Conferences. The following year Wauchope worked with the Cosgroves in Georgia. After graduating from college as an English major, he entered Harvard to study archaeology. In later years he specialized in Mayan as well as southeastern U.S. archaeology.

The Cosgroves were back in Cambridge for the spring, continuing their work in their basement office at the Peabody Museum. Burt and Hattie were writing a formal report of their five seasons of work at Swarts Ruin, but with the growing body of material from the caves, they realized that a second report would be necessary to present all the findings of the earlier Basketmaker occupations and cave artifacts. After several months of work, the Cosgroves took off a few weeks from work in June to visit Samuel J. Guernsey, an associate at the museum who had spent several seasons with Ted Kidder in the Four Corners country. Hattie and Burt spent part of June with Guernsey and his family at their beach cottage in South Bristol, Maine. From there they started west by train, stopping in Atchison to visit their families and then continuing on to New Mexico and Silver City, where they got their car and other equipment out of storage in preparation to go into the field. For the past five seasons Burt and Hattie had used their own automobile for field work, but years of carrying heavy loads and bouncing about in the rugged backcountry had taken a toll on the little auto. So with Dr. Kidder's support, and a check from the museum, they made a visit to El Paso to purchase a much-needed Dodge three-quarter-ton truck. The commercial truck had wooden spoke wheels and chain-linked wire sides. Its rugged and heavy duty assembly served much better for the Cosgrove's backcountry work than their old passenger car.

On the first of August they picked up Jacinto Compos, a local resident who had worked with the Cosgroves for several years, and traveled northwest of Silver City to the area of Cliff, New Mexico, to make inquiries about local ruins. In the town of Gila, they met with Steve Villareal, who gave them permission to excavate a ruin on his ranch. But before work could begin, the summer "monsoon" rains arrived and they were held up in Silver City for nearly a week waiting for better weather. One of the goals of the excavations done in 1929 and 1930 was to establish the boundaries of the Mimbres frontiers. Consequently, much of the work they did that first summer was in the Gila River Valley, an area northwest of Silver City. Work began on the Villareal Ranch in mid-August. The site is on the east side of the Gila River, just a few miles north of Gila, New Mexico. The pueblo consisted of two main house blocks with adjoining rooms and walls constructed of coarse rubble from the round river cobbles. At one time the site was much larger, but a road had been cut through a portion of the ruin, and much of the eastern side was under cultivation. The sherds and pottery were mostly Mimbres, but there were a few examples of sherds from the Rio San Francisco.

After nearly a week at the Villareal Ruin, Burt and Hattie left Compos in charge, packed the material they had excavated up to that point and left for Silver City. From there they drove to Pecos, New Mexico, where Ted Kidder was hosting the Second Pecos Conference. Because Kidder did not work at Pecos in 1928, there was no conference the previous summer. However, there was so much new material being researched and with more than forty archaeological excavations being conducted that season in the Southwest, the time was very appropriate for another Pecos Conference.

Another development was the discovery of wood beams that would extend the chronology of tree-ring dating to a period of more than a thousand years. After many decades of meticulous work researching tree-ring samples, archaeologists had at last worked out a continuous chronology from the present to 1,200 years into the past. This meant that occupation dates of a site could be learned from the year when a tree was cut for a roof beam. Richard Woodbury wrote that

Buffalo pictograph at Pierce Ranch, east side of Alamo Mountains, Hidalgo County, New Mexico. 1930.

Cimarron Valley Caves, Cimarron County, Oklahoma. September 14, 1930. Uncle Billy Baker and family, also the Cosgroves.

Camp above Red Rock, New Mexico. October 19, 1930. Burt and Hattie.

Deep Indian petroglyphs in floor of cave. Saddle Mountain. Catron County, New Mexico. October 26, 1930.

it is hard to imagine the excitement that this breakthrough caused, but at the time it meant that many hundreds of ruins could be accurately dated to within a few years. This development was certain to be a major topic of discussion at the conference.[4]

An additional attraction were the air photos of numerous sites taken by Charles and Anne Lindbergh, who had spent a part of that summer in the Southwest. Lindbergh and Kidder became friends, sharing a mutual interest in archaeology. Kidder was very enthusiastic about the possibilities of aerial surveys to locate and map sites and collect data about water systems and an area's geography. Through his affiliation with the Carnegie Institution, Kidder arranged for Lindbergh to fly him over Mayan sites in the Yucatan in the fall of 1929.[5] Sadly, after the tragic kidnapping of the Lindberghs' baby two years later, Charles Lindbergh's priorities shifted away from archaeology. This ended his affiliation with the Carnegie Institution. Kidder's enthusiasm for the possibilities of incorporating aerial technologies with archaeology was ahead of its time, but it was typical of Kidder's foresight in bringing nontraditional people and technology together with archaeology to further that science. Lindbergh did have a strong interest in archaeology, which in different circumstances might have aided the discipline. But for a short time after his record-setting flight across the Atlantic, several southwestern archaeologists benefitted from his interest in their field and gave generations of their descendants colorful tales to relate about meeting an American hero in a remote southwestern canyon or ruin.

One favorite Cosgrove family story relates that one day when Hattie answered a a phone call, the caller identified himself as Charles Lindbergh. Like Ted Kidder, who had received a similar call from Lindbergh, Hattie was very disbelieving about the true identity of the caller. Kidder had answered, "Of course you are Lindbergh, and I'm Theodore Roosevelt." But the caller did prove to be Lindbergh, and Hattie's family teased her for some time over her reaction to what she had believed was a practical joke. Lindbergh and his wife, Anne, had recently flown over the Mimbres country and had taken a number of photographs showing ruins and other archaeological features that they wished to share with the Cosgroves. It is very likely that some of Lindbergh's Mimbres photographs were shown at the conference.

Of the nearly sixty participants at the 1929 conference, twenty-three had attended the first conference in 1927. Women were in a distinct minority at the second Pecos Conference. There were a dozen women, but half were spouses of archaeologists, although Ann Morris and Hattie were both known for their own contributions to southwestern archaeology. Three of the women were archaeology students from the Lab of Anthropology training program of which Kidder was a co-director, but clearly it was a male-dominated gathering. The weekend meeting was very informal, with most participants camping out in tents they brought along with them, and seating was generally just the ground or a bedroll. Madeleine Kidder did have a kitchen staff to feed the crew and the conference attendees, but Hattie and several of the other women always helped with food preparation. This was also a time for Hattie and Madeleine to visit and renew their long-standing friendship and catch up on their families' activities. The conference ended on a Saturday, and the following day the Cosgroves followed Wesley Bradfield home to Santa Fe, where they stayed the night. On that Sunday the Cosgroves and the Bradfields went out to visit San Ildefonso Pueblo. Sadly, Bradfield's promising career in archaeology was cut short just three months later by his sudden and early death.

On the drive back to Silver City the Cosgroves stopped to investigate a cave in Nogal Canyon, where they found pictographs and other evidence of prehistoric occupation. By Wednesday they were back in their camp on the Gila, where they opened a room block on the southern edge of the site. Here they found mostly San Francisco Valley ceramics, from which they surmised that there had been two cultures at the Villareal Ruin, the earlier being the Mimbres. On the second of September they finished their work in Gila and moved to Hill Top Ruin on Duck Creek about four miles northwest of Cliff, New Mexico. Ted Kidder had previously worked briefly at this site, where he also found evidence of two occupations. The earlier people had been Mimbres, and the later culture he called the Middle Gila Phase. In his excavations he found Classic Mimbres black-on-white sherds in the walls of the rooms of the later occupation and also under the floors. The Cosgroves' excavations also supported this theory of two distinct occupations.

The Cosgroves spent a week excavating Hill Top Ruin. Their 1929 field notebooks give detailed information on the daily work of the expedition, listing artifacts and features and including maps and drawings.[6] Burt kept much of the daily journals of each of their expeditions, and he included visitors and side trips and other interesting, but not necessarily archaeologically related, details. Hattie is always "Mrs. Cosgrove" in Burt's field journals, and she was always exploring and working alongside her husband. Partway through that project Burt was hit by a porcupine and he noted that he had to go into Silver City to see a doctor for treatment, but he was back on the job by noon. After completing the

No. 3 Langdon Place. Hattie and Burt. Cambridge, Massachusetts. 1930.

Yucca Plant—Playas Valley, New Mexico. H. S. C. October 1930.

Hattie. 10 Sacramento Street, Cambridge, Massachusetts. July 1931.

work on Duck Creek, they spent three days resting in Silver City before heading back into the field. On September 14 Burt left for Cliff, while Hattie stayed behind. He spent the night with a local rancher before going on to Mule Creek on the Arizona and New Mexico border. Burt had learned of a large ceremonial cave in the valley, and after hiring a guide and pack horses, he rode into the backcountry to search for the cave. Six miles into the rugged canyon they located the shrine cave and climbed down a two-hundred-foot cliff to reach the nearly inaccessible site. Although it had been badly dug by treasure hunters, Burt found hundreds of painted pahos and reed arrows. Mule Creek Cave is a large cavern with three main chambers. It had never been used for permanent occupation, but Burt surmised that it had been used as a shrine for centuries. He worked in the cave for five days, mapping and excavating. He uncovered ceremonial bows, hundreds of arrows, painted pahos, painted wood tablitas, cordage, sandals, and numerous other artifacts.

After finishing up at Mule Creek, Burt spent a day resting in Silver City before he and Hattie headed back to the Cliff area to do more explorations. They had planned to search for a sealed cave that was rumored to be in Utah Bill Canyon, but the Gila River was flooding, so they had to wait a day or two for the water to recede. They explored some small ruins in the area and mapped the large Woodrow Ruin on a bench above the Gila River, seven miles above Cliff. When the water in the river was passable, they set off once again. Ten miles above Cliff they had to leave their truck and pack up the Gila, following the riverbed and crossing the river forty-four times. They went up Hell's Canyon and crossed the ridge into Utah Bill Canyon after a long, hard day of bushwhacking through the rugged country. After all their hard work they found only some small shelters with a few artifacts. The "sealed" cave was only a natural depression in the side of the canyon that water had washed rocks into, giving it the appearance of masonry. After two days of exploring numerous small ruins and shelters, they came down the river and drove into Silver City at midnight, ending their sixth season of reconnaissance in southwestern New Mexico.

After half a dozen years of shuttling back and forth across the country, putting their belongings into storage and paying for caretakers and rent, Burt and Hattie decided to sell their house on Black Street. Their plan was to eventually find a house in Santa Fe that would be more accessible to the railroad and more convenient for travel. It would also put them closer to their many friends and professional associates who were also working in southwestern archaeology. They felt that they were somewhat out of touch living in Silver City, a long day's drive from Santa Fe. They did continue to rent a large flat in Cambridge at Number 3 Langdon Place, where their lodgings comprised an entire floor. But the end of the 1929 season was also the end of their twenty-two year residence in Silver City. They left their truck and camping and excavation gear in a garage in Silver City, but they put all their personal belongings into storage in Albuquerque, including their Mimbres collection from Treasure Hill, which was stored in a fireproof vault.

When Burt and Hattie left New Mexico that year they intended to settle in Santa Fe upon their return the following season. They continued to store their camp equipment in Silver City, planning to carry on their work in the Mimbres country. After settling the details, they went to Tucson for a visit with Burton Jr. and Mrs. Silliman, who was again residing at the Desert Sanatorium through the winter. But Hattie and Burt never relocated to a place in Santa Fe. With the onset of the Depression, funding for archaeology was drastically reduced, and many of the wealthy benefactors who had sponsored the expeditions were now unable to contribute. Burt and Hattie spent a few weeks in southwestern New Mexico the following year, and there was a brief expedition to the boot heel country in the extreme southwestern corner of the state in 1933, but the golden age of southwestern archaeology of the 1920s had come to an end. Very few universities and institutions had money to fund expeditions, and when the national economy began to recover in the mid 1930s, the world was facing another devastating international confrontation, which brought an end to virtually all archaeological work for nearly another decade. Hattie and Burt continued to work on their notes and collections and write reports, but after 1930 their work in the Mimbres country was essentially at an end.

In the fall of 1930 the Cosgroves made a six-week trip back to New Mexico to finish their work in establishing the boundaries of the Mimbres culture. In September they excavated a cave in the northwest corner of Cimarron County, twenty-six miles from Boise City, Oklahoma. Earlier in the year William E. Baker, the agricultural agent for Cimarron County, sent several specimens, including a dart foreshaft and a fragment of an atlatl, to Dr. Kidder. These artifacts came from a previously unexcavated cave and represented an eastern extension of Basketmaker cultural material. Burt and Hattie stopped in Boise City on their way to New Mexico, and with Mr. and Mrs. Baker they excavated a number of caves in the sandstone cliffs. From Boise City they drove down to El Paso and spent a day with Eileen Alves exploring the Hot Wells Ruin before continuing on to Silver City. From there they drove south to the Playas District in

Thanksgiving at A. V. Kidders. November 25, 1932. Deric Nusbaum, H. S. Cosgrove, Hulda Haury, Madeleine Kidder, Alfred Kidder, Emil Haury. Front row: Bob Wauchope, Jamie, Barbara, Dr. A. V. and Randolph Kidder, Harry Roberts.

Hattie at work in her Peabody
Museum office. June 1933.

Burton Jr. and Mildred Cosgrove. Married September
30, 1931. Tucson, Arizona. November 1931.

Hidalgo County in the southwestern corner of New Mexico, the boot heel country. Here they surveyed a number of ruins, made sherd collections, and mapped six caves, including Buffalo Cave, named for the eight-foot-long black pictograph that had been painted on the back wall of the cave. There were also a number of red-painted pictographs on the walls. Buffalo were not known in this country in historic times, but they occasionally roamed the extreme eastern portion of the state, and some relic populations of buffalo were present in southern New Mexico and northern Chihuahua, as bison bones were sometimes found in prehistoric archaeological sites. So it is not unlikely that a prehistoric wanderer or artist did see one of the unforgetable animals and recorded his impression of the beast for eternity on the wall of a cave in the barren playas country. Hattie made detailed renderings of the pictographs for their records; ultimately to be published in their cave survey report. But her drawings were more than just accurate reproductions for scientific records; her work had a unique artist's sensitivity. Kidder once referred to her drawings of cave specimens as "wonderfully beautiful."

From the dry playas region the Cosgroves went north to Red Rock, where the Gila River comes out of the high mountains and crosses the low desert country into Arizona. Here they surveyed a large village site, the Hulbert Ruin, on the bank of the river before going on into Silver City for a night and then continuing their reconnaissance northward along the western boundary of the state. In Catron County they explored a fortified cave near Saddle Mountain. The cave is nearly twenty feet above the base of the cliff, so a ladder was built from two pine trees to gain access to the ruin. Still, it took a bit of physical exertion and daring for Hattie and Burt to climb up the cliff face on the crudely improvised ladder. A masonry wall six to seven feet high ran across the front of the shelter with six windows or beam sockets (the Cosgroves called them "portholes") and a doorway on the east end. This cave was probably not used for habitation because the nearest water was more than a thousand feet below. But the Cosgroves felt that the presence of the wall indicated that it was a place of refuge as well as a shrine. In the floor of the cave, tracks of bears, turkeys, and humans as well as several trail-like patterns, had been carved.

Even though the weather began to turn cold, as it was nearing the end of October, and they often awoke to a layer of frost on their tent and equipment, the Cosgroves continued to search for caves that they had been told about by local ranchers and Mr. Steel, the government trapper. South of Brushy Mountain along Pueblo Creek, they surveyed another series of caves, and then rode on to the San Francisco River, where they located nearly another dozen caves. Most of the shelters and shrines had been vandalized in the past or had been mined for the guano deposits, but the Cosgroves were able to retrieve enough artifacts and information to determine cultural occupations. In their annual report to subscribers, they added a plea to the Peabody Museum to use its position to work through the channels to urge the forest rangers to be more vigilant in arresting pothunters and halting the terrible vandalism of caves and ruins. Heading back to the south, they stopped at the W. S. Ranch Ruin near Alma, New Mexico, where they made a sherd collection in the dump piles left behind from the diggings of pothunters. When Hattie and Burt arrived back in Silver City late on the night of October 31, they had completed a 1,356-mile reconnaissance of southwestern New Mexico. When they stored their camp material and packed the cave artifacts for shipment, they had no idea that it would be three long years before they would be able to go out into the field again. After a few days of visiting with the Bennetts and the Cosgroves in Silver City, they went to Arizona to see Burton Jr., who had taken the position as the first manager of the Tucson Municipal Airport. While in Tucson, the Cosgroves had dinner one evening with Byron Cummings, director of the Arizona State Museum and the University of Arizona's department of archaeology. Frank Roberts and his wife were also pre-

sent at the Cummings dinner. Roberts was a young southwestern archaeologist who had received his doctorate from Harvard a few years earlier. He knew Ted Kidder well and had met Burt and Hattie at the 1927 and 1929 Pecos Conferences. In a December letter to their old friend Neil M. Judd, the Cosgroves mentioned that they had met Judd's mother at the Cummings dinner. The highlight of the evening was the fried chicken, which tasted especially good to them after being out in camp for six weeks.[7] After their visit in Tucson, the Cosgroves returned by train to Cambridge.

Burton Jr. was married the following year, and he and his new bride, Mildred, spent a year's honeymoon in China. They had traveled to the Orient to visit a friend who was assigned by the American

The two Harriet Lovejoys—Silliman and Cosgrove. July 20, 1933.

J. B. Silliman residence, Atchison, Kansas. July 1933.

Southeast from Stewart Ruin on Cloverdale Creek, Animas Valley. Hidalgo County, New Mexico. November 15, 1933.

Ready to leave Lordsburg, New Mexico. Mrs. A. V. Kidder, Mrs. C. B. Cosgrove, C. B. Cosgrove Jr., Jimmie Kidder, Dr. A. V. Kidder, C. B. Cosgrove. October 13, 1933.

government to a position in Peking. His government-furnished home was in a large, walled compound with guest rooms, landscaped gardens, and a complete staff of servants. When he was recalled to the United States he invited Burt and Mildred to stay on as long as they wished because the house would otherwise be empty. The newlyweds stayed nearly a year. Because of the Great Depression, there was little chance of finding work in the States, and if they stayed on in Peking they could live rent-free in fairly luxurious surroundings. A friend of Burt Jr.'s let Burt use his Ford Trimotor airplane whenever he wished, and he taught Mildred how to fly. Mildred became a very competent pilot and often took sightseeing trips by herself in the airplane. Mildred Cosgrove had the distinction of being the first woman to pilot a plane in China.

Shortly after their return to the United States, Burt Jr. joined the air force and subsequently enjoyed a very distinguished and much-decorated career. Though he was sent by the military to many spots around the world, he always returned to his home base in New Mexico, and he always maintained close and loving ties with his parents. The family affection is apparent in a letter in the New Mexico State Archives written by Ted Kidder, visiting in Santa Fe, to his wife, Madeleine, on the occasion of his first meeting with the newest Mrs. Cosgrove. Ted wrote that he and Jesse Nusbaum went down to the De Vargas Hotel after Burt Jr. had telephoned that he was in town. He found Mildred to be very pleasant and "extremely nice-looking," but she "won my heart by her evident enthusiasm about Burt and Hattie."[8]

Back in Cambridge, Hattie and Burt began work on their cave survey, but still there was no chance of getting out in the field. Funds for archaeological expeditions had nearly dried up. Previously well-off subscribers sent regretful letters to Kidder telling of their own business troubles and explaining that it would likely be years before they would again be in a position to contribute funds to support archaeological expeditions. The Cosgroves were kept on at the Peabody

From left to right:
C. B. Cosgrove Jr., Big Boy Taylor, Dr. A. V. Kidder, Floyd Caldwell, Mrs. Kidder, Laddie Pendleton, Mrs. C. B. Cosgrove, Sam Snider, Mrs. Tom Pendleton, C. B. Cosgrove. Jimmie Kidder.

Museum, and in spite of their "amateur" status, their Swarts report, published in 1932, was garnering high praise. The museum also published the Swarts pottery folio. The folio contained individual sheets printed from the drawings that Hattie had done of every Mimbres bowl that had been excavated at Swarts Ruin. The printed sheets were reduced to about one-half the size of Hattie's original drawings, which generally had measured thirteen inches by fourteen inches. The folio collection came packaged in a stiff-boarded container with sides that folded up and across and tied with a ribbon. Many copies of the Swarts report were distributed to universities and museums, and in addition to positive reviews, the Cosgroves received many complimentary letters from their archaeologist friends. Ever their friend and champion, Ted Kidder, in a letter to Donald Scott, director of the Peabody Museum, expressed glowing approval of their work: "I was greatly encouraged by your interest in the Cosgroves and their work. They get through a most astonishing amount and it is all high class stuff from the technical side, such as mending, cataloguing, etc. to the working up of their report. And I have never seen better field notes. Also, they have good, sound (if not brilliant) minds."[9] The museum continued to fund about one-third of Burt and Hattie's salary, with the rest raised through

Pendleton Ruin to northeast, figures indicate extent of ruin. Cloverdale, New Mexico. October 1933.

Pendleton Ruin, to east. Rooms 3 to 10 along north side cleared to floors. November 1923.

Pendleton Ruin, to east. Cloverdale, New Mexico.

Mr. and Mrs. A. V. Kidder and Jimmie Kidder. Mr. and Mrs. C. B. Cosgrove.

increasingly vanishing contributions. Kidder was unceasing in his correspondence and contacts. He cheerfully called it "panhandling," managing each year to coax enough donations to continue the Cosgrove's employment and to fund many other museum projects. In the delightful, less formal language of the early years of archaeological work, Kidder wrote a hearty letter of thanks to a subscriber who had sent in a contribution commenting, "You are a brick to back this grave robbing job so consistently."[10]

The Cosgroves and the Kidders had a unique relationship. Kidder was their mentor and champion, but of course, over the years Hattie and Burt earned the well-deserved respect of Kidder and the archaeological community. The two families had a professional association that spanned much of their adult lives, but they also shared a deep personal friendship. Over the years they camped and worked together, gathered with their two families for Thanksgiving and Christmas holidays, and enjoyed a unique, supportive association. In Cambridge they often shared casual, family-style dinners. Kidder made many references to these evenings in his journals, where they discussed a little work and often talked of the Southwest. When Hattie could get some fresh blue corn meal, they enjoyed one of her "unequalled enchilada suppers."

The Southwest was deep in the blood and hearts of Kidder and the Cosgroves. Ted sometimes called it the "Southwest virus," even though he ended his work in that part of the world in 1933 and went on to work in the Mayan area. But Burt and Hattie always longed to get back into the field in the Southwest. They made inquiries about the possibility of working at Galaz or at the NAN Ranch Ruin, large Classic Mimbres village sites on the Mimbres River, in the event that money for an expedition could be raised. Many of their friends, such as Emil Haury, Kenneth Chapman, Neil Judd, and Earl Morris, were southwesternists, and while they worked in the East, the Cosgroves kept up a lively professional and social correspondence with many of them. And always, there was their well-founded concern for the state of the rapidly disappearing Mimbres sites. In correspondence with a friend in Silver City, Hattie wrote of the "sickening vandalism" in the Mimbres country and lamented at another time that with the "tremendous vandalism" going on in the area, "soon there will be nothing left to tell stories from." Burt sent in brief reports to *Teocentli* twice a year, which plainly illustrate his longing to be back in the field. In the June 1932 issue he wrote, "As to plans for a dig this season, we are living in hopes which may or may not materialize. There is no comfort in the fact that others are in the same boat." And in December, "Here's hoping…we may outlive these times and be able to burrow again into old Mother Earth for archaeological treasures." In the following year, as the era of Prohibition came to an end, Burt wrote to a friend that it was a shame that the museum couldn't go into the brewery business, for then they would surely have no problem raising funds for archaeology.

In 1933 another summer field season went by with Burt and Hattie working on their cave material at the Peabody. As disappointed as they were at being stuck in an office, they were both grateful for the work. Burt wrote in the June issue of *Teocentli* that he had hoped for field work, but "luckily there is museum work to do and I am happy not to be idle." But midway through the year some funds came in that opened the possibility of doing another session of work in the Southwest. In July while the Cosgroves were visiting their families in Atchison, they learned about the donations and that they would be able to return to work in New Mexico. In a letter to Donald Scott of the Peabody Museum Burt wrote, "My breath was nearly taken away when I received Dr. Kidder's letter. I see lots of work ahead and it is a joy to look forward to."[11] Not only would Hattie and Burt be working in the Southwest again, but their dear friends Ted and Madeleine Kidder were joining them for this expedition. The two families were very enthused about working together out in the field in New Mexico, and they spent many hours at the museum and evenings at their homes talking over plans for the trip. Burt

always preferred the Southwest to the East, and although he dutifully worked on the reports with Hattie, writing up their field notes and analyzing data in their basement office, he longed to be out West, excavating a prehistoric site. Digging was his first love, and through the Depression years it was an unending frustration that lack of funds kept him and Hattie far away in an office while the irreplaceable Mimbres villages continued to be looted and destroyed forever.

In 1930, while working on their cave reconnaissance, Burt and Hattie had located what appeared to be typical Chihuahua sites in the extreme southwest corner of New Mexico, the area known locally as the boot heel. This region promised to be extremely significant because it was at the southern limit of the Mimbres culture and the northern boundary of the Casas Grandes civilization, which extended down into Mexico. Hidalgo County was the center or the meeting point of several prehistoric groups. In a surface collection they had gathered El Paso polychrome and Chupadero black-on-white sherds from the east, Mimbres pottery from the north, and Salado and Hohokam wares from the west. It was hoped that an investigation in this area would answer many questions about the origins of various cultural

Burrow and Eileen Alves, Hattie and C. B. Cosgrove, Ted Kidder. Pendleton Ruin. October 23, 1933.

Burton Cosgrove Jr., Emil Haury, Hattie Cosgrove, Hulda Haury. Pendleton Ruin. November 26, 1933.

traits and determine the extent of influence and trade relations between some of these cultures.

In mid-October of 1933, Ted, Madeleine, and young Jimmy Kidder met Burt, Hattie, and Burton Jr. in Silver City to start off on their Hidalgo County Expedition. The work of the next few weeks would be the last that any of the expedition members would ever conduct in the Mimbres country, and for Kidder it would be his last excavation in the Southwest. It is curious that Kidder never came back to work in the Southwest because from the eloquent descriptions in his personal journals it is obvious that he had a deep love and appreciation for the barren, windswept country. Driving down to Silver City, on the oiled dirt road that would eventually become Interstate 25, he noted that there were almost no cars on the road, just an occasional cluster of adobe homes adorned with red strings of dried chilis, and he was "revelling in the great sweeps of barren country."[12] Kidder did not need green grass and trees to appreciate the beauty of the land. He felt the attraction of the open vistas of bear grass broken by an occasional oak or big-tree yucca. On October 12, the group traveled from Silver City to Lordsburg, where they spent their last night in a bed

and took their last real baths for almost two months at the Hidalgo Hotel.

The following morning the Expedition to Cloverdale, Hidalgo County, New Mexico, set off in two vehicles, the Cosgrove's Dodge truck and Kidder's "Pecos Blue," his expedition car, which had been a fixture for years at the Pecos excavations. They explored several likely sites, but their first choice of a site at the Timberlake Ranch proved to be impractical because there were no workers available for hire, since all the ranch hands were involved in a cattle roundup. The group continued south to Pendleton Ranch, nearly fifty miles south of Animas and just four or five miles east of Arizona and north of the Mexican border. The Pendletons were happy to rent their site to the Peabody scientists. In addition, Mrs. Pendleton agreed to cook for the expedition, and their young son, George, "Laddie," was hired as a laborer, along with three other ranch hands. Mrs. Pendleton was a fine cook; her steaks and enchilada dinners were later a favorite with the archaeologists, and they even enjoyed the venison from a white tail deer that George shot one Sunday. The group was often invited over to the Pendleton ranch house for an evening of cards. In spite of the great differences in their lifestyles, the Harvard archaeologists and the boot heel ranchers all got along very well.

From the very first days of digging there was an unspoken and growing feeling that the high hopes of great finds and new information on prehistoric cultures and trade and migration routes would not materialize at Pendleton. The site proved to be much later than originally thought, well after the Mimbres era. Although the digging was thorough, the site produced very little in the way of artifacts except for quantities of broken, unpainted, reddish brown sherds. Manos and metates were also found in great numbers, and the growing consensus was that the prehistoric inhabitants of Pendleton had abandoned the site, carrying off anything portable, while leaving behind the heavy stone grinding tools. One small consolation was that as the weather turned colder each day, these smoothed stones proved to be perfect bed warmers when heated in the fire and placed at the foot of a bedroll. Hattie even stitched up small flannel bags with drawstring closings to hold the stones. But Ted Kidder noted very early in his journal that the site was exceptionally barren of artifacts ("Don't believe this ruin is going to be worth a damn.") and several entries indicate that even though it would probably not produce any great finds, he wanted to continue the work. Because the Peabody Museum was arranging the funding for the Hidalgo Expedition, there was somewhat of an expectation, typical of that time, that a nice collection of artifacts suitable for eventual display was a proper return for the opportunity to do this work, and perhaps could even be the basis for future funding.

As the weather turned colder, the group set up tents for sleeping, one for working, and another for cooking. The winds were ferocious, and sometimes visibility was so poor from the blowing dust that work had to be halted, but if it wasn't too cold, it was often more comfortable to sleep out on the ground. The flapping of the canvas tents in the wind made sleep difficult and even tore huge rips in the tents. But if the blowing dust wasn't trial enough, there was sometimes

Pendleton Ruin, to east. Cloverdale, New Mexico. 1933.

Pendleton Ruin. Manos, rubbing stones, metates, and mortar.

Pendleton Ruin. Rubbed indented corrugated olla in fill of room.

Old Garcia Ranch at International Line, head of Animas Valley, New Mexico. Sierra Madre Mountains in background. November 15, 1933.

Half in and half out of the U. S. Mildred, Hattie, and Burton Jr. November 15, 1933.

wind combined with heavy rain or even sleet. One stormy night the wind blew so hard that the tent stakes pulled out of the wet ground and the tents collapsed. At three in the morning everyone was out in the freezing and dark rainy night resetting the stakes to hold up the tents.

Kidder was also bothered from the start with health troubles. At first it was an eye infection that kept him from much of the excavating, but soon a more serious illness developed. Kidder became extremely jaundiced, and a doctor in Douglas, Arizona, diagnosed that he had gallstones. The doctor prescribed some medicine and Kidder went back to Pendleton hoping to recover. But it was not an easy project. The winds continued night and day. The nights got colder and the campers often woke to find frost on their blankets and ice in their water buckets. Most evenings the group gathered in the cook tent around the little sheet metal stove. They played card games—little Jimmy especially loved a game of Salvo—Madeleine sewed, Burt read (sometimes it was a "thriller"), and Hattie typed up the day's work notes.

There are two small red notebooks in the Peabody Museum archives containing field notes from the Pendleton excavations. One book is a room-by-room accounting of data and materials located in each room. The other book is a daily diary of the expedition and includes a description of the work accomplished, visitors to the site, and visits and survey trips made by the expedition members. One area that especially fascinated them was "Shrine Flat," a site a few miles north of Pendleton. The shrines consisted of rocks piled into a round or oval shape with one or two pieces of quartz placed in the center of each shrine. The unusual site covered an area of about three acres.[13]

As remote as the Pendleton Ruin was in the 1930s—it was a long drive over ungraded and sometimes washed-out dirt roads—there were several who made the trip to tour the site or just to visit. Burton Jr. even had a friend who flew his airplane over from Tucson, landed next to the site, and stayed for lunch before flying back to Arizona. Mr. and Mrs. Harold Gladwin, who directed the excavations and research at Gila Pueblo, drove down from Globe, Arizona, in their Ford and spent a night. Jo Brew, a young Harvard archaeologist, came in Kidder's old 1923 Ford, "Pecos Black." Emil and Hulda Haury also came for a night. And of course, local residents came to visit and look over the work, but according to Kidder, they did not consider the distances too long; anyone within a radius of twenty miles was a neighbor. The ladies were invited several times to visit at the homes of local ranchers.

Another couple who came to visit were the Cosgroves' old friends from El Paso, R. B. and Eileen Alves. Mrs. Alves was perhaps the more unusual of the two, especially for her time. Kidder recorded that R. B. was a kindly, humorous gentleman, while Eileen was the one with the interest in archaeology; she organized and led the El Paso Archaeological Society for many years. Eileen's husband sold fine china and culinary supplies to hotels and restaurants. Eileen drove and maintained the automobiles that they used to drive about the Southwest on notoriously primitive roads, visiting ruins and Indian pueblos and on R. B.'s extensive selling trips. She was also fascinated with desert creatures and had filled her home with a collection of snakes, scorpions, gila monsters, and other exotic animals. One treasured Alves family heirloom is a table runner that Hattie made for Eileen. Around the edges of the cloth are embroidered snakes, lizards, turtles, yucca plants, cactus, and other plants and animals of the Southwest. Hattie designed and embroidered the original motifs knowing that her friend would appreciate the unusual embellishments. Hattie and Burt both held Eileen in fond regard, and when she left Pendleton, Burt made a gift to her of a beautiful and precisely crafted reproduction that he had made of a Basketmaker atlatl.

Like many archaeologists, Burt and his son were fascinated with the beauty and perfection of the ancient arrowheads, or projectile points, and other artifacts they found at most prehistoric ruins. These intriguing points are found in a marvelous variety of colors and minerals, ranging from glassy black obsidian to pinks, mustard yellows, light blue, greys, browns, the rusty red of jasper, and the clear or creamy white quartz. Many an evening the Cosgrove men sat around the fire knocking flakes off a core stone in an effort to learn the skills of the ancient flintnappers, an endeavor that often resulted in bruised or bleeding fingers when a strike was misdirected. Burt also developed a talent for creating other handcrafted artifacts, such as the atlatl he presented to Eileen Alves. He was especially good at crafting handmade bows and arrows and loved testing his skill and weapons on straw targets. Sadly, Hattie and Burt never saw Eileen Alves again. She passed away after that last visit, and her husband left El Paso and moved back to the East. Hattie's southwestern embroidered table runner was passed along to Eileen's adopted daughter, who cherishes it as a remembrance of her mother's interest in desert animals and archaeology.

Because of Kidder's health problems, Burt increasingly took over the direction of the excavation. Hattie and Madeleine washed and sorted sherds and reconstructed pots. When the winds weren't too strong, Hattie worked outside under an old brown umbrella, washing and then acid-cleaning the pottery. All water had to be hauled to the site so it always had to be used sparingly, which made work more difficult for Hattie and Madeleine. Things definitely improved when a used fifty-gallon gasoline drum was found for holding water. Burt and Burton directed most work at the site, with Burt Sr. photographing rooms and features. Hattie wrote up the field notes, making typed copies each night, and everyone worked on the 3"-x-5" field cards that were made for each artifact found during the excavations. Hattie also sketched potsherds, rims, artifacts, and various features of the ruin. Before Ted became too ill to work, they were a compatible group of old friends who worked well together and enjoyed the time spent in each other's company. Burt constructed a flagpole, and with a dedication ceremony they raised a United States flag and a Peabody Museum flag. They

christened their site Camp Kidgrove. But Kidder did not recover from his jaundice. Finally, three weeks after the group had cheerfully set off from Silver City, Ted, Madeleine and Jimmy left for Santa Fe, where they could stay with their old friends the Nusbaums and Ted could get treatment for his gallstones.

The Cosgroves stayed at Pendleton for another four weeks to complete the excavations. Burt's wife, Mildred, arrived in early November just before the Kidders left to spend some time at the camp, although Kidder noted that the beautiful and stylish Mrs. Cosgrove did not look like a "campy sort of person." But the site continued to produce few artifacts and little information. They dug more than thirty rooms and partially excavated over fifty more. Only six burials were located, so what was done with the dead remained a mystery. Ted Kidder did not return to Pendleton, although Madeleine and Jimmy returned for a few days in early December while Ted went on to Gila Pueblo in Globe, Arizona. The Cosgroves finished at the site in the first week of December, returning to Silver City to put their truck and camping equipment into storage, paying four dollars per month to the Abrahams Garage. A letter from Kidder to Donald Scott at the Peabody gave very high praise to the Cosgroves and told how "magnificently" they had carried on the work at Pendleton. Kidder went on to comment that although the site was interesting, "our rosy expectations of good museum material were bitterly disappointed. I have seldom seen a more barren site, as far as specimens for museum display are concerned. This has worried me a good deal, as I had hoped to turn in a dandy collection to recompense, in small degree, the Museum for letting us have the Cosgroves. Without them the whole thing would have been a perfect flop."[14]

Ironically, the expedition that had begun with the highest expectations ended in many respects with the greatest failures. Occupation of the site proved to be too late to reveal the hoped for information about southwestern prehistoric cultures and trade routes. Pendleton Ruin is now dated at post-1300 A. D., well after the height of the Classic Mimbres phase, and it is a northern "outlier" of Casas Grandes, rather than a southern extension of Mimbres. As noted, the site failed to yield any exciting or unusual artifacts for the museum. And of course, the opportunity for the two families to camp and work together in their beloved southwestern state of New Mexico was marred by the freezing nights and furious winds and by Kidder's illness. Even the planned early report faced obstacles. In an admirable effort to publish a timely report of the Pendleton Ruin, Burt and Hattie wrote an introduction in August, before they went into the field, hoping to shave a bit of the writing time off the finished report. Unfortunately, circumstances intervened and it was more than fifteen years before the report of the Pendleton Ruin was published.

W. C. Roberts trading store, Hopi reservation. Jeddito, Arizona.

◀ AWATOVI EXCAVATIONS ▶
Sherds and Sand-Dune Skiing

During the fall of 1933, and before they met the Kidders to begin the Pendleton work, Hattie and Burt spent several weeks in Las Cruces, New Mexico, in order to sell several pieces of property that had been in Burt's family since the early years when his father, Con Cosgrove, had the mail and freighting business between Santa Fe, Mesilla, and Tucson, Arizona. Burt was acting as attorney in his family's business dealings, and while he did have his modest income from his work at Peabody (and Hattie's inheritance from Blish, Mize, and Silliman), he also supported his widowed mother, Amanda Bennett Cosgrove, now in her nineties and living in Atchison, Kansas, along with Burt's unmarried sister, Kitty. The income from the sale of any properties and possessions would be a very important supplement to the meager incomes of the pair of women.

Consequently, Burt approached Jesse Nusbaum, director of the Laboratory of Anthropology in Santa Fe, about selling the two Navajo blankets that had been given to his mother and sister nearly sixty years earlier by Governor W. F. M. Arney. Nusbaum felt that the addition of the "Governor Arney" blankets to the lab's collection was a high priority. The larger blanket, which had been presented to Mrs. Amanda Cosgrove, had a sage green striped background, which was extremely rare. Nusbaum felt that it was one of the two or three most important blankets that the lab had come across in several years. It was in perfect condition, and he referred to it as a "gem piece." The unusual color and the blanket's unique and datable history made it a very desirable acquisition for the museum. In a March 20, 1934, letter to a patron of the lab, Nusbaum noted, "We know of no

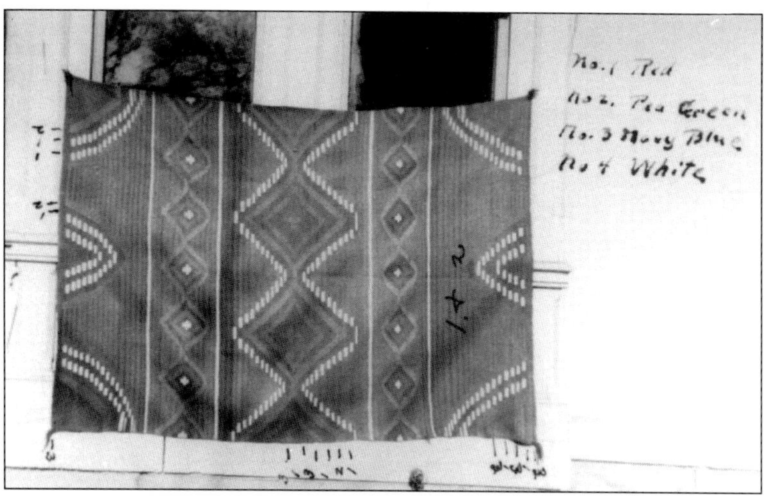

"Governor W. F. M. Arney blankets." Labeling in the photo margin indicates that the colors in the blanket are: No. 1 Red, No. 2 Pea Green, No. 3 Navy Blue, and No. 4 White.

other blanket in any collection of this type of color combination, nor are any blankets in better state of preservation." Burt wrote Nusbaum that because of their personal friendship, and his professional association with the lab, he wished he were in a position to just make a gift of the pair of Navajo weavings, but because of his mother and sister's financial circumstances he hoped that the laboratory could locate some funds to purchase them. Initially, Burt asked for fifteen hundred dollars for the pair of blankets, but when Nusbaum found a donor to put up the funds, the selling price was settled at eight hundred dollars, and the sale was made on July 28, 1934. Nusbaum knew that the blankets had been treasured possessions in the Cosgrove family for sixty years, but he also knew that Burt was selling property in Las Cruces in order to pay the taxes and that he needed cash. The money for the blankets came from Mrs. Frances Stewart, a wealthy patron of the lab with a strong interest in Indian textiles. The two Governor Arney blankets are still in the collection of the Laboratory of Anthropology, along with a few other artifacts from various locations that the Cosgroves donated at about the same time. Nusbaum was a friend of Burt and Hattie, but the low selling price of the blankets, at a time when Burt was trying to raise funds to save the family properties and support his elderly mother and sister, opened a rift in the friendship that was never healed.

While Burt and Hattie returned to their office in the Peabody Museum, after spending the Christmas holidays in Silver City, Burt Jr. found temporary employment with the Laboratory of Anthropology. As the assistant of Dr. Harry Mera, an old friend of the Cosgroves, Burt Jr. worked at the Petrified Forest National Monument in Arizona. Hattie and Burt now had all the new material from Pendleton Ruin to sort and catalogue, in addition to writing their report on the extensive information from the caves of the Gila. In the middle of May the Cosgroves took a month off from their writing and cataloguing to drive out to Atchison to visit their "aged mothers." Their western route took them through Pennsylvania, and on their return they traveled through Kentucky, West Virginia, and Washington, D.C. As Burt reported in the June 1934, *Teocentli*, they also stopped along the way for visits with several southwestern archaeologist friends, including Walter Hough, Neil Judd, Frank Roberts, and Frank Setzler.

Another friend with whom the Cosgroves corresponded and kept close ties was Emil Haury. It is likely that Burt and Hattie first met Haury at the first Pecos Conference in 1927, and as with the Kidders, that early meeting began a life-long friendship based on mutual regard and their deeply shared interest in southwestern archaeology. In the 1930s, Haury worked extensively in the Mimbres country, and he eventually became well known for his work defining Mogollon Culture, which included the prehistoric Mimbres people. Perhaps another link in their friendship is that all three of them were Kansas natives. Surviving correspondence between Haury and the Cosgroves, archived at the Arizona State Museum, first begins in 1931 and ends with Emil's last surviving letter to Hattie in 1967. Hulda Penner, who also attended the 1927 Pecos Conference and was another Kansas native, became Emil's wife the following year and was included in the enduring friendship. Much of their early correspondence is professional, with Emil inquiring about aspects of Mimbres sites, such as notched stones, "grass rubbed" pottery, mica as a temper in pottery, or the identity of an owner of a particular Mimbres site. But in the early 1930s, while working as a staff member of the Gila Pueblo in Globe, Arizona, Emil took a leave of absence to earn a Ph.D. at Harvard University, where he became better acquainted with Hattie and Burt. In spite of the rather large difference in their ages (Hattie and Burt were nearly three decades older than the Haurys), the two couples became close friends during those Cambridge years, and whenever the Haurys returned east to visit, they were always invited to stay with the Cosgroves.

Emil was promoted to the position of assistant director of Gila Pueblo in the spring of 1934, and he stayed with Burt and Hattie when he returned to Harvard later that year to take his final exams. Much of their correspondence was eventually of a more personal nature, such as the letters mentioned between Hulda and Hattie later that summer, with the news that the Haurys were expecting their first child. Unfortunately, most of those informal, personal communications, especially those between Hulda and Hattie, were not saved, but even in the more formal exchanges, which were a mix of archaeology and news of people in their field, there is a definite sense of the affection shared by the two couples. The Cosgroves did not do any field work in 1935, but the following year they were offered an opportunity to work in Arizona, and they immediately contacted Emil at the Gila Pueblo to tell him of their plans to make a detour to visit the Haurys while on their way to their new site. On June 1, 1936, Burt wrote that they would pick up their truck in Silver City, and rather than head straight up to northern Arizona, he and Hattie planned to head west first to visit the Gila Pueblo and Snaketown, the famous Hohokam site where Emil worked for many seasons. Burt then added, "Of course we are not interested in Mr. and Mrs. but we do want to see that boy, so please tell the authorities that some undesirables will appear in their neighborhood for a days visit sometime after the middle of July."[1] Emil Haury went on to have a distinguished career in archaeology, serving as head of the Department of Anthropology at the University of Arizona for twenty-

C. B. Cosgrove,
Castle Island, Boston,
Massachusetts.
May 1934.

nine years and concurrently as director of the Arizona State Museum for twenty-eight years. Though the Haurys and Cosgroves were separated by the distances between their homes and work and the differences in their ages, their mutual respect and enduring friendship lasted throughout their lives.

The great opportunity to work again in the Southwest came in the mid-1930s when three wealthy supporters of the Peabody Museum offered to organize and finance an expedition to dig at the famous Hopi site of Awatovi. In addition to serving as director of the Peabody Museum, Donald Scott was the owner of a large publishing business in New York City. Later in his life he returned to the academic world to study anthropology, and about that time he developed a strong interest in the American Southwest. Raymond Emerson was a friend of Scott's who had partially financed an expedition that conducted several years of survey and excavations in eastern Utah. William H. Claflin was a broker and owner of varied businesses, including a sugar plantation in Cuba. In his later years he was treasurer of Harvard University, and he had a lifelong interest in archaeology. In addition to being a friend of the Cosgroves, he had provided the financial backing for their earlier work at Stallings Island. Claflin had made many trips to the Hopi country over the years and had visited Awatovi

Pueblo Grande Museum and Ruins. Phoenix, Arizona. 1936. On the drive from Silver City to Awatovi, Burt and Hattie stopped in Phoenix to visit Old Halseth, curator at Pueblo Grande Ruins.

Camp at Awatovi. A corner of Hattie's cactus garden can be seen in the open area between the tents. Photo courtesy of Jenny L. Adams.

Ruin several times. He also maintained friendly ties with several Hopi families, which was later an asset in locating workers and obtaining the necessary permits for digging. Hattie and Burt had also made at least one visit to the site in 1923, when they had taken one of their summer motoring trips, stopping along the way to visit at various excavations. Other archaeologists, such as Fewkes, Russell, Hough, Kidder, Gladwin, and Morris had taken short field trips to Awatovi. There was great interest in the area because of its many sites and the unique blend of cultures and peoples who had come to the area over the centuries.[2] Because of Claflin's association with the Hopi and their country, and because of the long inhabitation of Awatovi and its unique historic record, the site was chosen by Claflin, Scott, and Emerson as the area to be studied.

Awatovi was an abandoned Hopi village site located on what is now the Hopi reservation in northeastern Arizona. The large ruin at the southwestern edge of Antelope Mesa covers many acres and was inhabited for about five hundred years until violent confrontation brought its history to an end in A. D. 1700. In 1629, a small group of Franciscan priests had arrived at Awatovi and established a mission, eventually building a large church known as San Bernardo de Aguatubi. The Awatovi church was a mission, one of many that formed the primary influence of Europeans (Spaniards) on southwestern native cultures for the first one and a half centuries of European colonialization. Smaller churches were later built in other villages, but Awatovi had the largest church and the largest group of converts following the religion of the Spanish Franciscan priests. Traditional Hopi leaders viewed this spread of foreign ways and beliefs with alarm and feared that if the priests were not stopped it would lead to the demise of Hopi culture. In 1680 the Hopi and other pueblo people in northern New Mexico drove the Spanish out of Arizona and New Mexico. This violent uprising was known as the Pueblo Revolt. The Spanish priests and explorers returned twelve years later and resettled Awatovi, but the Hopi

Al Lancaster at Awatovi. Photo courtesy of Jenny L. Adams.

would not let them extend their influence any further west. Seventy years after their initial arrival, the Spanish priests, along with many of their converts, were murdered during a second uprising of traditional Hopi and their leaders in 1700. The church was destroyed and the entire village site was abandoned for the next two centuries until the arrival of the Peabody Museum's Awatovi Expedition.

The first year of work in 1935 was a small reconnaissance to map and test excavate the area. In charge of the expedition was a young Harvard graduate student who often worked under Ted Kidder, John Otis (Jo) Brew. Jo had previously worked on other southwestern projects funded by Claflin and the Peabody and later in his notable career would serve nearly twenty years as director of the Peabody Museum. Second in command was Al Lancaster, a Colorado farmer with a remarkable instinct for uncovering the mysteries of a prehistoric

The small side altars were later additions to the San Bernadino Mission church at Awatovi.

Baptismal font of church.

site. Like Burt and Hattie, Al had no formal archaeological training, but he had worked at Lowry Ruin for the Field Museum in Chicago and with Jo Brew at Alkali Ridge. He also went on to have an outstanding career in archaeology, which included many years of work at Mesa Verde in Colorado. But for much of his life, in spite of his brilliant work in southwestern archaeology, he had to deal with the handicap of being a self-taught archaeologist in a field that was becoming increasingly professional. One example of this was the friction that arose over Al's formal title on the Awatovi staff. Brew felt that Al should be officially known as assistant director of the Awatovi Expedition. Out in the field, Brew saw that Al had a special feel for archaeology and an instinct for reading a site that sometimes went beyond the reach of a formal education. Al shouldered a great deal of responsibility at Awatovi, both in the excavations and also in the general business of running the camp. But Donald Scott, with his more privileged and traditional background, could not agree to give such a prestigious title to a poorly educated farmer who completely lacked university and archaeological training. Scott believed a more appropriate title would be assistant to the director. This small but symbolic conflict existed between Brew and Scott for the entire five years of the Awatovi Expedition, but in the end Jo Brew prevailed, and Al was listed as assistant director in all the Awatovi publications, a small but significant step toward recognizing the high quality of the work Al did at Awatovi.

Strangely, this lack of education and professional training did not hamper Burt and Hattie. Burt, of course, had a university degree, although his was in law, but Hattie had no college experience at all, and the respect that she commanded as a ceramic specialist is especially remarkable because she worked in an age when it was believed that ceramics held the key to dating and unraveling the mysteries of vanished civilizations. In any archaeological expedition, the accuracy and professional level of her work would have been a vital and pivotal component of the project. Clearly, Hattie's experience and skills were highly respected and a valuable contribution to each project she worked on. An additional hurdle for Al Lancaster that did not seem to hinder Hattie and Burt, was that many of the professional archaeologists were easterners, often wealthy, who came from backgrounds and environments that were extremely different from his rough and somewhat frontier-oriented upbringing. This clash between the perceived aloof and privileged manner of the easterners and the easygoing, casual style of the westerners often created a barrier when the two came together out on the southwestern excavations. Al took to Hattie and Burt immediately because in spite of their Harvard and eastern affiliations, they were New Mexico people, and their meeting at Awatovi began a lifelong friendship.[3] Indeed, Hattie and Burt were two of the few people who successfully straddled the two worlds of East and West at a time when the differences between the two were much greater than today.

It should be remembered that the

Southwest in the 1930s was a vast and sparsely settled country, and, especially on the Hopi and Navajo Reservations in the Four Corners region, communication was difficult and roads were often little more than wagon tracks wandering across windswept mesas and down through rocky arroyos. The differences between East and West, between the people and their landscapes, would have been magnified to the small group of workers of the Awatovi Expedition. In his delightful book *West of the Thirties*, anthropologist Edward T. Hall, writing of the years during the mid-1930s when he worked on the Navajo and Hopi reservations, described the unique character of the country, recalling that it was the "last gasp of the nineteenth century." It was still "frontier." Surely Al Lancaster was not the only one in camp who keenly felt the differences among the group of Hopis, eastern scientists, and a few westerners who worked at Awatovi.

Another important member of the team was Lindsay Thompson, a Mormon from southern Utah, who served the vital role of cook to the archaeologists. Every day Lin prepared volumes of food for the many project workers and for the carloads of scientists and visitors who arrived to look over the site, although sometimes Hattie had to cajole him into agreeing to cook extra portions for the often unannounced visitors. The noon meal was generally a hearty serving of roast beef, potatoes, vegetables, gravy, biscuits, and beans. The noon dessert was pie, and reconstituted milk was served at each meal. But Lin's speciality was hotcakes, served every morning, half a dozen for each person, with an unspoken message that consuming any less than that number was an insult to the cook.

After a few weeks of work in the fall of 1935, the expedition members returned in early August the following year to begin the four-year work of excavating Awatovi. The vision of the organizers was that the project would extend for several seasons and would encompass scientists from many disciplines, including botanists, ceramic specialists, geologists, architects, and other interested scholars. Indeed, people with varied scientific or casual interests were welcomed at the site, and Awatovi was the last and culminating expedition of a golden era of southwestern archaeological expeditions. Over the five years of its existence there was a stream of visitors, scientists, and tourists, including movie stars, Indians, aviators, graduate students, wealthy easterners, and artists. Unlike many of today's sparsely funded archaeological digs, Awatovi's backers were relatively

An Awatovi crew party in the pottery tent. Hattie is seated on a chair to the left side of the photo. On the table is the slide projector that Mott Davis and Carlos Garcia-Robiou created with a battery, an automobile light bulb, and a nail in a bowl of saltwater. Photo courtesy of Jenny L. Adams.

Luke and Vivian Kawanyousi relaxing in the pottery tent. Photo courtesy of Jenny L. Adams.

San Bernadino Mission. Altar. Stairway at right was built later. (Hattie's photo captions use an earlier version of the mission's name. San Bernardo is the correct spelling.)

generous in providing for the needs of the expedition. Perhaps many of the amenities they provided, such as a full-time cook, would not have seemed luxurious to them. But beyond the needs of the staff, meals and hospitality were provided for a multitude of people in numbers that would severely strain the budget of a contemporary archaeological expedition. Hattie's guest book stands as evidence that over the five seasons of Awatovi's existence, seldom a day went by that did not include providing meals and even lodging for carloads of visitors. It was also a time when spouses, children, and other relatives were welcomed at an excavation. Burt Jr. went everywhere with his parents, and Ted Kidder's wife and five children spent all of their summers at Pecos. Madeleine Kidder's ceramic work at Pecos was an important contribution to the Pecos studies, but unlike Hattie, Madeleine never aspired to a full-time career in archaeology, and while she assisted at most of Ted's excavations, she did not work at the Peabody Museum when the family was at home in Cambridge. Nevertheless, it was not uncommon at the time for spouses to come along on an expediton and to join in the work, shouldering much responsibility, and often making a real contribution to an expedition. It was also not uncommon for younger siblings or the older children of eastern friends to be welcomed at Awatovi for some length of time. William Claflin provided substantial funds for the Awatovi excavations, and his three children, Helen, Kitty, and William Jr., spent part of several seasons working at the dig. Everyone seemed to be welcomed and most everyone pitched in with the work whether they were trained in archaeology or not.

Hattie and Burt were invited to join the excavation when the expanded second season began in August 1936. In his delightful, privately published memoirs entitled *One Man's Archaeology*, Watson Smith, who joined the project later the first season, wrote that the Cosgroves were the "elder counselors" of the expedition. Officially, Burt was excavation supervisor and Hattie was field supervisor of pottery analysis (Smith refers to

Hattie at work in the pottery tent. Over the four years that she worked at Awatovi, Hattie supervised the sorting, cleaning, and cataloguing of a half-million potsherds. Photo by Carlos Garcia-Robiou. Photo courtesy of Evelyn Nimmo Brew.

her as "chatelaine of the pottery tent"), but privately, among the expedition's organizers, there was a feeling that while Brew was an excellent archaeologist, he was still young and relatively inexperienced to run an excavation of this size. Therefore the older and more experienced Cosgroves would also function as senior advisors. Other specialists joined the crew over the next four years, and the working group generally numbered ten to twenty people, although at times it swelled to more than thirty. In addition to that group, there were between ten and sixteen Hopi laborers who did much of the excavating and one or two who helped Hattie in the pottery tent.

Hattie's secondary, but equally important, duty was as camp hostess. She maintainted a guest book for the next

Awatovi
August 8, 1936

Mr. Donald Scott
Peabody Museum
Cambridge, Mass.

Dear Mr. Scott,

Here I am very comfortably settled in my new quarters. Being the only woman in camp I seem to be a sort of privileged one for my house was the first to be erected after the temporary quarters were set up. The first two nights Burt and I slept in our truck bed so they did not have to put up a temporary tent for us. I chose the site for my house for I thought that after they had had a man's camp for the past years they might find it inconvenient to have a woman in their midst. [Several of the Awatovi crew members had worked on Peabody expeditions in previous years.] I thought it best all way around for our tent to be slightly apart from the general row of quarters and am glad we did so for it has worked out splendidly. Every one seems better satisfied. The work of camp building is going on well though it naturally is slower to build house tents than to put up a pegged-down tent. It is the only thing possible here though for the sand is soft and deep and we would soon be buried in it if we did not have floors.

I have been cook since noon yesterday as Joe [Jo Brew] took the cook in to Holbrook to buy a new stove. The little stove he has been cooking on is too small for this sized camp. He is such a wonder that he deserves good equipment. His food is delicious, not the camp food we have always been used to having. I had only Burt and Al Lancaster to cook for so it was not very strenuous work. We think Al is such a fine fellow, such a worker and so pleasant to have around. We are expecting Joe back tonight and he is bringing Mr. Wheeler with him. The roads have been so bad every where that plans often go astray. Such bad floods in all directions. We have not had enough rain here to interfer in any way. Most of the storms have gone around us. This has been the hottest day since we arrived, the sort that burns right into one. We find we are pretty "soft" having been housed up so long.

Our vacation trip was very satisfactory and we have saved a few days of the vacation time to stop off to see the son again and my mother on our return but of course everyone was away. Mrs Haury took us over to the Pueblo so we could see the place and we gathered what information was possible with everyone away-very little I'll admit. From there we started for Montezuma Castle and Montezuma Well. After passing through Roosevelt Dam we blew out a cylinder head gasket and had to stay in Payson all night and phone back to Globe to have another sent out on the mail stage the next day. It was a good place to be held up for it is right on top of the mountain, such a peaceful cool place. We spent one night in Flagstaff, going out to the museum the next morning. The Coltons have every reason to be proud of what they have done. After seeing the museum we went to call on Dr. Colton at his office, which as you may know is not at the museum but at his home place. I tried to absorb their pottery types but it is very bewildering. However, I feel that after we get to handling the pottery here it will come easier.

From Flagstaff we went to the Canyon for a day (Burt's first glimpse of the Canyon) and then on to Tuba City where we were held up from afternoon till next day by bad flood in the Moencopi Wash. While stranded there we met Dr. and Mrs. Loomis of Amherst. He has the geology of the Park Service outfit. We enjoyed them so much for it helped pass the time while stranded. You may remember that their son, Fritz, helped me mend Mimbres pottery for a while a couple of years ago. As we came out of Tuba City that Sunday morn we stopped at Moencopi and saw part of the Cow Dance. It was very colorful and fine we thought. We felt lucky to have been stranded at that time for we have seen so few of the Indian dances.

The road from Moencopi to Keams Canyon was one big jolt; fortunately no mud, only the aftermath of it with ruts and bumps. In Keams Canyon we followed a big rain and the newly built road was one lob-lolly of mud. We slid all the way in, all ditches running full. We had no trouble getting to Jeddito from there and we found a welcome at the Roberts. They are such fine people. Mrs. Roberts insisted that we stay with them till Joe came instead of making camp as we had intended to. Mr. Roberts was in Holbrook and in trying to get home that night he had to sit at the side of a flood ditch until morn Joe and his men came in that afternoon too late to get to camp that night so spent the second night with the Roberts.

So that is the story of our progress here and we begin to feel very much at home now.

We are looking forward to your being here sometime later on. The Claflins are due before another week passes I believe. By then work will be started at the ruin I imagine. This camp building takes time but it is necessry time spent.

The only news we have heard from the museum seems to be of the matrimonial nature. Dr. Tozzer's remark that the museum is getting to be a matrimonial bureau seems to be holding good. He said that when Mary and Alfie [Kidder] were married.

Burt joins me in best wishes.
Hattie S. Cosgrove

Hattie Cosgrove to Donald Scott. Letter courtesy of Harvard University, Peabody Museum, Donald Scott Papers.

four years of work at Awatovi, greeted newcomers, and made sure that there was adequate food and lodging for them. Hattie also had her little folding box Kodak camera, very ancient, well used, and patched with adhesive tape, with which she recorded many of the visitors and other scenes of life about the camp. Her collection of informal photos now at the Peabody Museum is the most complete photographic record of daily life at Awatovi.

Burt and Hattie were thrilled at the prospect of working in the Southwest again. They had been at the museum for three years without a hope of field work, and the opportunity to go to Awatovi was a bit of long-dreamed-of good fortune. Burt's enthusiasm about the Awatovi project shows plainly in his June submission to *Teocentli* when he wrote, "Am delighted to report that this summer the Cosgroves are to be on the staff with Jo Brew at Peabody's Awatovi dig. Three years is a long time not to wield a pick and trowel with the Southwest always calling." That July Burt celebrated his sixty-first birthday on July 15 and Hattie turned fifty-nine on July 31. They took the train to Albuquerque and then traveled south to Silver City to get their Dodge truck and camping gear out of storage. Then they traveled west to Globe, Arizona, where they visited Hulda Haury (Emil was working out in the field) and toured the Gila Pueblo. From there the road took them north to Flagstaff, where they saw the Museum of Nothern Arizona and then called on Dr. Harold Colton at his home and office. After leaving Flagstaff, Hattie and Burt spent a day at the Grand Canyon and then drove northeast to Tuba City, where they were held up for a day because of an impassable flood in Moencopi Wash. From Tuba City to Keams Canyon, Hattie noted that the road was "one big jolt," but fortunately, it was fairly dry—just the huge ruts from the previous rain to contend with. But from Keams Canyon to Jeddito it was one "lob-lolly of mud" and they "slid all the way in."

The expedition camp was set up about one-half mile east of Awatovi in a low area, which gave some protection from the winds. The Hopi crew members set up their tents a bit apart from the main camp. Each Hopi group had a large army tent, and as the workers were always equally divided between residents of First and Second Mesa, the young men generally shared the tent with others from their own village. The crew worked Monday through Friday afternoon, when the Hopi workers went home to their villages, returning to Awatovi on Sunday evening. The young men had no transportation; they ran the entire distance each Friday and Sunday, about fifteen miles each way.

Lin Thompson's cook shack was of board-and-tar-paper construction and contained two tables that seated about twenty people. There was no water at the camp site, but Al built a cement cistern to store water, which was hauled from a spring about a mile north in Tallahogan Canyon. This name comes from a Navajo word meaning "singing house," a reference to the Awatovi mission church. A gasoline generator supplied power to the camp. Next to the cook shack was Hattie's pottery tent, which was larger than the sleeping tents and served as the gathering area for evening talks and card games. The walls were lined with bins that held wooden apple crates. These crates could be filled with potsherds at the ruin and carried back to the pottery tent and placed in a bin along the wall until Hattie was able to begin the sorting and washing. Long tables in the center of the tent provided work areas. Al designed and built the bins and sherd carriers with apple crates he brought from Cortez, Colorado, and it was under his practical direction that most of the camp was constructed.[4] With the aid of a Hopi workman, Evans Poleahla, who worked under her supervision for all four years, and sometimes a student, Hattie washed, sorted, and catalogued half a million sherds. Sherds were boxed at the ruin, separated by room and level, and brought back to the pottery tent for study. Hattie recorded everything in her notebooks, washed, counted, and sorted the sherds, and selected which would be bagged and returned to Peabody for further study and possible reconstruction,

Cornelius Burton Cosgrove
1875—1936

and which would be reburied in a trench behind the tent. Evelyn Nimmo, a student who came to Awatovi in 1938, recalled that the pottery bags all had linen tags because mice would eat any paper left about.

The thirteen tents that made up the encampment were arranged about a central plaza with a circle drive and a cactus garden, planted and maintained by Hattie. The canvas-walled sleeping tents were erected over wooden plank floors, each tent measuring nine feet by twelve feet. Each tent had one or two metal cots, a washstand and water pitcher and basin. When the weather turned cold, small sheet-metal stoves were set up in each tent, and Hattie cut and hemmed openings for the stove pipes. There were Navajo rugs on the floors and nails on the wooden tent frames to hang clothing. The camp was built over the summer, and when excavations formally began on August 3, there was great optimism at the prospect of several seasons of well-funded excavations and scientific testing. A carefully chosen group had been brought together, and there was great enthusiasm about the future. For some, like Burt and Hattie, there was joy at being able to "burrow again into old Mother Earth." They were back again in their beloved Southwest, and perhaps it was even a sign that the Great Depression was finally coming to an end. But the optimism was not to last long. Before the first season ended a dreadful tragedy struck the camp.

Digging began at the western edge of the ruin, at what was suspected to be the oldest part of the site. A mound at the cliff edge rose twenty-five feet above the bedrock, and as this area was excavated rooms were exposed, with the newest habitation being near the top layers and the earliest occupation at the deepest level. Pottery found in the fill of these rooms helped to date the habitation sequence. Potsherds were placed in the boxes, separated by rooms and levels, and then carried back to camp. Hattie then washed and sorted the sherds for tabulation. The enormous work this involved becomes clear in the ceramic charts Hattie kept. By the middle of the season 80,000 potsherds had been tabulated, and some days as many as 5,000 sherds were brought to the pottery tent. Records were kept of the sherds from every room with vertical records in fifty-centimeter blocks. In the 131 rooms that were excavated that season, 440 levels were recorded.[5] In addition to excavating the rooms in the western mound, the expedition also dug three kivas and eighteen test sites. The consensus was that there was evidence of habitation in the area on a continuum from Basketmaker times to the present, a span of two thousand years or more.

Work proceeded for the next three months, and as October ended and the weather started its turn to winter, the sucessful season began to draw to a close. Mr. and Mrs. Donald Scott had come out from Cambridge to see how the work was progressing, and Burt Jr. got a leave from his post in Albuquerque to take a short weekend visit with his parents. At that time Burt Jr. was a military officer serving as district adjutant. He oversaw about thirty Civilian Conservation Corps camps in the area. It was after dinner on the Sunday afternoon of October 25 when Burt Sr. began to complain of stomach pains. When it became apparent that he needed medical attention, Hattie and Burt Jr. drove him to the BIA hospital at Keams Canyon about eight miles away. Burt was cared for by a doctor, and his pain seemed to subside. When Hattie was assured that he was recovering from the attack, she agreed to leave Burt in the hospital overnight for observation. Burt Jr. drove her back to Awatovi and then had to leave because he had to report back for duty in Albuquerque the next morning. But shortly after he left, an Indian rider arrived from the hospital with the unexpected and horrifying news that Burt had suddenly taken a turn for the worse and died of a heart attack shortly after they had left. Al was the one who went to Hattie to tell her of the tragic turn of events.

Hattie got through the next few hours with an outpouring of help from her friends and coworkers at camp. Jo Brew tried to get a message to Burt Jr. before he reached Gallup, but Burt did

Letter from Hattie to her friends at Awatovi, written from the Clark Hotel in Silver City two weeks after Burt's death. Letter courtesy of Harvard University, Peabody Museum, Awatovi Expedition, J.O. Brew Records, Folder, "Awatovi Staff—Cosgrove."

not learn of his father's death until he arrived at the base in Albuquerque. The Scotts helped Hattie make arrangements to take Burt back to Atchison, but their location made it a very difficult process. There were great distances to travel over dirt roads that were often washed out, and telephone service was nearly nonexistent. But with the help of people at Awatovi, Hattie took Burt's body to Winslow and boarded the eastbound train. Burton Jr. and Mildred met the train in Albuquerque and the somber little group journeyed to Atchison, where Hattie buried her beloved husband. Hattie and Burt had been married for thirty-five years. In addition to having a warm and loving relationship, they had been working partners out on their excavations, packing into wilderness areas, exploring remote canyons, and spending hours together in their Peabody office sorting artifacts and writing their reports. With Burt's death, Hattie lost more than a husband; she lost her life's companion and soulmate. It was a loss that would ease a little with time but would forever leave a void in her life.

After Burt's death Hattie was left with much unfinished work and many legal responsibilities. Their Swarts report had been published four years earlier, but they had never finished writing up the material from the Gila cave survey and the Pendleton site. Additionally, Burt did not leave a will, and there were many details to attend to before his estate could be settled. He did not leave much financially, but Hattie had always been able to count on a fair amount of money from her share of the Blish, Mize, and Silliman hardware business. It was a small comfort to know that with her family money and her small Peabody salary she would not be in financial distress. Burt's mother, Amanda, had died in Atchison a year earlier at the age of ninety-six, and her estate had never been completely settled. This was an additional responsibility that Hattie shouldered. There was also Kitty Cosgrove to consider. She had always lived with her mother, and now Hattie planned to continue to help her seventy-year-old sister-in-law financially and in any other way she was able.

After a short stay in Atchison, Hattie went to Silver City to begin probate, and she also began the huge task of writing thank-you notes to the many people who had sent flowers and letters of sympathy. In a letter to Jo Brew, Hattie wrote that the florist in Atchison told her that in twenty years of business he had never had so many orders to fill for a funeral. The telegrams had come from across the entire country. Hattie also mentioned that she had nearly one hundred thank-you letters to write, but she especially wanted everyone at the camp at Awatovi to know how deeply she appreciated the outpouring of love and thoughtfulness in the hours after Burt's death and in deciding on the many arrangements that had to be made. Hattie got right to work because it helped her get through the days, but she confided to Jo that the nights were difficult and she had a great deal of trouble sleeping since Burt's passing.[6] She had many arrangements and decisions to make in Silver City and Atchison, but she planned to spend the holidays with

Burton and Mildred in Albuquerque and then return to Cambridge soon after the first of the year. Mr. Scott had assured Hattie that he hoped she would return to Awatovi the following season, and that was a special comfort to Hattie, because she felt so close to her old friends at camp, and like most archaeologists, she was always happiest out in the field. Indeed, Hattie's close friendships with the crew at Awatovi and with a great many archaeologists across the country probably derived from the casual intimacy of living and camping together for days and weeks out at some remote site. There is a closeness that comes from spending twenty-four hours together outside, eating every meal together, and sharing evening talks in front of a flickering campfire. These people shared her love of the Southwest and her fascination for digging in the ground. In many respects they were as close as any family. Donald Scott must have known that even though Hattie was still in the dark abyss of grief, it was still a great comfort and a reason to go on to know that there would be another season of field work for her.

When the December 1936 issue of *Teocentli* was sent out just a month after Burt's passing, it contained an obituary written by Carl Guthe that is not only a tribute to Burt, but also to Hattie and to the exemplary work that they had conducted and reported as a devoted and hard-working team. In words that conveyed not only respect and regret, but also a remarkable warmth and affection, Guthe noted that: "The Cosgrove name will always be linked with the Mimbres culture. Their kindliness and unfailing good nature made them ever welcome companions in the field and the laboratory. Their scientific enthusiasm and attitude won the respect of their co-workers. They were a real archaeological team. We shall miss Burt Cosgrove as a friend and a colleague. Yet our loss is small compared to that sustained by Mrs. Cosgrove. So we record here our sympathetic understanding and our best wishes for her success in carrying on the good work."

One other bit of unfinished work was to find a good repository for the Treasure Hill collection. Hattie and Burt had always intended to donate it to the Museum of New Mexico, but after their dealings with the sale of the "Governor Arney blankets," the Cosgroves did not feel that Santa Fe was the right place for their collection. Perhaps because of the Depression and the fact that Nusbaum falsely believed that the Cosgroves were living on the "ragged edge," he felt that the museum could purchase the blankets for about half of Burt's asking price. But the fact was that the money was not for Burt at all; it was for his mother and sister. Hattie had always kept a low profile about her inheritance and very few people knew that she actually came from a wealthy background and had a substantial inheritance. She and Burt always lived so modestly that no one suspected that they survived on more than their small salaries from the Peabody Museum. They were unhappy about the sale of the blankets because they had always been very friendly with people from the museum, and for twenty years they had been members of the Santa Fe Archaeological Society, an affiliate of the Museum of New Mexico and the Laboratory of Anthropology.

Hattie and Burt always believed that they would return to the Mimbres

On September 5, 1937, Father Victor Rose Stoner held a service in the ruins of the mission church. Hattie is seated second from the right, wearing her work clothes and, in honor of the solemn occasion, a formal black hat.

Five of the Dennis brothers from Second Mesa worked on the Awatovi crew. They are from left to right: Elwood, Leland, Emery, Chester, and Alec. Photo courtesy of Jenny L. Adams.

Everett Dennis and wagon. Photo courtesy of Jenny L. Adams.

country and finish their work at Treasure Hill. They had a great deal of writing to finish back in Cambridge, and with the Depression going on it was nearly impossible to get out in the field. But they both believed that an opportunity to do more excavations at Treasure Hill was coming in the not-too-distant future. They were very concerned about the tremendous looting going on at Mimbres sites, so their land was posted and friends kept watch on the ruin while they were away. But in an attitude typical of their time, they felt that they had done too little work at the site to even begin to write a report. Today it is common practice among archaeologists to leave part of a site untouched for future excavations. With the many scientific advances, it is believed that new technologies will always be coming along that will unlock even greater secrets of prehistoric cultures. But in Hattie's time a ruin was not complete until a site had been dug from one end to the other, so there was much unfinished work for them to conduct at Treasure Hill.

With Burt's death Hattie realized that it was very unlikely that she would be returning to work in Grant County, and even though she was looking forward to another season in the field, without Burt alongside her it would have been too painful to return to their special ruin in the Mimbres country. After discussing with Burton and Mildred that Thanksgiving the matter of where to place the Treasure Hill material, Hattie wrote to her old friends Mary and Harold Colton in Flagstaff, Arizona, to ask if they would be interested in taking the collection for the Museum of Northern Arizona. Dr. Harold S. Colton was originally a marine biologist and professor of zoology at the University of Pennsylvania. His wife and son both had health problems and the family moved to Arizona in 1926 with the hope that the drier climate would be beneficial. After settling in Flagstaff, Harold became interested in the many ruins of the prehistoric cultures in the area, and his artist wife, Mary, discovered the rich heritage and beautiful artworks of the nearby Indian groups. Dr. Colton became the director of the Museum of Northern Arizona, formed in 1928, and both Coltons devoted themselves to the museum and to research in northern Arizona. It was to this recently created museum, and particularly because of the friendship and respect that the Cosgroves had for the Coltons, that Hattie wished to present the collection of artifacts that had been lovingly gathered over the early years of their archaeological careers.

The Treasure Hill collection consisted of "seven barrels and a box," mostly Treasure Hill material, but also some cave material, some pieces that they had purchased from pothunters, and other artifacts that they had collected and documented over the years. In her November 24 letter, Hattie noted that if they were interested in taking the material she would like to ship it right away, but she would also like to go to Flagstaff to go through the material as it was unpacked, because in the initial packing, Burt had tucked in a number of personal and household items if they fit into a space in the barrels, and she would like to retrieve them.

Harold wired back that they would be delighted to accept the collection, and that Hattie was to stay with them when she came to Flagstaff. He could not promise that the collection would be on permanent display, but he thought it would be excellent research material. Hattie shipped the barrels soon afterward, and the Treasure Hill collection found a permanent home at the Museum of Northern Arizona. In all, there were more than 1,400 items that Hattie donated. Besides the Treasure Hill material there was pottery that the Cosgroves had purchased from pueblos in northern New Mexico, Apache baskets, and some prehistoric material that had been gathered during their early years in Silver City, such as pahos and bows and arrows from Greenwood Cave. There was even some very old Apache material, such as bows and arrows, that Burt had inherited from his father, who had collected it during the 1880s. From Treasure Hill there were turquoise pendants, shell bracelets, arrowheads, potsherds, stone tools, grinding stones, and the "usual lot of

beads, pendants, etc. that go with a Mimbres collection." But the great treasure of the collection was in the hundred or so Mimbres bowls that Burt and Hattie had dug from the floors of Treasure Hill. Today the bowls reside on shelves in a dimly lighted corner of a warehouse-sized room, along with row upon row of pots from sites across the southwest and Mexico. But the bowls still work their magic power when a visitor or researcher goes back to that special corner and lifts down a plain, dark-sided pot and looks down into an ageless scene of polliwogs swimming eternally about the rim of a bowl, of a beetle about to scurry off, or romping antelope and big-horned sheep, or even a whimsical, checkerboarded elk. Hattie left a legacy that has been preserved and will continue to enchant and delight researchers and visitors for years to come.

Another small bequest that Hattie made in the spring of 1937 was to the

Charles and Madeleine Amsden at Awatovi. Photo courtesy of Jenny L. Adams.

Hattie at Awatovi.

Kansas State Historical Society. Over the years Burt and Hattie had investigated many sites in their travels betweeen Cambridge, Atchison, and Silver City. One historic site that particularly fascinated Burt since his boyhood days was the old Pensoneau Trading Post on Stranger Creek near Atchison, in the country where he had spent much of his youth. Paschal Pensoneau married a Kickapoo woman and built the stone trading post in 1839, on a southern-sloping hill with a broad view of the Stranger Creek Valley. Pensoneau and his family lived there until 1855, when they sold the farm and moved out of the area. In addition to the ruins of the old trading post, there was also a Kickapoo cemetery and a Woodland culture site. Burt made some surface collections around the area of the old trading post, and among the items that Hattie gave to the Kansas State Historical Society were strings of trade beads, a box of small bones, and a blue porcelain mug. There was no information among the records, however, of when the material was collected, and even the donated items have disappeared from the museum's inventory over the passing

years.

Hattie celebrated her sixtieth birthday at Awatovi the following summer, but she had no thoughts of slowing down or retiring. The crew arrived in mid-July, and Hattie's guest register recorded 428 visitors to the ruin during the next three and a half months. More than five hundred meals were served to those visitors. In her guest register Hattie noted each visitor's name and hometown along with the length of their stay, such as Over night, Dinner, Lunch, Supper, or "S.V.," for short visit. With all the guests dropping in at Awatovi, and a number of scientists and archaeologists working at various sites and studies, it took a great deal of organization to keep things running smoothly. The four people upon whom responsibility fell (Watson Smith refers to them as "The Quadrumvirate") were Jo Brew, Al Lancaster, Lindsay Thompson, and Hattie Cosgrove. While Jo directed operations, Al figured out how to keep things going in camp and at the excavations, Lin cooked and fed the multitudes, and Hattie, being in camp much of the time working in the pottery tent, greeted visitors, showed them about, and made arrangements for their stay. She also injected a female point of view to the camp organization, and as an older woman she seemed to have been looked on fondly as a sort of matriarch to the expedition. E. Mott Davis, a young expedition member, fondly called her the "Awatovi Den Mother." Certainly she gave advice, since she had many years of archaeological experience to draw on. But she was also decades older than anyone else in camp, and the combination of her age and experience gave her an acknowledged, although unofficial, authority. Hattie was also a very gracious lady; she instinctively knew how to put people at ease, and in her role as camp hostess she became well loved and respected. Watson Smith gives Hattie a good deal of the credit for the happy and congenial atmosphere at Awatovi. He notes that there was a remarkable lack of jealousy and irritability among the camp workers, and Hattie's humor and wisdom seems to have been the main contributing factor to the "happy, wholesome, pleasant social milieu."

Many of the people who worked at Awatovi were young Harvard archaeology graduate students. Richard Woodbury, E. Mott Davis, and Richard Wheeler worked with the stone and bone artifacts, and John Hack made geological studies. William Claflin's daughters, Helen and Katie, and his son William, spent time working with the expedition. Other camp residents were Volney Jones, who came with his wife and son, Alden and Marion Stevens, Ned and E. Boyd Hall, and Mott Davis's sister Penrose. In his Awatovi diaries, Jo Brew refers to this changing group of students, siblings, and spouses as the Young People's Society. Between the young, energy-charged students and the unending stream of visitors, Awatovi was the center of much social activity and stimulating evenings of games, music, and conversation. Pinochle and other card games were most popular, but one item that definitely set Awatovi apart from other archaeological encampments was the Kimball piano in the pottery tent. Carlos Garcia-Robiou was a student studying archaeology at Harvard as a Guggenheim Fellow. He came to Awatovi at Mr. Scott's invitation, planning to stay just a week or two. Carlos was immensely popular and a gifted archaeologist, and he ended up staying for the remainder of the season and returning for following seasons. One of Carlos's talents was his musical ability. He sang beautifully and was an accomplished pianist. When Brew learned of his ability, he made arrangements to purchase a used piano from Jim and Mary McKenna for fifteen dollars. Jim and Mary operated a furniture store in Winslow and were frequent visitors to Awatovi. The McKennas brought the piano to the camp in the back of their truck and moved it into Hattie's pottery tent. With Carlos's singing and playing, there were many enjoyable hours passed in the evenings after a long day of digging in the ruins. Watson even recalled when Mr. and Mrs. Scott made a visit to camp shortly after a trip to England, where they had learned to do the Lambeth Walk, a newly popular dance. With Carlos on the piano, the Scotts aban-

doned some of their New England restraint and led the entire camp in the cakewalk dance around the tent.

Another unusual activity engaged in by the Awatovi crew was "sand-dune skiing." Toward the north end of the mesa were one-hundred-foot-high sand dunes that sloped down into Tallahogan Canyon at a gentle angle. The brave participants would run to the edge of the escarpment and jump over the side, hoping to land on their feet and slide downward to a graceful stop at the bottom of the dune. Watson noted that that was the objective, but long tumbles resulting in scrapes and bruises were an accepted part of the event. The climb back up the loose sand to the top of the mesa was equally strenuous, but according to Smith, Hattie was as enthusiastic a participant as any member of the Young People's Society in the sand-dune skiing evening competitions and that she "probably outperformed all competitors."[7] It goes without saying, that it was a most remarkable activity for a well-bred lady in her sixties.

Other off-duty pasttimes involved visits to local people and attending the marvelous dances at the Hopi villages. Jo Brew drove into Holbrook or Winslow once a week for supplies, but more frequently visited was the Jeddito Trading

Hattie and Harriet Harris. When she gave her name to the Harris baby (one of several names the infant may have been given at a naming ceremony) Hattie became an honorary grandmother to the child. Photo courtesy of Jenny L. Adams.

Mound on edge of Guatemala City.

Carnegie station wagon. Guatemala City. 1938.

Mildred and Burton. Guatemala. March 19, 1938.

Post about seven miles from Awatovi. Mail was held at Jeddito for the Awatovi camp, and trips were made three times a week to gather the mail, telegrams, and buy a few supplies. The post also had a telephone, which provided the nearest link with the outside world. Wilmer "Chi" and Alma Roberts operated the trading post and heartily welcomed visits from the archaeologists. On many evenings they fed and entertained the whole Awatovi crew. The Roberts also had a piano, which Alma played, although not with the concert-like perfection that Carlos did. Chi played the drums, and there were usually several neighboring Navajos who joined in the music making with native instruments. And of course, the Hopi dances were a great attraction. The Awatovi workers enjoyed very friendly relationships with the Hopi and were often invited to visit the villages when the dances were being performed. Hattie always tried to maintain a bit of propriety, and when she went to a dance she generally changed out of her camp attire of pants and knee-high, laced boots into a dress and silk stockings. But she became the object of a long-standing joke when a Japanese photographer visiting Awatovi to gather material for a magazine article joined the group on their way to a Hopi dance. As the group climbed out of the truck, Mr. Natori looked blankly for a moment at Hattie, then bowed and apologized. In his accented English he then explained that he hadn't recognized Mrs. Cosgrove "without her

pants on."

Over the five seasons of the Awatovi Expedition many lasting friendships were formed between the archaeologists and the Hopi workers and their families. Besides attending the dances, the campers received frequent invitations to visit families in the villages, and many Hopi visitors came to Awatovi to tour the ruin. Because many of the Hopi women were potters, they often spent time with Hattie at the pottery tent looking for designs and ideas to incorporate into their own work. Hattie became especially friendly with the Harris family, who had a boy working at the camp. When a baby girl was born into the family, she was named Harriet after their friend who worked with the ancient Hopi pottery. Evelyn Nimmo Brew recalled that when you were asked to give your name to a new baby, that child became your grandchild. In this way, Hattie became "grandmother" to a Hopi granddaughter.

An Awatovi event that has gained a small bit of fame in southwestern lore over the years was the mass that was held in the ruins of the mission church of San Bernardo de Aguatubi in the early fall of 1937. Father Victor Rose Stoner was an occasional visitor to Awatovi while he made rounds of the Civilian Conservation Corps camps in northern Arizona, ministering to the young men and holding services for them. Father Stoner's home base was in Tucson, where he was known for his strong interest in archaeology. On the occasion of one of his visits to Awatovi the altar of the Franciscan mission had been excavated, and the plan was proposed to hold a mass upon the main altar, the first mass held on the site since the church was destroyed two centuries earlier. Accordingly, the mass was conducted on September 5, with Father Stoner attired in his priestly vestments. In the photography archives of the Arizona State Museum there is a silent movie made by a visitor to the ruin who filmed various parts of the site and a portion of the mass. For the service, a few folding chairs were set up on the dirt floor in front of the altar. Hattie was one of the participants that day, and she arrived in her usual work clothes, a man's long-sleeved shirt, pants, and boots. But in honor of the event, rather than appearing in her old straw sun hat, she wore a black Sunday hat with a half-veil and ribbon and feather decorations. Undoubtedly it was her attempt to show a properly somber and respectful demeanor for the service, but in the silent film her formal, black hat looks strangely foreign among the workmen and the dirt and sand of the ruins.

The second full season at Awatovi ended in early fall before the weather turned cold. Barrels of pottery were shipped to the Peabody Museum, along with other artifacts and information gathered through the summer. The piano was trucked to Winslow, where the McKennas stored it for the winter. The camp was partially dismantled, the tents taken down and placed in storage, and everyone scattered to their respective homes, jobs, and universities until the next season. But this year Hattie did not return to another cold winter in Cambridge and her office in the Peabody Museum's basement. Dr. Kidder was working on a major excavation in Guatemala, and he invited Hattie to accompany him, along with Madeleine and some of their older children, when they returned to Central America in January.

The Guatemala trip was certainly not just a vacation. Kidder obtained funding from Donald Scott, director of the Peabody Museum, and Dr. Clark Wissler, curator of anthropology at the American Museum of Natural History, to bring Hattie and Paul Richard to Guatemala to restore pottery and other artifacts.[8] Once again, it was Hattie's expertise, and not friendship alone, that resulted in this chance to work and travel. Hattie was very pleased to be invited to join the Kidders. She was enthused about the opportunity to work with very different kinds of ceramics and a rich cultural assemblage that was quite different from the southwestern material she had always worked with. But it was also a good time for a change in her life. Burt had been gone for just over a year, and Hattie was beginning to build a new life, filled with work and friends. This change of place, climate, and work came at an

March 15, 1938

Dear Earl:

Ted has told me of your mother's death and I want you to know that you have my deepest sympathy. It is so hard to give up one's mother no matter how long in advance you know that it is coming to you. I think that you have known for some time that the inevitable was not far distant but that does not help when the time comes for parting. I have been more fortunate than most for I still have my mother at almost 90 years of age.

We are all so busy down here that time goes all too rapidly. I know that when going-home time comes I will hate the boat that takes me away from here. I love it all so much. I have been fortunate in getting about the country for the Kidders have seen to it that I have had most of the Sundays out—a new direction each time. I have often thought of your remark to me about buying textiles. You said to buy all I could for as soon as I got home I would wish I had more. They are hard to resist. I am getting quite a few but the ones I want the most I find on the backs of the women and they wont part with them.

Burton and his wife have been with me here since the 27th of Feb. They are in Panama right now, however. They flew down there Saturday morning and are returning tomorrow afternoon. It has been such a nice trip for them. They are thrilled with it all. They return to the states Sunday.

This has been an exceptionally cold season here, everyone is complaining. I had thought that I was coming to a tropical climate but I have been truly miserable with cold many times since I came. I have worn summer clothes only a very few times. It is supposed to be the hot dry season and we have had much cold rain and dreary weather. Like California "it is very unusual".

How are the two fine little girls? Give them a hug for me. They were so dandy at camp last summer. I am looking forward to a repetition of that trip next season.

This letter is for Ann too, but I wanted you particularly to know that I was thinking of you and sympathizing with you in your sorrows.

Much love to all four of you-
Hattie S. Cosgrove

Letter from Hattie Cosgrove, Carnegie Institution of Washington, Guatemala Research, to Earl Morris. Letter courtesy of the University of Colorado at Boulder.

Dr. Kidder at work.

Madeleine Kidder. Guatemala. 1938.

Faith Kidder and Francis Richardson recording sculpture at Victoria coffee finca.

Reginald Crampton getting orchids.

opportune moment. Hattie was at a turning point, and she was aware that she had to carry on without Burt working at her side as he had for so many years. Of course the opportunity to go to Guatemala was based on a working trip, but Hattie's dear friend Ted Kidder would have known how beneficial the work and the change would be for her.

For much of Kidder's early career, he had been a southwestern archaeologist. He had worked at Pecos for fifteen years, but that era ended in 1929, largely because of the national economy and a growing lack of funds. Kidder had been an advisor to the Carnegie Institution's Maya program for several years, and in 1929 he was appointed chairman of Carnegie's Division of Historical Research, where he supervised all of the institution's archaeological programs. With the exception of his brief time at the Pendleton Ruin in southwestern New Mexico with Hattie and Burt, Kidder never returned to the Southwest to do archaeology. From this time on his focus largely turned to Middle American archaeology, in addition to directing archaeological programs for the Carnegie Institution for the next two decades. By the mid-1930s, Kidder was able to also take direct part in excavations, and he began to travel to Guatemala each winter to do field work. On the outskirts of Guatemala City there was a large prehistoric ceremonial center known as Kaminaljuyu, "Hills of the Dead." Kidder and his associates first began excavating in 1935 and worked here for the next two decades. It was to this enormous site, containing more than two hundred mounds, that he brought Hattie to work in sorting, restoring, and cataloguing pottery. This was tedious and exacting work because some of the ceramic vessels were broken into hundreds of pieces, and reconstructing them took immense skill and patience.

Hattie traveled with the Kidder family south from Massachusetts by train, then by boat to Puerto Barrios, and again by train to Guatemala City, where they all lived in a large compound of rooms and work areas. In addition to work, there was time on the weekends for side trips

May 2, 1938

Dear Evelyn:

Your letter came to me Saturday night and I did want to get an answer off to you on the early morning plane but I didnt manage it so this will have to take the Thursday plane out.

First of all I want to say how delighted I am that you are going to Awatovi. It is simply great. I am hoping that you will like it as we all do. I dont see how you can help it. Of course, I'll admit it is a <u>far cry</u> from New England. At first you may feel strange. Never having been in the desert country you may wonder at the vastness of it all but even so I feel that you cant help but grow to love it. I have never seen anyone yet who didnt.

I had heard in a letter from the museum that Mr. Scott had asked you if you would like to go but never having heard anything further about it I decided that you had turned him down. Has Dottie Newton given up going? I know that she was on the fence about it. If she is not going I will miss her greatly. She is great fun to have about.

Dont worry about your never having been able to shut closet doors. Some time you will wish you had a closet to have a door to shut. It is always a question <u>where</u> we can hang things. If we dont keep things off of the floor we cant walk in the tent and if we do keep them off the floor we wonder which nail in the tent beam will hold another garment, all being full to overflowing. Dottie and I managed it so I am sure we two can.

I am afraid that someone has been stuffing you about the temperature in camp. It is <u>not</u> 115 in the shade. It may get that in the sun and more too perhaps but that is the strange thing about the desert, no matter how hot the sun is one can always find coolness in the shade. Of course it isnt chilly by any means but I have never really suffered with the heat unless in the sun. Our tent opens at both ends and faces south so there is always a north-south breeze through it and I find it very comfortable. My tent is the only one like that. Marion and Dottie both used to take naps at noon but that is never comfortable for me for the bed seems hot, but when I am up and about I never feel the heat. I wish I was there so we could have a good gab-fest about it all but it wont be long now before I am there and then we will "go to it" in great shape. There is one big thing to remember—no

one wears decent looking clothes. We all are <u>awful</u> looking. It is a great place to wear out old underwear, shoes etc. I am trying to make up my mind to wear skirts this year instead of the old pants I usually wear, but when I think of it I just dont see how it will be possible. I have gone through this same thing for three years and always come right back to the pants so I suppose I will do the same thing again this year. I think as long as I am not as young as I once was I should "be my age" but I know I wont. So be prepared!

No doubt Marion and Dottie have told you much about everything but when I get back we can get right down to making lists and all such things. I have some bedding out there but not quite enough for two beds. And of course if Dottie is going out some of it is hers too. All such things can be settled later. It is enough now to say that I think it is just fine that you are going. You will be a great help to Jo I am sure. He needs some like you who can take dictation.

I am sorry that I will not see Alice again before she leaves. Tell her please that I will miss her when I return. It would be fun if she could get to Awatovi. Unless she has a car of her own to drive it is rather a hard place to get to for it is only about <u>80</u> miles from the railroad and getting in to meet people is quite a task.

About forwarding my mail. We plan to leave here Monday May 30th. Ordinary mail takes at least ten days to get here and more often two weeks. The last boat that could bring in ordinary mail would get here on May 26th so you could do as you think best about sending anything. If mail misses a boat it takes so long before another boat comes in. Air mail of course comes through in 24 hours (if it makes close plane connection). It is really wonderful how quickly it comes at times. I doubt if there would be any to send down any way. Most of my mail has come direct here. Please tell Mr. Scott that I was mistaken when I said we landed June 6th. It is June 6th that I get to Boston. Not that the one day makes much difference but I just wanted to correct myself.

Give all the girls my love. Tell them they have been great about writing to me and I have appreciated it <u>very much</u>.

Much love to you,
Hattie Cosgrove

Letter from Hattie Cosgrove, Carnegie Institution of Washington, Guatemala Research, to Evelyn Nimmo. Letter courtesy of Evelyn Nimmo Brew.

Burt Cosgrove.

Hattie and Paul Richard mending pottery. Guatemala. 1938.

to markets, other prehistoric ruins, and local attractions. And as usual on most major excavations, there were many visitors, archaeologists and tourists, who dropped by the excavations for a tour. Several of Hattie's old friends in archaeology came to visit, and Burton and Mildred came for a few weeks in March. Hattie also kept up her usual correspondence with old friends from home. She had exchanged letters with Earl Morris for several decades, and on hearing the news of his mother's death in the spring of 1938, she sent a letter conveying her sympathy.

Another correspondent was Evelyn Nimmo, Mr. Scott's secretary at the Peabody Museum and a recent college graduate. Evelyn wrote with the news that she would be joining the Awatovi Expedition in the coming summer. Her responsibility would chiefly be to type and take notes for Jo Brew. She would also help out in the pottery tent and at the excavations as needed. Hattie was pleased to get Evelyn's news. The two women had known each other since Evelyn had joined the Peabody staff a year earlier, and they got along very well in spite of the great difference in their ages. In fact, Hattie and Evelyn would be sharing a tent at Awatovi, and Hattie wrote back that May with a lot of practical advice on what to bring and what to wear in camp. Evelyn confessed that she wasn't always tidy, and she didn't always remember to shut closet doors. Hattie replied that "sometime you will wish you had a closet to have a door to shut." All they had in the tents for their clothes were nails hammered into the wooden tent beams, and they were generally "full to overflowing," but Hattie was confident that they would work things out and get along just fine. Hattie reassured Evelyn that it really wasn't 115 degrees in the shade—out in the sun, perhaps, but "one could always find coolness in the shade." She also noted that even though the desert was very different from New England, she was certain that Evelyn would grow to love the country. A last bit of advice pertaining to what to wear at Awatovi reveals a good bit of Hattie's charm and character. She wrote that everyone in camp looks perfectly "awful," and Evelyn should not worry about wearing good clothes. Truthfully, it was a good place to wear out your old underwear, shoes, and so forth. Hattie had many old skirts and dresses that she thought she should wear, and wear out, at Awatovi, and each season she told herself that she should be her age and wear skirts, but then she added, "But I know I won't. So be prepared!" And every year she went back to wearing her old work pants.

Hattie stayed in Guatemala through the spring—work began at Kaminaljuyu in early February and ended in late May—but she never enjoyed the warm weather she had been told they would experience. Hattie had expected a tropical climate and had packed summer clothes, but she was seldom able to wear them because of the cold, wet, and dreary weather. She even confessed to having been "truly miserable" at times with the cold. Hattie and the Kidder family left for the States on May 30, about the time the cold, rainy season traditionally started, although they all felt they had already been through a winter, and they arrived in Boston on June 6. Four weeks later Hattie boarded a westbound train to Arizona to begin her third season at Awatovi.

Al Lancaster and Jo Brew began setting up camp the first week of July. Hattie and Evelyn arrived in Winslow on the ninth and Al and Jo drove down in "Pecos" to meet them. Over the years Ted Kidder had used a series of expedition cars that he named Pecos Blue or Pecos Black, according to the color. Along the way Jo inherited one of the Pecos cars and used it at Awatovi. Years earlier when the Cosgroves were working in the Mimbres country, they had purchased the Dodge truck with Peabody funds to use as an expedition vehicle. After the Awatovi work began, the Dodge was pressed into service and was used each season as a camp truck.

Hattie celebrated her sixty-first birthday in camp on the last day of July. She was escorted to the head of the long table at suppertime, and after everyone had eaten, Lin brought out a magnificent cake decorated with candles and "Happy Birthday" written in icing. Al led the group in singing to Hattie, and according to the entry in Jo's camp journal, she was quite pleased with the festivities.[9] True to her vigorous nature, Hattie did not let a small matter of another birthday slow her down; she regularly joined in with the evening camp activities, singing with the

Hattie celebrated her sixty-first birthday at Awatovi. On the back of the photo she wrote: "My birthday cake. You can see 'Hattie' written across it." July 31, 1938.

group or playing pinochle with Jo, Al, and Watson. There were also regular meetings of the Awatovi Bridge Club in Hattie's tent. And on more than one occasion Jo noted that Hattie had joined the Young People's Society for a session of sand dune-skiing or "sand-sliding." In addition to the camp amusements, Hattie and Jo were often invited as the senior personnel to attend a dinner or picnic held by one of the neighbors. They also called on hospital and government officials, tribal leaders, and the nearby traders.

Awatovi continued to be a destination site for archaeologists and assorted tourists, and as in the past seasons, Hattie maintained her guest book, logging in the names of visitors, the length of their stay, and meals and lodging provided by the camp. Most overnight visitors brought their own bedding and camping equipment, but hundreds of meals were provided by Lin in the Awatovi kitchen. Hattie's old friend Odd Halseth visited the ruin in August, a popular time for visitors because of the dances and festivals going on in the Indian villages. When Odd left Awatovi he gave Hattie a ride to Gallup, where she met Burton and Mildred for the weekend. Other archaeologists who visited that season were Carl Guthe with his wife and sons, Earl Morris and his wife and daughters, Charles and Madeleine Amsden, and Emil Haury, who brought a group of students from the University of Arizona. Dr. and Mrs. Colton drove in from Flagstaff and John Wetherill walked in. Peter Blos, an artist from California, visited and stayed to do some painting of the ruins and the camp. Even Barry Goldwater, who at the time was a traveling salesman for his family's Arizona stores, stopped by to see the famous site.

The hard-working archaeologists also took an occasional day off to visit neighboring attractions and to watch the dramatic and colorful dances in the Hopi villages. In October Hattie, Al, and Watson drove to Oraibi for a short visit. It was peach-drying season, and as they drove through Hotevilla and Bacabi they saw the peaches, halved and pitted, spread about on the rocks to dry in the sun. The whole camp went to the Navajo Tribal Fair in Window Rock, and through the late summer and early fall they attended the Snake Dance in Second Mesa, the Hunting Dance at First Mesa, the Basket Dance at Walpi, and the Butterfly Dance at Mishongnovi. Whenever they visited the villages Hattie bought some of the local arts, such as Hopi pottery and baskets. At the trading posts she shopped for Navajo rugs and silver and turquoise jewelry. These were often purchased as gifts for friends back at the Peabody Museum or to decorate her apartment in Cambridge, so even when she was miles away in the East she could enjoy a bit of the Southwest.

As September ended and the 1938 season drew to a close, a remarkable discovery was made in the church that changed all the plans for closing the camp. Charles Amsden was an archaeologist employed through the Southwest Museum in Los Angeles. He was a friend of Jo Brew and he also knew Hattie through Burton Jr., who had worked with Charlie for the museum at Casa Grande, Arizona, a few years earlier. Over the years of the expedition, Amsden made several visits to the camp and also dug a small ruin nearby. When excavation began on the mission church, Charlie advised Brew that it would be helpful to have an advisor who was an expert in the area of the history and construction of the mission churches. He recommended that Brew contact Ross G. Montgomery, an architect from California who had extensive knowledge of the background and architecture of the early Spanish missions in the Southwest. At Brew's invitation, Montgomery spent several weeks of each season at Awatovi as an advisor, and later he wrote a report as one of the Awatovi papers.

After the Franciscan church was excavated, Montgomery advised Brew that they should dismantle the altar and dig through the floor beneath it. In Montgomery's experience he had found that it was common practice for mission priests to build a church directly over a kiva or other sacred place to demonstrate their dominance over the native religion.[10] The altar was torn up with reluc-

tance, because in doing so the altar paintings that had been recently uncovered were destroyed, although drawings were made and a portion of the image was stripped off to later be preserved. But after the adobe bricks of the altar had been removed, workers digging beneath the floor came upon the intact roof of a kiva. Not only was the roof intact, but the entire kiva was complete. The Franciscans, recognizing that this was a sacred place, had filled the kiva with sand and had then built their church over the structure. The kiva was an exciting find, but even more notable was the discovery of beautiful paintings on the kiva walls. These remarkable paintings of human and naturalistic images still had bright and glowing colors and fine detail. Additionally, it was discovered that underneath the murals were more layers of plaster and more murals.

Watson Smith was put in charge of cleaning, recording, and stripping the murals, not only in the kiva under the mission church, but in several more kivas that were discovered nearby. Brew was reluctant to leave Awatovi before all of the murals were recorded. Either option, of refilling the kiva or leaving it open over the winter, carried a risk of losing the paintings, so he decided to winterize the camp and stay on with a small crew to finish retrieving the murals. Mr. Scott made a longer season a reality when he donated a thousand dollars to continue the work. Most of the crew and all of the Hopi workers left for the season (Hattie took pictures of all the young Hopi workers before they left), the extra tents were dismantled, and the rest were winterized as much as possible. Small stoves were set up in the tents, and Hattie cut and hemmed holes in the canvas for the stovepipes. Dirt was banked up against the wooden sides of the tents for additional insulation.

As it was now the end of October, the remaining crew, undaunted by the weeks of cold and strenuous work ahead of them, began planning a Halloween party. They had Jack-o'-lanterns, games, decorations, music, and a special dinner, and of course, everyone came in costume. Jo Brew recorded that Hattie was "made up

Parade. Navajo and Arapaho.

Jemez drummers.

Jemez buffalo dancers.

Indian Tribal Ceremonial, Gallup, New Mexico. August 1938.

extremely well as a Chinaman, with the typical long mustachios and a magnificent queue made from a black silk stocking." Jo was a padre, Charlie Amsden a French aristocrat, Mrs. Scott a Cossack, and Mrs. Chi Roberts told fortunes while the others bobbed for apples. The next day Al left to visit his family in Ackmen, Colorado, taking Hattie along with him. They arrived on a Saturday evening in time for a second Halloween party at the school. As Hattie had taken along the decorations, games, and Jack-o'-lanterns for Al's children, they all made a welcome addition to the party. The next day Al and Hattie went on to Mesa Verde where they were given a private tour of the magnificent ruins.

When Hattie and Al returned to Awatovi two days later, work on the lovely kiva murals was moving along nicely. A roof was erected over the kiva to

Mesa Verde. 1938. When Al Lancaster went to visit his family in southwestern Colorado at the end of October, he took Hattie along with him. Before they returned to Awatovi they also spent a day at Mesa Verde.

Donald Scott and Watson Smith at Awatovi. Photo courtesy of Lucy Cranwell Smith.

Watson Smith, New Hampshire. Photo courtesy of Lucy Cranwell Smith.

give some protection from weather to Watson and his helpers, but winter had set in with the first heavy snowfall of the season on the second day of November. Realizing that they were unprepared for cold weather, having packed for a summer season of work, Jo took Hattie and Evelyn to Flagstaff to buy winter clothes. Hattie took advantage of the trip to do some Christmas shopping and have her hair done. When Evelyn tried to find warm clothes to work in, she and Hattie decided to look in the men's department to find woolen shirts and warm work clothes, but they ended up in the boy's section of the store because all the men's clothes were too large for Evelyn. As a result of this shopping trip to the men and boy's department, Evelyn was thereafter affectionately called "Charlie."

Hattie soon had all her pottery sherds catalogued and boxed for shipping to the Peabody Museum. It had been an extremely rewarding season in which Hattie and her helpers had sorted, classified, and tabulated 203,871 sherds. By mid-November she began helping Watson with the kiva murals. Each one had to be photographed, drawn, measured, and recorded before it was peeled off and scraped to reveal the next image. It was grueling and exacting work. At one point Hattie strained her wrist after scraping at the ancient plaster hour after hour, so she took a day or two off to work on her drawings and analysis of all the ceramic ladle handles uncovered at the ruin. Hattie's study was later incorporated and published in Watson Smith's report on painted ceramics at Awatovi. The smaller group of workers celebrated Thanksgiving at Awatovi with a special dinner prepared by Lin of many delicacies that had to be shipped in by railroad and trucked over miles of dirt roads to the remote site. But Lin, who deserved his widely held reputation as the best camp cook in the Southwest, assembled a traditional feast of stuffed turkey, sweet potatoes, clam chowder, and pumpkin pie with whipped cream for dessert. As part of the festivities, Watson read a humorous poem, written by Evelyn, describing the more notorious facets of each crew member's character.

That night the temperature fell to zero, and although the days warmed up some, it was still very cold work out in the kiva, and the little sheet-metal stoves provided only a small bit of warmth in the canvas tents. Still, Hattie cheerfully stayed on at Awatovi until mid-December when the kiva work was finished. Each morning Evelyn lay in bed as long as possible, while Hattie arose early to start the fire and heat water for washing. Most days the water was frozen in the basin and the fire had died to just a few warm embers. Evelyn recalled that she always felt guilty about Hattie getting up first in the dark and cold; as the younger person she should have jumped eagerly out of bed each day to warm up the tent. But Hattie never minded about that chore falling to her. The two women always got along well, and they remained affectionate friends for many, many years.

By early December Watson was finishing work on the kivas, and the staff started to box the artifacts in wooden crates to be shipped back to Cambridge. When all the material was packed it amounted to nearly seven thousand pounds. Hattie, Evelyn, and Jo took a Saturday off from work to make the three-hour drive to Flagstaff, where they did some shopping at Babbitt Brothers' Curio Shop. They considered it the best place in the country to buy Indian arts. After lunch and visiting in Flagstaff, they returned that night to camp. Hattie often went along on these trips with Jo and Evelyn because the three were good friends, but as the two young people grew fonder of each other, perhaps she also began to function as a chaperone. Even though they lived out in a remote camp setting, there were strict rules of behavior at that time, and for all her non-traditional work, Hattie still held to very formal and conservative rules of morality. Sometimes her sense of appropriate behavior conflicted with the accepted practices she observed among the Hopi people she worked with every day, and there were times when it was a bit of a struggle for her to reconcile the differences between the two very different cultures.

As activity at the camp slowed down, Hattie and Jo paid several farewell visits to their neighbors, often sharing a last dinner and evening together. On December 6 Jo drove Evelyn and Hattie to the train in Winslow. Evelyn left on an afternoon train, while Hattie took the California Limited at noon and traveled to southern California. When Jo returned to Awatovi he worked with Al, Lin, and Carlos to take down the tents and pack as much gear as possible into the cook shack, where it would be safe until the following summer. The piano had been taken from the pottery tent to Hopi Superintendent Seth Wilson's house, where it would spend the winter.

In California Hattie stayed with Burt and Mildred for the Christmas holidays before she returned to her work at the Peabody Museum. Burt had recently been sent to the Los Angeles area to work with local film studios to make pilot training films for the Air Force. With another world war looming ever closer, the government recognized that air power would be a vital asset, and plans were conceived to use these films to train

Hattie, Tyrone Power, and Mildred Cosgrove. Burt Cosgrove met Tyrone Power and other well-known film stars when he was making pilot-training films for the Air Force. Power became a family friend and often visited the Cosgroves in later years.

On June 11, 1939, Jo Brew and Evelyn Nimmo were married at Awatovi. Hattie and the other women decorated the pottery tent with juniper branches, paper streamers, and wedding bells. Lin Thompson made the wedding cake, which was appropriately adorned with a tiny bride and groom. About fifty guests celebrated the event with Jo and Evelyn. Photo courtesy of Jenny L. Adams.

pilots as part of their education. Of course, with the many movie stars in southern California, it was only natural that they were recruited to act in the films, and Burt recalls the many legendary film stars he worked with over the years. Two actors who became close family friends were Gary Cooper and Tyrone Power. After the war when Hattie retired to Albuquerque to live near Burt and Mildred, Cooper and Power often visited them as they traveled across the country to make new films.

There was still a great deal of work to be done at Awatovi, but Brew was not able to get the Hopi elders to extend the permit to work beyond 1939, so he decided to begin the last summer's work in May to ensure a longer digging season. Hattie, Evelyn, and Penny Davis, a young student who would assist in the pottery tent, arrived in Winslow in mid-May and were picked up by Al and Jo. Al and his helpers had set up the tents, but the spring winds were so violent that tears and rips appeared every day in the

old canvas tents and flys. Hattie worked tirelessly to make enough repairs that the canvas would last through the final season. Within a week or two the winds had died down and work on the ruin could proceed, but there was one happy and noteworthy distraction before the crew could finally settle down to work. That memorable event was the marriage of Jo Brew and Evelyn Nimmo. There had not been an opportunity for the two to get married before they came to Arizona, but Donald Scott absolutely would not approve of the engaged couple living and working so closely together at Awatovi, so the solution was for them to hold the ceremony at the camp.[11]

Under Hattie's direction the pottery tent was cleared and juniper branches, paper wedding bells, and streamers were put up to create a wedding chapel. Lin baked a wedding cake, and Carlos played the Wedding March on the piano. Evelyn's mother was present for the service, but since her father was deceased, Al gave Evelyn away. Watson Smith was

Jo's best man, and Penny Davis was Evelyn's bridesmaid. With all the neighbors and local traders invited, there were about fifty people at the wedding. The young couple later left for a two-week honeymoon, and when they returned, work continued rather uneventfully at Awatovi for the fifth and last season. The occasional excursion for sand-dune skiing, in which Hattie was a regular participant, was offset with more sedate evenings of music and games in the pottery tent. Hattie, Evelyn, Penny, and Bill Claflin Jr. formed the nucleus of the Awatovi Bridge Club, which held regular sessions in Hattie's tent. Additional entertainment was provided by Carlos and by Mott Davis, Penny's brother and a Harvard graduate student, who constructed an ingenious projector (using a battery, an automobile light bulb and a nail in a bowl of saltwater) to show Kodachrome slides.

In July, Hattie, Jo, and Evelyn drove to Flagstaff to see the Hopi crafts show organized by the Coltons; this was the forerunner of the annual Indian arts and crafts show now held every summer. Two weeks later the three drove down to Show Low to visit Emil Haury, who was working in the Forestdale Valley. Haury was convinced that his work in the area was building a case for the existence of what he called Mogollon Culture, distinct from the Anasazi to the north and the Hohokam to the south, with the Mimbres being a southeastern extension of this phenomenon. It was some time before Brew and other archaeologists endorsed his theory, which has become widely accepted today.[12] The end of the month saw the approach of Hattie's sixty-second birthday, and the Awatovi crew, always ready for an excuse to have a celebration, decided to have a birthday party for her. Watson had to travel to Los Angeles, and a collection was taken so that he could purchase a special gift. Lin cooked a huge cake, the Amsdens gave Hattie a box of candy, and Watson returned that afternoon from California with a beautiful silver tray. There were other guests and special gifts. It was a memorable birthday for Hattie, and the last she would celebrate at Awatovi.

Hattie continued with her pottery work, taking a break at times to help Watson scrape and record his murals, and when Bill Claflin Jr. excavated an unusual burial with many artifacts, Hattie helped to pick out of the sand and string thousands of tiny stone beads that had been wrapped around the right arm of the skeleton. As August approached the usual guests arrived to tour the site and attend the spectacular Hopi dances. Emil Haury and Ted Sayles spent some time with the group and photographed many sites in the area; Charlie and Madeleine Amsden stayed to work; Frank and Brownie Hibben came in time for the Snake Dance; and the Coltons and Katherine Bartlett drove in from Flagstaff. And two decades after he had graciously invited two amateur archaeologists to visit his site at Hawikuh, Dr. F. W. Hodge, director of the Southwest Museum, was given a personal tour of Awatovi by ceramic specialist Hattie Cosgrove.

The end of the summer brought a close to five years of excavations at the famous site, and as the camp was dismantled for the last time, the somber group heard the foreboding news on the third of September that England and France had declared war on Germany. Not only was this an end to one of the most memorable archaeological expeditions ever mounted, but the coming of war in 1939 marked an end to a golden age of archaeology, a time when the young discipline was emerging, becoming a legitimate field of study, and searching to define itself. The early years of American archaeology represented a time when individuals such as Hattie and Burt, Al Lancaster, and Watson Smith could make the transition from interested amateurs to employed professionals. Even Ted Kidder, perhaps the most prominent early twentieth-century southwestern archaeologist, had a remarkable introduction to field archaeology as a twenty-two-year-old college junior. In 1907 he had volunteered (with no previous archaeological experience) for an expedition to the "cliff-dweller country of the Southwest." Kidder and two other Harvard students met Edgar L.

Hewett, who rode with them into a remote canyon area in southwestern Colorado. Hewett waved his arm around in a huge circle, told them to make an archaeological survey, and then rode off, saying that he would be back in three weeks.[13]

The last years of the 1930s marked the closing of a chapter in archaeological history when there was room for amateurs, spouses and children, friends, tourists, and any interested people who cared to visit and participate at one of the legendary expedition camps. It marked the end of a time when casual interest and amateur status could be nurtured to grow into professional expertise, without the prerequisite of a university degree. In many respects it also marked the end of a time of innocence and full-blown exploration and excavation in the Southwest with grand intents to answer the big questions regarding prehistoric time sequences and attempts to unravel the great mysteries of vanished cultures and peoples. In fact, most archaeology came to a complete stop for much of the 1940s, and when work resumed it was taken up by university trained professionals. It became a science with new technical methods that could be learned only through much study and advanced training. The entire archaeological process became much more formal, with government permits and regulations and proper credentials required at every step. Gone were the hundreds of visitors at a site, along with a budget to feed them all and a cook to prepare the meals. Never again would there be a piano in camp, a mass in a church ruin, or a wedding in a pottery tent. It was a sad day when that special group left Awatovi, and they would all have been sadder still had they known that they were dismantling and packing away forever a golden and treasured era in southwestern archaeological history.

As the camp was closed, each Hopi worker was given a portion of the equipment that was not shipped back to Harvard. This distribution of lumber, tents, stoves, and food was based on the length of work and level of responsibility each worker had with the expedition. The Cosgroves' old Dodge truck was disman-tled. Tires and other usable parts were salvaged and given away; the engine was later used as a generator motor. Al took the Kimball piano home to his family in Ackmen, Colorado. Hattie caught the noon airplane from Winslow and arrived in Los Angeles later that afternoon. For Hattie the close of the Awatovi Expedition was also the end of her active field work. Although she was to work in archaeology for many more years, she was now in her sixties, and she would never again have the opportunity or the vigor to work in the field, living for week upon week in a tent set up at a remote site. In a very real sense it was also an ending of a golden age of the archaeological life for Hattie. Burt was gone, and the two of them would never return to the secret caves in the isolated canyons of the Gila country, never uncover another magical painted bowl in a Mimbres ruin. Hattie loved the excitement and discovery that each new excavation brought, loved the feel of the dirt as it was slowly scraped away from a long-buried artifact, and most of all she loved the smooth, hand-polished feel of a potsherd between her fingers. Hattie loved the archaeological life. Truly, her heart was in the work.

The Cosgroves. August 1926.

◀LAST EXPEDITIONS▶

The end of the Awatovi Expedition left Jo Brew, Hattie, and the other staff members with a wealth of information and several tons of artifacts to catalogue and study before the tremendous job of writing up reports could begin. Hattie spent most of the next several years at work in her office in the basement of the Peabody Museum, organizing the pottery and supervising restoration. She also drew hundreds of illustrations of ceramic vessels. Because of World War II most archaeological work was interrupted for many years, but in 1971, three decades after work at Awatovi ended, the Peabody Museum published Watson Smith's *Painted Ceramics of the Western Mound at Awatovi*. The volume is dedicated to Harriet S. Cosgrove with "esteem and affection," and Watson notes in the acknowledgments, "The very special contribution of Mrs. Harriet S. Cosgrove has

been basic to the entire enterprise. Throughout four field seasons 'Hattie' Cosgrove sorted, counted, and recorded the myriad potsherds that erupted from the debris of Awatovi. Without her careful and exacting work there would indeed have been little from which to formulate the descriptions or adumbrate the conclusions that are herein presented."[1]

Hattie's work continued at the museum, and in keeping with her well-known affinity for young people, she befriended many students who were working on archaeology studies at Harvard. Her blue corn enchilada dinners were famous, and when she couldn't get fresh blue corn, or when there was a particularly large crowd, she served up quantities of Texas hash and homemade gingerbread. Among the students with whom she had affectionate ties were Edward Danson, Herbert Dick, Richard Woodbury, Robert

Lister, Mott Davis, and Raymond Thompson. Mollie Thompson recalled that Hattie was a sort of wonderful "mother hen" to the students and many of their wives, whom she often invited out to lunch. They loved to visit her apartment just off Harvard Square with its cozy southwestern decorations of Navajo rugs, baskets, and pueblo pottery. Mollie always thought that Hattie had a lot of spunk and a zest for living, and everyone loved to hear her wonderful stories of field trips and Awatovi days and digging in the Mimbres country. Hattie's old friend Emil Haury once remarked to southwestern archaeologist Joe Ben Wheat that Hattie was the one who kept the western students sane. They could go to her Cambridge home and enjoy the Indian crafts and southwestern decorating and get a real western meal. To many of the anthropology and archaeology students at Harvard, Hattie represented "archaeology in the West."

When Hattie could get time off from the museum she visited Burt, who was now assigned to March Field in Riverside, California. Hattie also maintained close ties with her family in Atchison. Her mother still lived there, as did Burt's sister, Kitty Cosgrove. In 1941 Hattie was asked to become a member of the board of Blish, Mize, and Silliman. She accepted that position and worked as a board member for the next twenty-one years. The old family business had grown significantly and now occupied a five-story office and warehouse facility that covered nearly a whole city block in downtown Atchison. The successful company, now in its third generation of management by family owners and directors, concentrated on wholesale distribution of plumbing and hardware supplies across the country. At a time when very few women worked out of their homes, and even fewer served on large company boards, Hattie assumed a very active and responsible role on the board, participating in decision and policy making for all the years she served.

In May Hattie took some time off from her ceramic studies to go out west. On the trip to California to spend some time with Burt and Mildred, she stopped off in Arizona for several days to visit Wilmer "Chi" and Alma Roberts, operators of the Jeddito Trading Post. Chi drove her around to see old neighbors and visit some sites. In the evenings Alma played her piano and Chi got out his drums, but of course, it just wasn't the same without all the old Awatovi crew. Hattie also made a nostalgic trip back to Awatovi and spent some time walking over the ruins and the old camp. In a May letter to Jo and Evelyn Brew she reported that the area was much the same as when they left two years earlier, but some of the walls in the ruin had fallen and some of the adobe had "melted a good deal." She had expected that her old cactus garden would have been "buried under a sand dune" from the constantly blowing winds, but it was "a thing of glory with its rich red blossoms." The following day she went to visit everyone at First and Second Mesa. Five of the Dennis brothers had worked at Awatovi, and when Hattie got to Second Mesa she wrote, "I thought Edith [Dennis] would hug the life out of me."

After going on to California, Hattie visited with Madeleine Amsden and stayed a few days with Ross Montgomery, who was writing his report on the Spanish Mission at Awatovi. On June 1, Burt was transferred to Albuquerque, where he worked on the building of Kirtland Field. When Hattie

HATTIE'S TEXAS HASH
(Courtesy of Mollie Thompson)

In a deep casserole saute one chopped onion and one green pepper. Add 1 to 1 1/2 pound ground beef and cook until browned. Add 1 cup of rice and cook and stir for 3-5 minutes. Stir in a large can of peeled, chopped tomatoes, 1 cup water, and a dash of powdered garlic, pepper and salt.

Bake uncovered 1 hour at 350 degrees. Check the dish periodically, some people like it dryish, some like it moist. For variations pats of butter on top can be added, also chili, tabasco or beef bouillon seasoning.

Dear Evelyn & Jo,

See where I am? Maybe you dont think it feels good to be here! It is like coming home. Alma & Chi send you their best. They are the same grand people. We talk constantly and last night the drums came out, but we missed the gang that always is associated in my mind with the drums.

Chi has made many improvements here, has put in a good Delco system, has lights all through the house & store and Alma can now have a vacuum cleaner, electric irons etc. Then too, they have done away with the old wood range in the kitchen, and have the most up-to-date gas stove I have ever seen. It is the last word in perfection It, as well as the refridgerator, are fueled (is there such a word?) from a tank buried in the back yard. It is a liquid gas, have forgotten the name of it. So you see how much easier things are for them. There is an abundance of water & they are again starting flowers & grass. Alma's flowers froze June 2nd. Its been very cold here, have a fire in fire place all the time. As Chi said this morning, instead of fixing fires this time of year he should be filling glasses with ice cubes and serving cooling drinks.

I went to Awatovi Tuesday. Everything at the ruin is as you left it with the exception of one very small wall in the Spanish-Indian section which had fallen some & the adobe walls of the "stables" have melted a good deal.

My cactus bed instead of being buried under a sand dune was a thing of glory with its rich red blossoms and Lelands Hopi house is in perfect condition. The winds from the bone & stone tent direction to the office site have worn quite a run way so the cactus bed is elevated about 1 1/2 feet. The cook shack has finally shed all of its paper covering and really looks better than when we were there. No one was there so I looked in the window and it was very neat & cozy. There is a solid partition through the place where Lin had his shelves, & a small clothes closet built in the front room. He has a book case against the partition and a cot bed, comfortable chairs & table in the front room and a good modern gasoline stove in the kitchen - 4 burner stove. It makes a very comfortable house. The cellar & cistern were still in good condition. There was water in the cistern but it was dirty & I dont think they use it. I looked in and saw that the walls were not cracked in the least. Al is a good cement man. His front steps to the shack are still holding well.

Yesterday I went to 1st and 2nd mesa. The old Namokis were out in the field but a neighbor woman told me they were O.K. Gibson is married to a Chimopovi girl & lives over there. Max is home with the old folks & works at the day school down below the mesa. Gilbert Namoki is divorced from his wife Irene (I liked her) and is married again. At the Nash house I found Mrs Nash, Deborah & another woman sitting on the floor

making pottery. They all seemed glad to see me. Mrs. N. said Sylvan is working at the hospital at Keams. I'll try to see him. I asked Deborah where Evans was & she just hung her head & said nothing so I guess she got rid of him.

At 2nd mesa I went to the Dennis home & saw the old lady & Edith. I thought Edith would hug the life out of me. I couldnt break her grip. Jake was out in the field as were the Dennis boys, Emory is again "in the east" with Mrs Sterling. They said his letter was from Leavenworth. What on earth they could be doing there I dont see for it is the most drab ____ town you ever saw. There is the army post near by & the big Federal prison also. Im wondering what its all about. They were very vague about it. Edith said Emory's wife was "running around with other men & he couldnt stand for it any more".

George Harris is living in the new house down on the lower level and I had hard work locating it for there are so many new ones down there just like it. George was out in the field and there was a new baby asleep on the floor, so George's family still grows on. Everett was in bed with a badly strained back did it about two weeks ago he said. He had the Hopi doctor care for it but I tried to persuade him to go to the hospital & have it taped well, but I doubt if he will. I could see that every move he made hurt him a great deal.

Chi stayed in Hale Lucakukuis store while I made the rounds. When I returned & was getting in the car a boy came out of the store to speak to me. At first I didnt recognize him. It was Douglas. He was all smiles. They all wanted to be remembered to you. Saw Randolph working on a bridge between Keams & Polacca.

I think that about checks up this part of the country. My California visit was great. I have lots to tell you when I get back. Had two days at Montgomerys. They are going down the Colorado river now. Saw Madeleine A. [Amsden] & she looks badly I think.

I spent five days at La Posada before I came over here. The McK's [McKennas] asked me to stay with them but I thought it best to stay at the hotel. I am not much of a moocher. I had most of my meals with them & spent all idle time at the store. They are great. Jim has had to give up all hard liquor, drinks only Sawtern wine now, eats very little but how he does work!! I dont see what he gets all his energy from. I will see them again when I go back from here, probably Monday. They are fine people.

I'll stay a couple of days in Winslow & then go to Albuquerque & Silver City, back to Albq. before going to Atchison. Burton is now in Albq.

Love to you both. How are the exams and the baby?

Affectionately,
Hattie.

Letter from Hattie Cosgrove to Evelyn and Jo Brew. Letter courtesy of Evelyn Brew. This letter was begun in May but was not completed and mailed for several weeks.

Hattie and Burt Jr.

left California to spend some time in Atchison, she also stopped off in Holbrook and got a ride down to Show Low to visit Emil Haury, who was working at Forestdale. Continuing on her way east she stopped in Albuquerque and then traveled south to Silver City to visit old friends and the Cosgrove cousins. Hattie's long vacation from the Peabody Museum and her nostalgic reunions with archaeologist friends in the Southwest were some of the last happy and peaceful weeks she spent for the next few years. The war began just a few months later, and Burt was at Clark Field when it was attacked in December. He spent the rest of the war flying bombing missions in the Pacific.

At Kirtland Air Force Base Burt was assigned to the Nineteenth Bombardment Group. In the fall of 1941 his group was sent to the Philippine Islands and was at Clark Field on December 8 when it was bombed by the Japanese, just a few hours after the Pearl Harbor bombing. Many of the men in Burt's unit were killed or wounded in the bombing and it was some time before he was able to get word to his family that he was safe. During those first days and weeks of December and January, Hattie was desperately worried about her son, and it wasn't until February that she received a letter from Burt, written on January 28 and sent from Java, that she knew he had survived the Clark Field bombing. Burt was safe, but everything he owned had

been burned or bombed. All of his worldly possessions consisted of "2 shirts, 1 pair of pants, 1 pair of shorts, razor canteen pistol" and a photograph of Mildred.[2]

Like every mother, Hattie feared for her son for the rest of the war. He flew dangerous bombing missions, and his few letters contained little information. In letters to friends Hattie wrote that the most difficult part for her was knowing that he was involved in dangerous operations, but the only communications were heavily censored letters that arrived weeks after they were written. Sometimes they made her "shudder" to learn of some of Burt's experiences. During all the years of the war, Burt was able to make only one telephone call to his wife from Australia, and that involved talking through military censors. After Clark Field, Burt made it safely through the jungles of Java in spite of bombs and machine gun strafing. He ended up in Australia, where he spent the rest of the war flying bombing missions. He was later awarded the Silver Star for his wartime actions.

Meanwhile, in Cambridge, Hattie found refuge from the war news and her unceasing concern for Burt in her work. The Awatovi ceramic work was going slowly, and most museum and archaeology work basically came to a stop as every able man was eventually called away to active military duty. A March 1942 letter from Earl Morris gave Hattie the impetus to return to some of the neglected reports that she and Burt had worked on years ago. Morris was known as an expert on prehistoric basketry, and in his letter he asked Hattie about the status of the cave report that she and Burt had worked on before Burt's death. They had finished their cave report in 1934, but it had been put aside after Burt died, and then Hattie became involved with the Awatovi project. She had great hopes of it being published, but Donald Scott, director of the Peabody, felt that it had little value because of the passage of such a great time, as well as new studies and finds on Basketmaker culture. Walter Taylor had done extensive work on caves in Coahuila, Mexico, and he hoped that the

Letter from Hattie Cosgrove to Earl Morris. Letter courtesy of University of Colorado at Boulder.

Cosgroves' cave material would soon be published; otherwise much of it would be published as his own work because of the similarities of the material. He joined in urging Scott to publish the study.[3]

Morris was asked to read the report and comment on its value. If it was published, it would be explained in a preface that the work was done ten years earlier, and although there were many new ideas and terminology had changed, the facts and material were still valid. Hattie saw the cave report as a tribute to Burt's memory, and even though they had worked together every step of the way, and Hattie had climbed a shaky tree ladder or been lowered by a rope into every cave in the Gila alongside Burt, this material would carry only Burt's name as a tribute to the fine work that he had done. Earl agreed to be a reader, and it turned out that he

had to postpone his own field work for lack of tires due to wartime rationing, so he had time to work with Hattie to prepare the manuscript for printing. After his first reading, a letter to Hattie indicates his high regard for the material when he wrote, "I wish I could shake Burt's hand and tell him what a remarkable job I think he has done. His verbal description is so clear that I think if it were necessary I could reconstruct even the most intricate techniques from it; and when the text is read with the wonderfully clear and simple drawings to refer to, the whole becomes the finest presentation of comparable material that I know of anywhere."[4]

Morris finished with the report at the end of the summer. He made minor changes in basketry terminology and classification, and he edited the entire

Looking down on camp from Cave #7. Hueco Mountains, northeast of El Paso, Texas. July 1928.

Pictographs in Picture Cave. Northeast of El Paso, Texas. July 1928. In addition to the large geometric motif to the right side of the photo, there is a large line drawing of a bird in the upper middle area and several small designs as well.

manuscript, and when Hattie read his finished work she immediately sent a glowing letter showering him with thanks and appreciation for his thoughtful and professional efforts. Unfortunately, in spite of Morris's fine work and the quality of Burt's original investigations, and even interest from others in seeing a finished publication, Mr. Scott again proved to be a hindrance, and the manuscript was put aside for several years. Scott never wrote a preface as planned, but Ted Kidder wrote a warm and admiring foreword in which he noted that the Cosgroves' work was "here reported with [their] characteristic thoroughness and accuracy."[5] He also noted that even though only Burton's name appeared on the report, it should be understood by all readers that Hattie had worked along with Burt in gathering, classifying, and reporting on all of the cave material, as she had over the many years of their shared career. Kidder wrote, "I have often spoken, in this brief foreword, of 'the' Cosgroves for, although Mrs. Cosgrove has wished the fruitful results of the excavations in the southern caves to stand as a memorial to her husband, they were the product, both in the field and in the preparation of the report, of the happiest and most complete of partnerships."[6]

In December 1927 Burton had written in *Teocentli*, "I investigated some caves in this part of the state and I am in hopes a well illustrated pamphlet can be presented showing the interesting collection taken from them." His *Caves of the Upper Gila and Hueco Areas in New Mexico and Texas* was published in 1947, two decades after he wrote those words. His "pamphlet" is nearly 200 pages long and in addition to the thorough and accurate text, it contains numerous maps, photos, and dozens of Hattie's illustrations of pahos, basket weavings, and pictographs. Like much of the Cosgroves' work, it is still referred to today by archaeologists and scholars, and in spite of new discoveries and ideas, the original material is a valuable resource in the study of the prehistory of the Southwest.

Hattie celebrated her sixty-fifth birthday in the summer of 1942, and although she was at an age where many people consider retirement, she stayed on at the Peabody Museum for four more years as a volunteer. Certainly there was a need for her help and expertise, as most archaeologists were called away by the war. But Hattie was also blessed by good health and remarkable energy, and it simply did not occur to her to stop working in the field that she so loved. She just kept going to the museum each day, working on the endless material gathered at Awatovi. Her mother, Harriet Silliman, passed away two years later in 1944 at the grand age of ninety-six. Undoubtedly, it was from her that Hattie inherited her energy and longevity, for Hattie enjoyed nearly three more decades of work and good health, remaining remarkably active and keeping abreast of work in southwestern archaeology and her old friends in the field.

In 1947 Ted and Madeleine Kidder returned to the Southwest, where they attended the Pecos Conference at Chaco Canyon. Later they toured the San Juan country with Jesse Nusbaum and spent some time at Emil Haury's University of Arizona field school at Point of Pines on the San Carlos Indian Reservation in eastern Arizona. That old "southwest virus" flared up again and Ted wrote that when he returned to Cambridge he "asked Mrs. Cosgrove to get out our old collections [from the Pendleton site]. That started us off. We went over the field notes, the plans and photographs. The first thing I knew I had temporarily ditched the Maya and was happily at work with Mrs. Cosgrove in her room in the Peabody basement."[7] Hattie and Ted spent the fall analyzing the Pendleton material and writing a report. They consulted with Emil Haury and Harry P. Mera on some sherds that they had difficulty classifying. By November they had finished the writing, and their collaborative Pendleton report was finally published in 1949.

Hattie then accompanied Ted and Madeleine to Guatemala, where they spent the last weeks of 1947 and the entire spring of 1948. For this trip the weather was lovely, and Hattie escaped the snow and cold of a Massachusetts winter. Emil Haury was planning to host the Pecos Conference at Point of Pines later that summer, and when Hattie returned to Cambridge she found his invitation to the conference waiting for her answer. All winter Ted had been urging Hattie to attend, but she felt that she needed a formal invitation. Hattie's reply to Emil was that she would love to attend the conference, but it was a long journey for just the two meeting days. She wondered if she could come out early and spend a week or so helping at the field school. Besides being interested in Point of Pines because of Emil's involvement, Hattie was also a regular contributor to the field school scholarship fund. She wrote to Emil, "I realize that probably my expedition days are about over with and I can think of no better way to top them off than to have a week with your camp workers."[8] She lamented that she had no camping gear but would certainly bring her own bedding if Emil could provide a tent, and she hoped that she could help out around the camp and not be a burden to anyone. Emil heartily invited Hattie to come out and spend as much time as she liked at his camp. Hulda and his two sons were at the camp, and the Kidders would be coming for the conference. It would be like old times for them all. So at seventy-one years of age, Hattie again was looking forward to spending a week or two in an archaeological camp.

She took the train to Flagstaff, where she visited with the Coltons and then went on to Globe, Arizona, arriving on August 13. She stayed at the old Dominion Hotel until one of the camp trucks came into town for supplies and gave her a ride back to camp. The trip out to the field school was an adventure in itself. Not at all for the faint of heart, it covered about ninety-five miles over a dirt road and crossed the creek twenty-three times. Emil said it could be dangerous if there was much water running, and Mollie Thompson called it "desperate." But Hattie had no fears about the trip, and she thoroughly enjoyed her time at Point of Pines, her last experience with living in a working camp. Besides seeing Emil and Hulda, Hattie visited with many old friends, and when the

Hattie at Point of Pines. 1948 Pecos Conference. Photo courtesy of Evelyn Nimmo Brew.

As more work was done in the area, more archaeologists came to support the concept of Mogollon culture, which included the Mimbres country, as distinct from Anasazi and Hohokam, but a few, such as Jo Brew, still felt that there was not enough evidence to give it a separate identity. Although Hattie was not a formal participant on the panel, her opinions as a pioneering worker in the Mimbres country were still a valuable contribution to the discussion. Years later Richard Woodbury noted in his Pecos Conference history: "There have been other Pecos Conference symposia on contested issues, but probably none more important in defining the issues of a major controversy."[9]

With 136 registered participants at the conference it was a chore to feed everyone. There were two seatings for meals, and when the discussions were over, Hattie and Madeleine Kidder could be found by the kitchen sitting outside in the shade, chatting and peeling potatoes by the barrelful. Hattie loved the talk and the old friends who gathered at the conferences each August. Over the next two decades she attended a great many of them and always got a special acknowledgment as one of the participants in the original Pecos Conference in 1927.

Now that the war had ended and there was no longer a shortage of staff at the Peabody Museum, Hattie gradually ended her volunteer services and took more time to travel and visit her friends and family. After eighteen years of marriage, Burton and Mildred had a little boy whom they named Cornelius Burton after his father and grandfather, but he was fondly known as "Corky." Hattie adored her grandson, and her new role as grandmother may have played a part in her decision to move to Albuquerque to be near Burt and his family. At seventy-one Hattie admitted to slowing up a bit, and while she did have many friends in Cambridge after residing there for more than twenty years, Burt now had a semi-permanent post with the air force in Albuquerque, and Hattie would have an opportunity to spend time with him and her new grandson. She packed her belongings and went to New Mexico,

conference began on August 24, she took part in discussions during the conference and evening gatherings around the fire. The Kidders attended the meetings, and Jo Brew, who had just succeeded Donald Scott as director of the Peabody Museum, also came out from Cambridge. Other old friends that Hattie spent time with were Odd Halseth, Earl Morris, the Coltons, and Watson Smith.

Emil's 1948 meeting was the first held outside of New Mexico, and since that time it has been held in a different site each year, sometimes returning to an earlier site. It was not until the following year that its name formally became the Pecos Conference, in honor of Dr. Ted Kidder, who had organized the first of the southwestern archaeology conferences two decades earlier. The most important part of the conference was a panel discussion of the Mogollon culture.

where she spent Thanksgiving with Burt and Mildred and Corky. Of course, she didn't plan to live with her son—that would be imposing—and Hattie enjoyed her freedom too much. She soon found a little apartment near Burt's home and settled in quickly.

Albuquerque was an ideal choice for Hattie's retirement. It was in the heart of the Southwest, surrounded with the prehistoric ruins and contemporary pueblos that she so loved. And in a time before people flew about the country as they do today, it was on a major train line, and many of Hattie's old friends would stop off in their travels to spend a little time with her as they went across the country or traveled out to the Southwest for their summer field work. In a letter to Evelyn Brew she wrote, "I've seen so many friends that way, enroute east or west." Albuquerque's central location also gave Hattie much easier access to the annual summer Pecos Conferences, which were much like reunions to the old "Southwesterners." She attended the 1949 conference in Santa Fe, and stayed with Harold and Mary Colton in Flagstaff when the Museum of Northern Arizona hosted the event the following year.

Hattie did not attend the 1951 conference at Point of Pines. Burton had been sent to Washington and then on to Europe, and she had planned to spend some time in Cambridge and then go on to Washington and stay with Corky while Mildred joined Burt in Europe. Instead, she fell from a ladder while pruning some bushes, and broke both legs and an arm. Doctors told Hattie she would not walk again, and when she was released from the hospital she hired a housekeeper and three nurses to give her twenty-four-hour care. After her casts were removed several weeks later, she was allowed to sit in a wheelchair for a while each day, but she was not allowed to try to stand for another three months. But Hattie did not have the patience to be without the use of her legs. For all the years that she had lived in Cambridge she had not had a car—she walked everywhere—and certainly walking and hiking had been major parts of her life when she was out on a dig. She told her doctor

that it was "nonsense" to think that she would never walk again, and when the three months had passed and she was allowed to put weight on her legs, she worked a little each day to get her strength and mobility back.

Hattie not only regained the use of her arm and legs, she also joined another archaeological expedition. She had known Frank Hibben since he was a young graduate student. As a zoologist he had spent the winter of 1933–1934 in the Mogollon Mountains near Silver City studying mountain lions. There he had met Burton and Hattie. Later he turned to archaeology and had called on Hattie in Silver City. Together they visited several caves and Mimbres sites in the Gila country. Hibben also worked briefly with Hattie at Awatovi. In the 1950s and 1960s he was director of the archaeology field school for the University of New Mexico, which was held at Pottery Mound, about forty miles southwest of Albuquerque on the Puerco River. After moving back to New Mexico, Hattie often visited with Frank and his wife, Brownie.

Hattie spent the next year regaining her health and mobility, and when Frank and Brownie Hibben began making exploratory visits to Pottery Mound, she often joined them on the day trips. When the University of New Mexico field school began excavations at Pottery Mound in 1954, Hattie came along as a volunteer at Frank's urging. Each morning a busload of students left the campus for the drive out to the site, and if Frank was not able to pick up Hattie in his car, she got a ride on the bus. During several seasons in the 1950s, she worked along with the students every day.

Volunteering with the field school was a wonderful opportunity for Hattie to remain active in archaeology, and her experience was especially valuable when murals similar to those at Awatovi were discovered on the kiva walls at Pottery Mound. Hibben stated that Hattie was "just a peach" and "a real campaigner," but he also had great respect for her field work and her precise laboratory techniques. Her advanced years did not stop her from climbing down into a kiva each morning for the demanding work of

cleaning and recording each mural, even though some walls had as many as thirty-eight images on each panel. Hattie became very interested in the identities of the various artists who had painted the murals. She saw identifying styles in certain paintings, such as the "master of the parrot ladies" and the "painter of the spotted women." Because of the detail in some of the clothing, she suggested that perhaps some of the artists had been women. Frank recalled that they had many ongoing and lively arguments about the identity of the artists, but in spite of their congenial differences of opinion, Hibben had great admiration and affection for Hattie. This fondness is demonstrated in his book *Kiva Art of the Anasazi at Pottery Mound*, "affectionately dedicated" to Hattie, one of the "most beloved and respected figures in all of American archeology."

For many years the Hibbens had a cook and housekeeper, Nora Chino, who was from Acoma Pueblo. Nora's father, a much respected elder at Acoma, was a frequent and interested visitor to the excavations at Pottery Mound. Although he was reluctant to discuss the possible meanings of the kiva paintings, he sometimes offered valuable comments on the murals. Over the years at Pottery Mound and in the Hibbens' home in Albuquerque, Nora and Hattie became great friends and talked often, and because they both enjoyed cooking, they traded many recipes. A favorite of both women was watermelon pickles; Nora insisted that the best watermelons to use were those with thick rinds, such as the ones grown near her home in Acoma.

Pottery Mound was the last site where Hattie actually worked in the field, but she kept up with developments and with her friends in archaeology. She received reports as they were published by her colleagues who kept her on their complimentary mailing lists. She attended meetings of the Albuquerque Archaeological Society, where she was named an honorary life member. John King was an amateur archaeologist from Silver City who served on the board of the Albuquerque Archaeological Society, and he recalled a meeting that Hattie attended; upon her entrance to the meeting room, she received a standing ovation from the members. She was greatly loved and respected and King related that all of the society members wished to honor her great contributions to New Mexico archaeology. Hattie also attended meetings of the New Mexico Archaeological Society, and she was an honorary life member of the Northern Arizona Society of Science and Art as well.

Hattie attended St. John's Episcopal Cathedral and volunteered at the St. Johns Cathedral Thrift Shop. Through her board membership at Blish, Mize, and Silliman, she cajoled her nephew John Mize into making substantial donations of useful materials from the plumbing and hardware company to the thrift shop. She made occasional trips back to Cambridge to visit old friends, always staying in hotels because she valued her independence, and she often said that "old folks are not good visitors." Besides,

HATTIE'S WATERMELON PICKLES

Pare and slice the rind from one or two watermelons. Use a thick-rind melon. Let stand overnight in a weak brine. Drain and put in clean cold water and bring almost to a boil, but do not boil. Put rinds in clean water again with a little alum, about the size of a medium sized hickory nut to a gallon of water. Boil until tender. Put again in cold water, boil in a rather strong ginger tea, and cool again in cold water.

Mix the following ingredients together and boil for a few minutes before adding seven pounds of rinds:

    4 pounds of sugar
    1 pint of vinegar
    1 level tablespoon each of cinnamon, allspice, and ginger
    1 teaspoon each of cloves, mace, and nutmeg
    6 bay leaves

For the melon I find it is hardly enough liquid, so use 5 pounds of sugar and 1 1/2 pints vinegar—spices, etc. same. Boil rind in the syrup until clear and tender. Use old fashioned thick rind watermelon for pickles. Fine for peaches and pears.

she had many people to see—old friends who corresponded and sometimes visited Hattie when they came to New Mexico. The Kidders often came out to the Southwest, and Madeleine regularly spent a few weeks with Hattie each summer at her home in Albuquerque. Hattie traveled to California and had a visit with Ross Montgomery and Madeleine Amsden, and she often traveled to Atchison to visit her family and spend some time with her sister-in-law, Kitty. Hattie was her legal guardian until Kitty's death in 1959 at the age of ninety-four. Hattie just seemed to keep going on, her tremendous energy and optimistic spirit holding off old age. She wrote Evelyn Brew in 1956 that "from the looks of me, I think I'll be on hand sometime yet. I can't say I enjoy the prospects of being eighty next time, but as long as I can keep up as I am now I don't suppose it makes much difference."

When Hattie turned eighty in 1957, the University of New Mexico's *New Mexico Quarterly* contained a warm and praising article about the Mimbres work done by Hattie and Burt that was written by their old friend Ted Kidder.[10] Kidder chronicled their lives and many achievements and told how their love of the Mimbres country went beyond an impersonal, academic study. He wrote that from their earliest work at Treasure Hill, "long before they had the slightest idea of going into the work professionally, they acted as archaeologists rather than pothunters." Locally, they had worked for protection of Mimbres ruins. They encouraged archaeologists to work in the Mimbres country and helped them to obtain permission from ranchers and Chino Copper Company to excavate sites. Kidder praised the work they had done at Swarts and in the cave survey, mentioning their scientific methodology and precise reporting and Hattie's beautifully accurate drawings of the Mimbres bowls. He recalled that they were fun and easy companions in camp and that both Cosgroves were remarkable human beings. In a touching and extraordinary tribute, Ted Kidder wrote that his old friends Harriet and Burton Cosgrove should be called "Mr. and Mrs. Mimbres."

The Kidder family. 1929. Hattie, Madeleine, and Ted Kidder remained close friends for all of their lives and visited often between their homes in Massachusetts and New Mexico.

That 1957 issue of *New Mexico Quarterly* was illustrated with pages of Hattie's drawings of Mimbres bowls. Two years later, because of the "warm response" by readers, the summer issue of the quarterly contained more of Hattie's Mimbres bowl drawings. In her typically modest way, Hattie wrote to Ted that she and Burt owed all of their successes to him, for without his interest and support they would not have gone so far in their field. On June 3, 1957, on the occasion of Kidder's fiftieth anniversary of work in archaeology, Hattie wrote: "I understand that this week is the 50th anniversary of your first 'sherd picking-up.' Congratulations on all the wonderful results you have passed on to all of us. Some of us would not have gone far if it hadnt been for your interest and boosting. You beat me by two years. I picked up my first sherd 48 years ago and it was on Treasure Hill! Someway I felt so proud of myself. And I still own Treasure Hill."[11]

In 1958, when she was eighty-one years old, Hattie received an honorary doctor of science degree from the University of New Mexico. In a letter to Burt's cousin in Silver City, Inez Cosgrove Ford, Hattie wrote that she was "floored" when she received the notice about the honorary degree, and she added, "It was about the last thing in the

Looking north to the Twin Sister Mountains from Treasure Hill, east of Silver City, New Mexico. 1919. Hattie owned Treasure Hill from 1919 until 1962, when she sold it just a few days before her eighty-fifth birthday. The Mimbres village ruin is now owned by a foundation formed to protect and preserve the ancient site.

world I had ever dreamed of having." In her customarily modest style, she felt that she was getting the award more for Burt than for herself, "even though I always worked with him." [12]

Four years later when Hattie's old friend from Awatovi, Al Lancaster, received the Distinguished Service Award from the National Park Service, Hattie flew to Boston with Al and Alice and they had a reunion of many of the old Awatovi crew members.[13] Hattie stayed with the Kidders and the Lancasters with Jo and Evelyn Brew. The Claflins hosted a dinner for nearly two dozen of the old friends and coworkers. They toured sights in the area and visited the Peabody Museum, which Al had never seen, although like Hattie, he had been a Peabody employee for several years.

Hattie did not go to Washington, D.C., with the Lancasters and Brews. Her sight was failing and it was becoming more difficult to travel. When she wrote to old friends she placed one finger along the paper as a guide, and her last letters show those extra wide spacings between each line. She had to limit her writing to just one or two letters a day because it was so very tiring to her. In a letter to a friend she wrote, "I hope you can read it —I cant!" A magnifying glass helped Hattie to read a few papers, but it was a tremendous strain on her eyes to read with the glass. She borrowed recorded books to listen to every day, and her favorite topic was southwestern history. Burt drove to Santa Fe to a special lending library for the blind to get the books, which were played on a record player. She never completely lost her sight; she could always see indistinct shapes and colors, but she was considered legally blind. Hattie missed the field work of her younger days, and when Emil Haury wrote that he was retiring from administration and returning with Al Lancaster to do some additional excavations at Snaketown, Hattie replied that she knew "just how good it will feel to you to get away from the desk and into dirt archaeology again. I wish I could lop off 30 or 40 years of my age and get busy digging again! There is so much to be done."[14]

Hattie still held the deed to Treasure Hill, the site were she had picked up her first potsherd in 1909. It had always been her dream to go back to that special place and continue the work that she and Burt had begun half a century earlier. Of course, Hattie realized that with her advancing age and loss of sight that would never become a reality, so when she was approached by a young Silver City woman about buying Treasure Hill, she quickly agreed to the sale. LaVerne Cloudt Herrington had grown up in the shadow of Treasure Hill and even today makes her home within a mile of the site. Like Hattie, LaVerne always had an uncommon love and appreciation for the ruins that she wandered over near her home in the Arenas Valley. And like Hattie, she realized that the only way to protect and preserve such a special place was to acquire knowledge and professional training. When LaVerne bought Treasure Hill from Hattie for five hundred dollars, it was with the promise that she would always care for the site. Today Hattie's original two acres, along with several more acres of land that LaVerne has purchased over the years, comprise the Treasure Hill Foundation, which has a board of directors of prominent archaeologists and carries the stipulation that the site be held in trust for research and education relating to the Mimbres culture.

LaVerne went on to school to earn a doctorate in archaeology from the University of Texas at Austin. Her dissertation, "Settlement Patterns and Water Control Systems of the Mimbres Classic Phase, Grant County, New Mexico," contains a special acknowledgment to Harriet Cosgrove "who, by entrusting the author with Treasure Hill, prompted this long journey." LaVerne remains scrupulously loyal to her original promise to Hattie and is fiercely protective of all the prehistoric sites in the Mimbres country. Like Hattie, she has worked at sites and surveys throughout the area, and she continues to be a liaison between archaeologists and local landowners. LaVerne and Hattie met only once, but Hattie would be pleased to know that her legacy of respect and care for the Mimbres culture lives on in LaVerne's capable hands.

Indeed, Burt and Hattie's legacy will endure for many generations. Some contemporary archaeologists have derided the Cosgroves' work and are quick to remind that they were amateurs, even though the work of many early archaeologists was more along the lines of collecting rather than scientific examination when compared with today's advanced techniques. Even the name of the the ruin where the Cosgroves first worked at archaeology has been mocked and belittled. Indeed, Treasure Hill's name does come from a more casual and perhaps naive time, and considered in that light it does have a rather charming connotation. And the Mimbres ruin on Whiskey Creek did prove to be a real and lasting treasure to Hattie and Burt. It introduced them to the marvelous new world of archaeology and led them into a wonderful career, their own "long journey," doing important and lasting work. After the Cosgroves left the Mimbres country, very little work was done there for nearly half a century. But as scholars and archaeologists have recently come back to do new surveys and excavations in the Mimbres, Hattie and Burt's work is being rediscovered and examined, and today's Mimbres archaeologists have warm praise for their work and methods. Dr. Steven LeBlanc, who directed the Mimbres Foundation, a modern organization of professionals who endeavored to survey all Mimbres sites and material and document all known Mimbres bowls and artifacts, wrote of Burt and Hattie, "The quality of their recording and digging is quite impressive. They employed procedures that have not become common until quite recently."[15] Their Swarts report has become a classic volume. A contemporary southwestern writer noted that a half-century after its 1932 publication, the report was still cited in the Smithsonian Institution's prestigious *Handbook of North American Indians.*[16]

There is a momentum gathering today, focusing on the Mimbres culture and art, with professionals taking a new look at the Mimbres country, and popular interest is awakening through art gallery and museum shows. Images from Mimbres bowls that the Cosgroves and others dug from the ground, and that Hattie reproduced in her ink drawings, are appearing across the country in books and artwork, on T-shirts, bags, dishes, fabrics, and other decorating and household goods. Thanks to researchers like Hattie and Burt, the marvelous paintings

1966 Pecos Conference at Flagstaff, Arizona. Hattie is standing to the left of Emil Haury. To her right are Paul S. Martin and Harold S. Colton. The fourth man is unidentified.

Camp at pueblo ruin, north of El Paso, Texas. April 1924.

Cave shelter, Cornudas del Alamo, north of El Paso, Texas. M. L. Crimmins. In 1924 and 1925 Hattie and Burt worked in the El Paso area with support and funding from the El Paso Archaeological Society. Their report was published by the society in 1965.

that flourished only for a few generations in southwestern prehistory will live on and continue to charm and delight people everywhere.

Hattie was to receive one last honor for her work from the very group that had hired her and Burton forty years earlier to do some of their first professional excavations. Several members of the El Paso Archaeological Society came upon the original notes and records of the Cosgrove's survey of the El Paso area and their excavations at Three Rivers. Vernon Brook and others assembled the material into a finished manuscript ready for publishing. A copy of *The Cosgrove Report: A Preliminary Survey of the El Paso Pueblo District*, published by the El Paso Archaeological Society, arrived at Hattie's door on her eighty-eighth birthday on July 31, 1965. And in a thank-you letter to Edmund White, president at the time of EPAS, she wrote that she never had a better birthday gift. In addition, the El Paso Archaeological Society established the Cosgrove Memorial Publishing Fund, named for Burt and Hattie, to publish archaeological papers.

Hattie attended her last archaeological meeting in Tucson just days after her ninetieth birthday. Emil Haury, along with the Arizona State Museum and the University of Arizona's department of anthropology, hosted the Pecos Conference in 1967. It was the thirtieth Pecos Conference and the fortieth anniversary of the first conference in 1927. In the spring of that year Hattie had sent Emil the original photograph taken by Burton of the first Pecos Conference attendees. Hattie wrote to Emil, "I am sending you the original photo & listing of the first Pecos Conference, 40 years ago. I have cared for it all these years and feel that it should pass to the younger generation of S.W. archaeologists. So I am turning it over to you. I know of no one I'd rather give it to."[17]

Hattie and seven other of the "originals" attended the Conference: Harold S. Colton, Alfred (Alfie) Kidder II, Hulda Haury, Paul S. Martin, Madeleine A. Kidder, Faith Kidder Fuller, Neil M. Judd, Emil W. Haury, and Clara Lee Tanner. Emil, who had been a student at the time of the first conference, was now a retired director of the Arizona State Museum and one of the foremost southwestern archaeologists of the time. As he gave a recap of the last four decades of the conference, the changes and advancements in the field must have been apparent to many of the founders and participants. From that first outdoor meeting with casual talks under shady trees, bedrolls stashed in Model A cars, and spouses and children wandering about the camp, to the professional talks on the university campus, southwestern archaeology had come a long way and experienced many changes. The students were now distinguished professors, many of the old friends were gone, Harold Colton's museum was nationally known and respected, and Hattie Cosgrove, the amateur archaeologist and hardware store heiress, was the distinguished Mimbres and ceramic expert. When Hattie picked up that potsherd one warm Sunday afternoon on Treasure Hill more that half a century earlier, she could never have predicted the journey she was about to begin, the canyons and caves she would explore with Burt, the months spent camping in a tent beside a ruin, the campfire talks with Hopis and Navajos and fellow field crew members, the trips to Harvard, and the company of eminent professors and archaeologists. Hattie's life was a grand adventure, and when she was interviewed in her ninetieth year for a book about the Gila Cliff Dwellings, she recalled "riding pack horses in from the Sapillo to the Cliff Dwellings. She had never ridden horseback previously, but says she had developed some strong muscles from slogging through the sand and climbing a 100-foot cliff at Hueco Tanks near El Paso where they had been doing some excavating." And her comment on her marvelous life with Burt and all the places they had dug and explored was: "I wouldn't have missed a minute of it—I'd like to live it all over again!"[18]

As a result of the contacts with Hattie in 1965, Vernon Brook and other EPAS officers resolved to do something to further honor the "pioneering" El Paso archaeologists, and in 1969 Hattie and Burt and their old friend Eileen Alves, who had died in 1935, became the first recipients of the El Paso Archaeological Society's Hall of Honor Award for their many outstanding contributions toward the advancement of archaeological knowledge. Hattie flew to El Paso to accept the plaques for her and Burt at a banquet held at the University of Texas at El Paso, where she was also made an honorary life member of EPAS. Hattie seemed to have impressed the EPAS members not only with her professional expertise, but also with her unique spirit. A report of the banquet and awards in *The Artifact*, the EPAS newsletter, noted that "Mrs. Cosgrove, now 92, being perennially youthful and indomitably energetic, still exhibits the quality of independence by flying alone in airplanes and attending archaeological meetings."[19]

Hattie passed away on July 7, 1970, just a few weeks short of her ninety-fourth birthday. The young girl who had been raised in a mansion on the banks of the Missouri River had lived a life that was rich in experiences very different from what might have been expected for a typical, wealthy young woman of her time, but her courageous spirit and gracious style opened her life to many opportunities and endeared her to everyone she met. Hattie's obituary in the El

Cliff dwellings, west fork of the Gila River. October 1909. When Hattie made her first visit to the Gila Cliff Dwellings there was no easy access to the ruins. She made the long trek into the site on horseback and camped near the Gila Hot Springs for several days. Twenty years later she and Burt returned to the area as professional archaeologists and made a survey of ruins and cave shelters in the valley where three branches of the Gila River join.

Paso Archaeological Society's newsletter is a warm tribute to her life and her achievements. The writer was speaking from his heart when he wrote: "Those of us who knew her will have an emptiness that will last for a long time."[20]

Hattie's life was blessed with many friends, and one of the most notable was Ted Kidder, who aided and encouraged Hattie and Burt, the amateur archaeologists from Silver City. His support gave them the backing to work in archaeology, but in the end it was Burt and Hattie's own skill and professionalism that earned them the respect of their contemporaries. The Cosgroves came into the field at a time when southwestern archaeology was in a golden age. Wealthy backers from the East supported the memorable expeditions, often arriving to spend some time themselves helping with the work. Spouses, children, and other family members were welcomed and often recruited to help with the digging or cataloguing. Archaeologists visited each other's camps and shared gossip and information over hearty meals prepared by a camp cook. Lifelong friendships that went a great deal beyond the usual professional associations were formed. It was a congenial time and an unforgettable time, a time that has passed into the lore of the great Southwest. Hattie made the dreams of her life come true with her meticulous work and her ageless spirit, but she was also fortunate to have lived in her time. Richard Woodbury, who knew Hattie from the old Awatovi days when he was a graduate student, wrote that Hattie was a "dear friend and a marvelous person," a sympathy held by all those who knew and worked with her. He also noted that "the Cosgroves are stellar examples of what could be done by bright and dedicated people in the years when avocational archeologists could become professionals, without people fussing about academic credentials."[21]

Hattie was indeed fortunate to have lived in a time when an amateur's desire to do archaeology would not be thwarted by a lack of formal training and university degrees. Because she was given the opportunity to study the field techniques of the foremost southwestern archaeologists of her time, as well as the opportunity to put that knowledge to work, not only did she become a much respected archaeologist herself, but the early work that she and Burt did in the Mimbres country is among the few complete records of Mimbres culture that exist today. Hattie's contributions to the science were great, but in doing the work she also found her bliss. She loved her vocation with a passion that went beyond the common efforts that many people put into their daily endeavors. Truly Hattie summed up her life when she wrote near the end of her years to a friend who was going out to do field work: "My days for such things are over but my heart is still in the work."

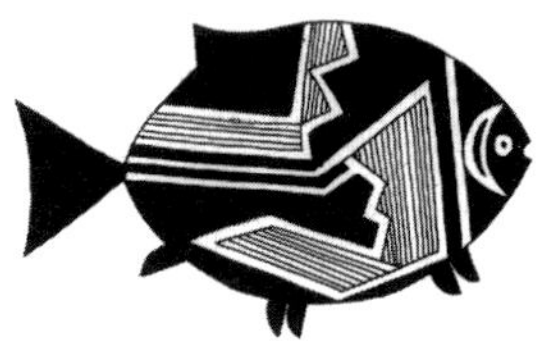

Hattie S. Cosgrove

HATTIE'S MIMBRES BOWLS

Hattie and Burt felt a deep connection to the Mimbres culture and the village sites scattered across southwestern New Mexico. They did everything possible to stop unauthorized digging in the ruins. They met with landowners and encouraged them to post their property against trespassers. They spoke before government boards hoping to pass laws against pothunting. But they could not stop the digging. The only alternative was to make a record of the beautiful painted Mimbres bowls that were being taken from the ground and sold into private collections. Hattie and Burt made a tremendous effort to seek out collectors in order to document the Mimbres ceramic art. Hattie made full-sized pen-and-ink drawings of the bowls, sometimes from photographs, but most often from the original piece of art when she was allowed to visit a collector. In the corner of each drawing Hattie noted the site where a bowl was found. More often, because the bowls were dug by amateurs who did not keep records of their digging, only the name of the collector was recorded.

Hattie's drawings are careful and accurate renderings of the original bowls. She used a compass and pencil to begin the drawing, and India ink, pens, and brushes to finish the image. If a portion of a bowl was missing, Hattie left that area blank, rather than fill it in. She did not presume to imply that she knew what was in the vision of the Mimbres artist who had created the bowl. Missing portions were indicated with dotted lines. Many of the drawings were made out in the field after a long day of digging. Two surviving photographs in the Cosgrove albums show some of the drawings hung to dry on a clothesline and secured with clothespins. The light Hattie worked under to make her drawings was provided by kerosene lanterns. When Earl Morris camped with the Cosgroves and dug McSherry Ruin in 1926, Hattie was drawing the bowls as he was piecing them together each evening. Morris dug over two hundred Mimbres bowls, but only eighty-one of the drawings have survived.

The images on the bowls were often very complicated and difficult to draw. The figures are intricate and the geometric motifs contain hundreds of fine lines and shapes. Each bowl would have taken a great deal of time to reproduce. Hattie's surviving portfolios contain over four hundred drawings. There are several hundred more from Swarts Ruin in the Peabody Museum collections. In addition to the bowls, Hattie drew hundreds of broken sherds, bone objects, stone tools, pictographs, and other artifacts. Her Mimbres bowl drawings are a beautiful and haunting legacy of an extraordinary culture. Hattie's efforts to leave a permanent record of the Mimbres art represents a tremendous investment of time and work, and a remarkable and enduring love of the vanished Mimbres people.

"Chums" May 18, 1919. Treasure Hill.

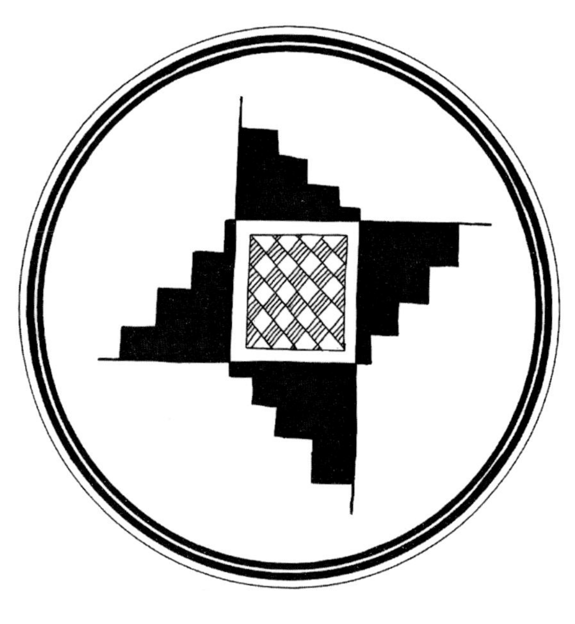

A. M. Cosgrove. September 18, 1921. Treasure Hill.

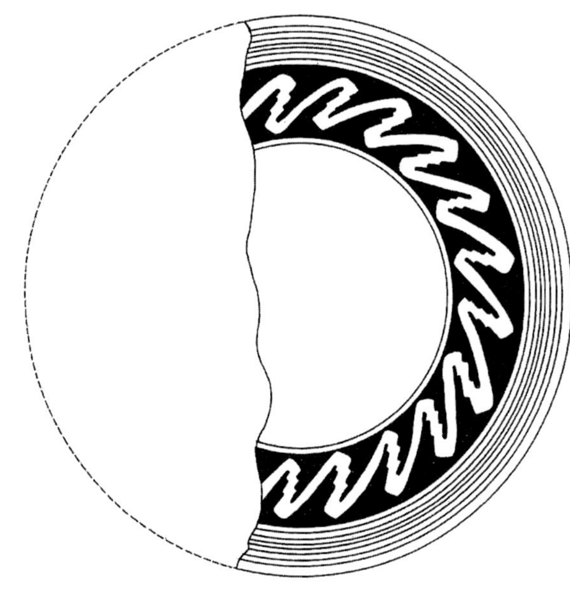

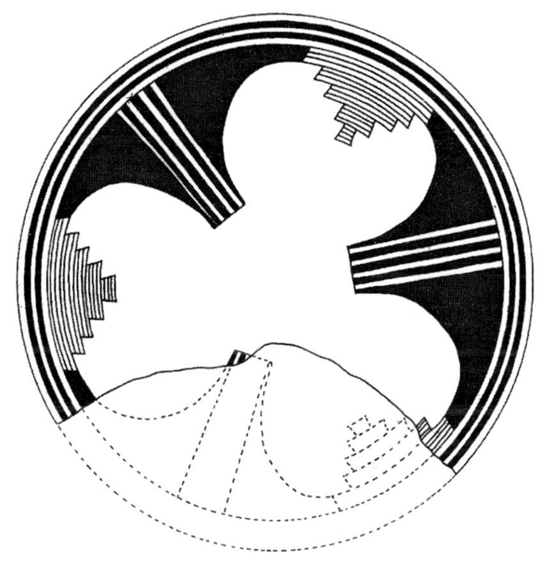

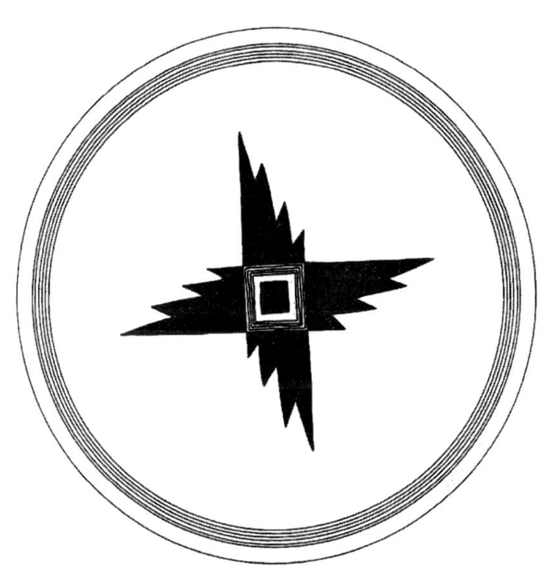

Petroglyphs, Ojo del Alamo (Cottonwood spring). N. E. of El Paso, Texas, in New Mexico.

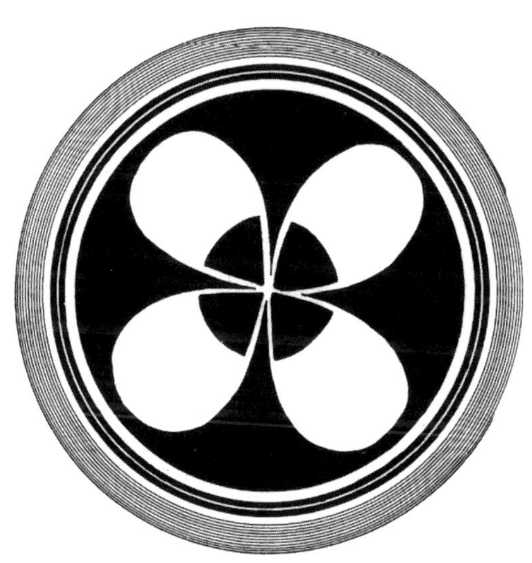

Seed bowl.

Ruin on NAN Ranch. East side of Mimbres River 4 miles above Dwyer, New Mexico.

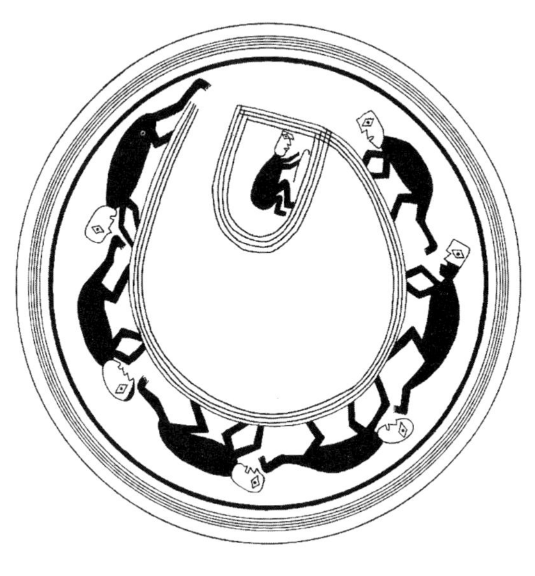

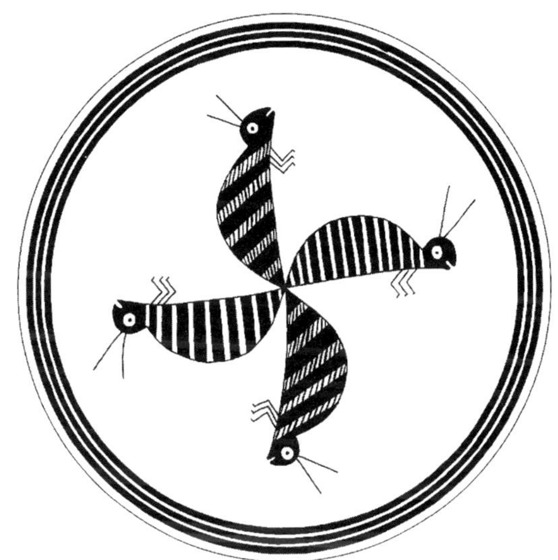

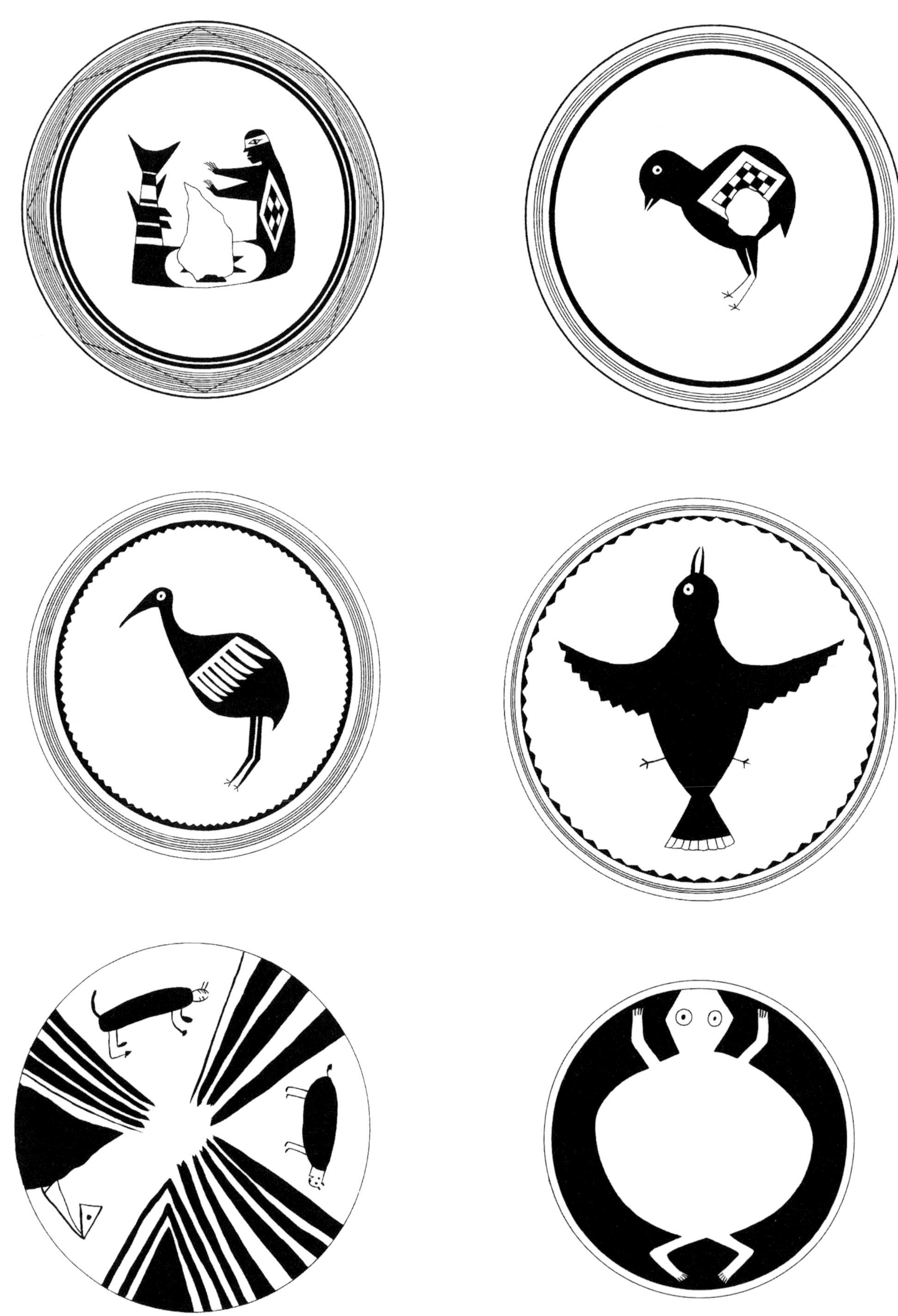

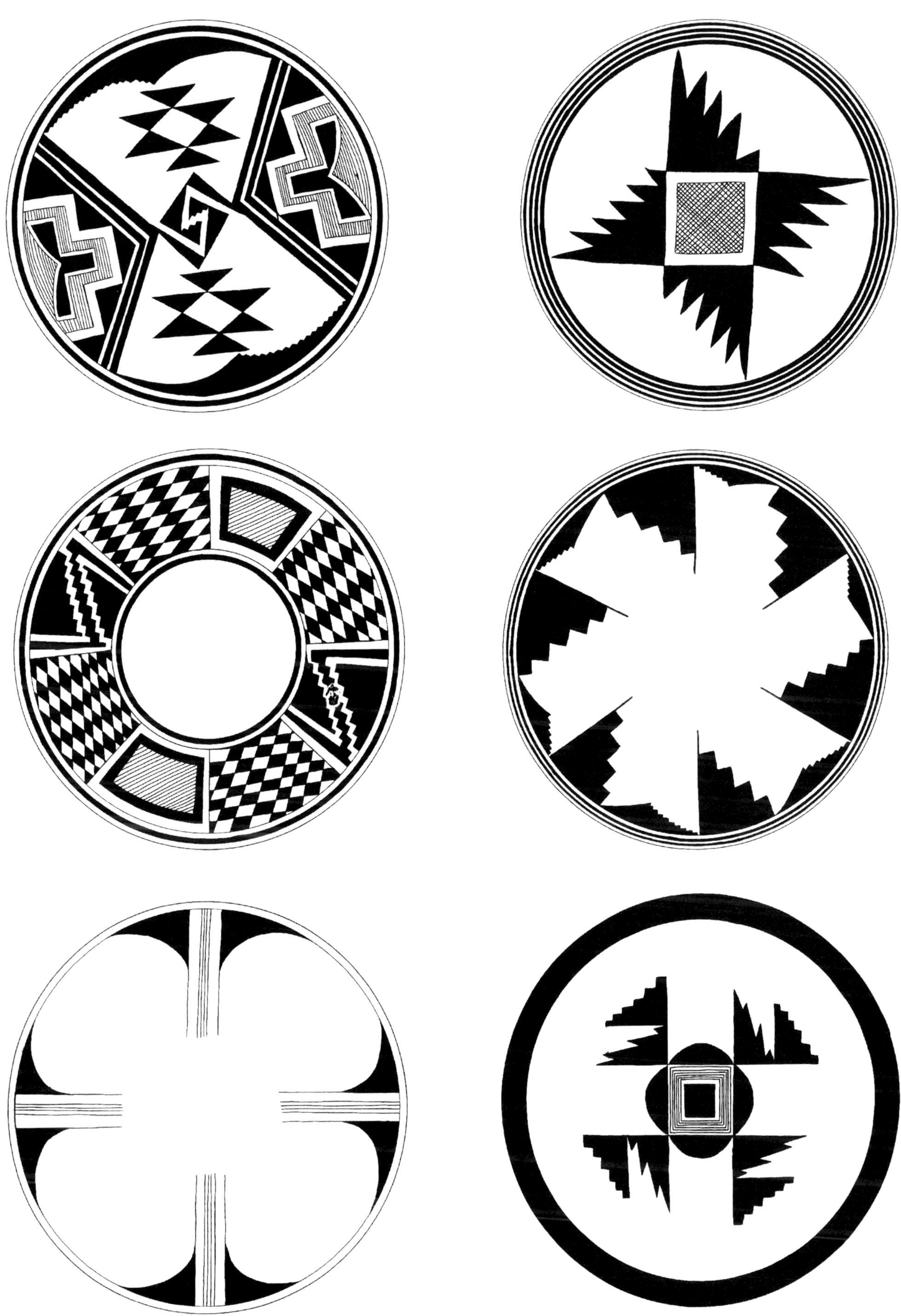

EISELE COLLECTION

170

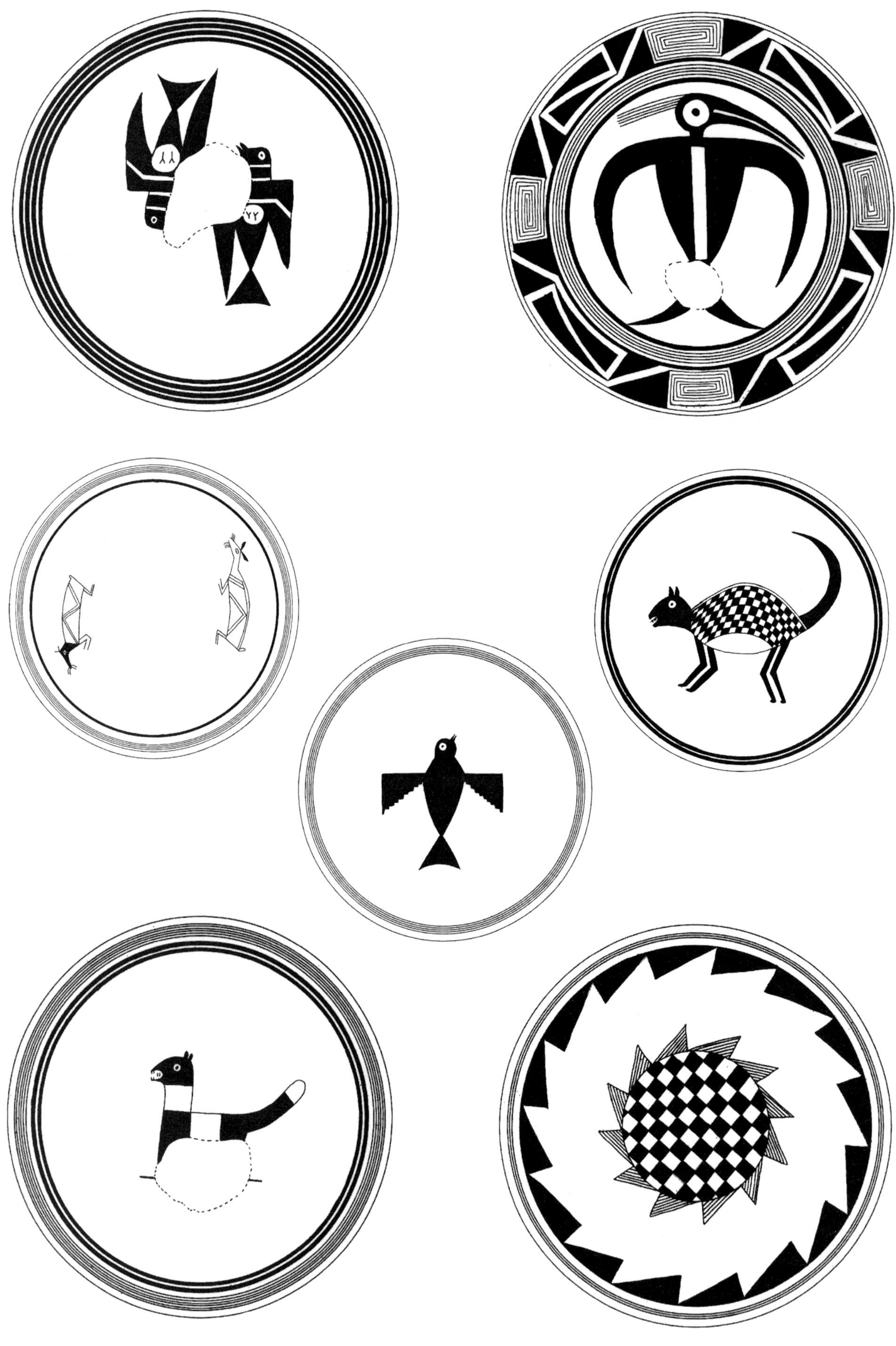

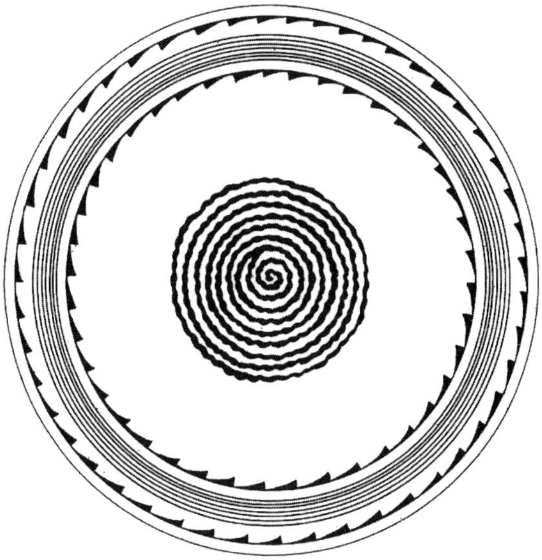

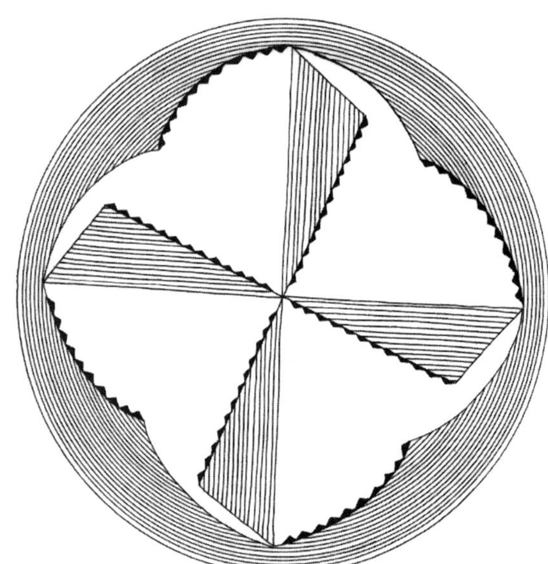

Three Rivers, New Mexico.

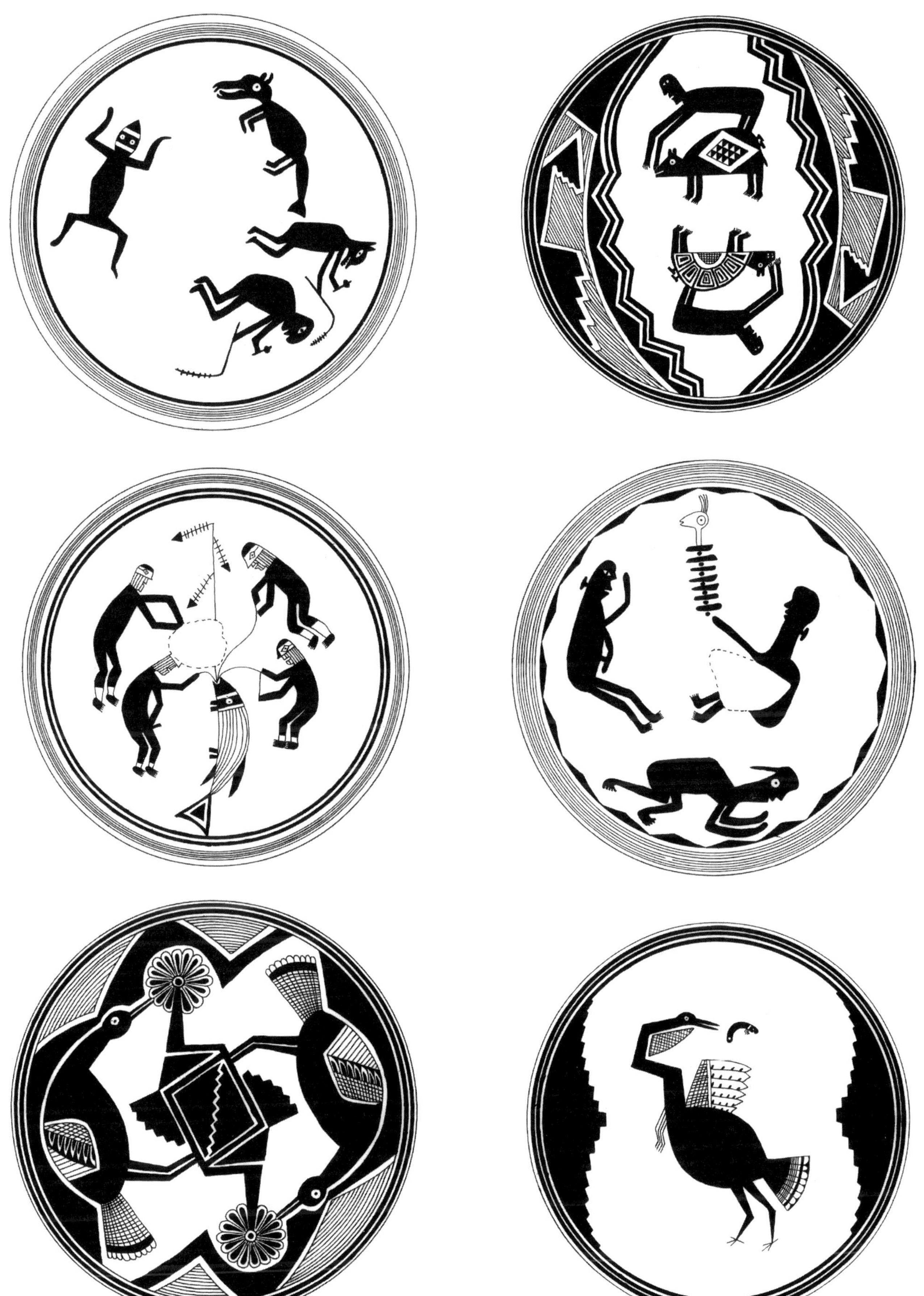

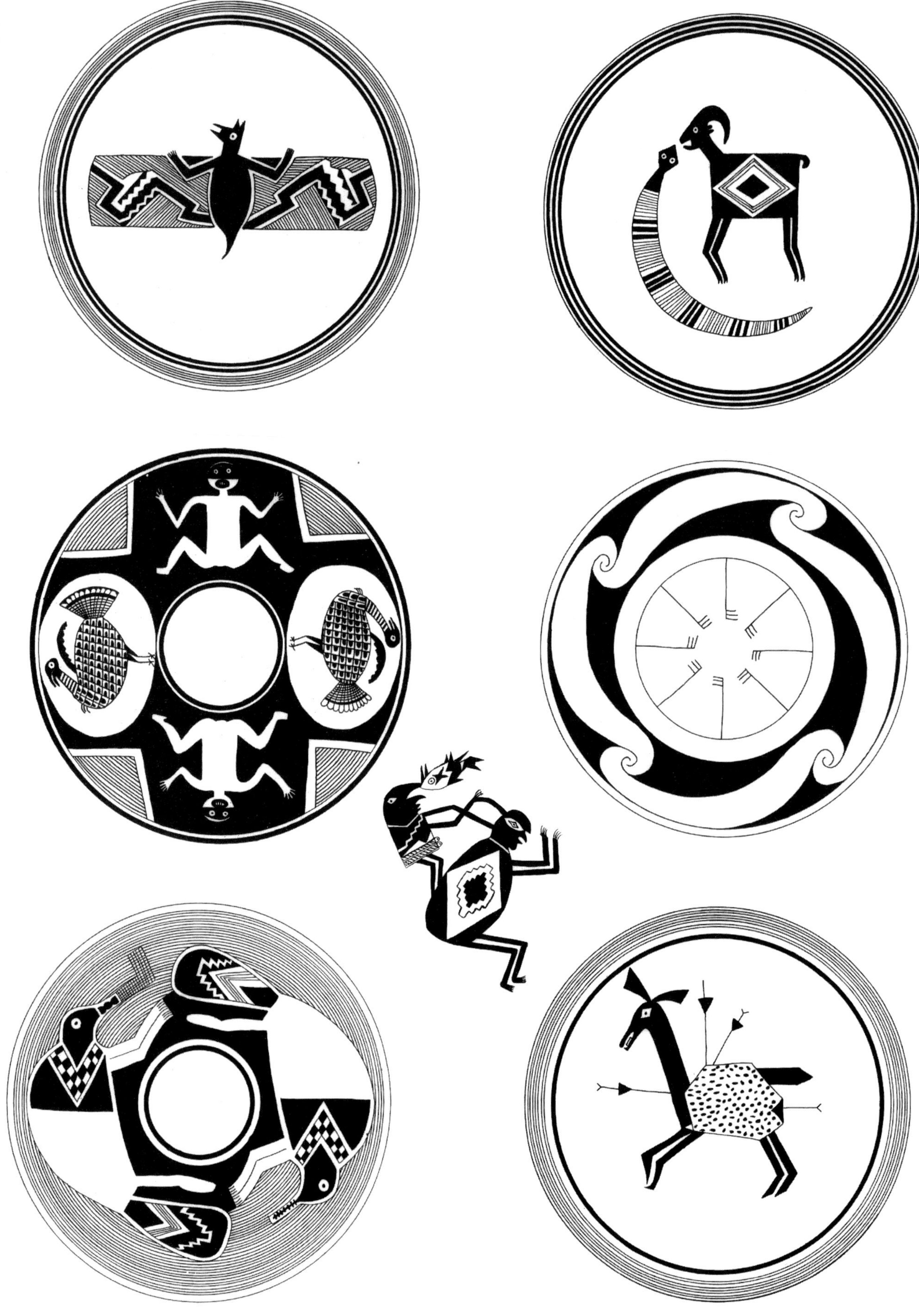

HEYE FOUNDATION COLLECTION

Doolittle Cave—Mimbres Valley.

Old Town Ruin on Mimbres River east of Faywood, New Mexico.

Frederick Pleasants Collection.

Stovall Collection from Cold Springs Creek Ruin—1 mile north of Mimbres Hot Springs.

189

Ledwedge Collection.

Ledwedge Collection.

Chas. Fry Collection—Fort Bayard, New Mexico.

Dog Springs, New Mexico.

Metcalf Ruin—Mangas Valley, New Mexico.

Swarts Ruin—pot-hunted by West.
Alves Collection.

Ruidoso, New Mexico. Alves Collection.

Swarts Ruin—pot-hunted by West.
Alves Collection.

Fort Bayard, New Mexico.

Chupadero Black-on-white. La Luz, New Mexico.

Cameron Creek Ruin.

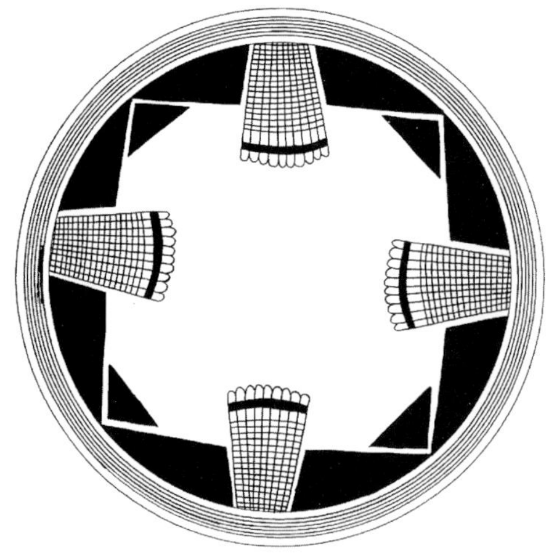

Cameron Creek Ruin.

Cameron Creek Ruin.

William H. Claflin Collection.
Fort Bayard, New Mexico.

Hulbert Collection.

Hulbert Collection.

Swarts Ruin. Drawn from sherds.

Swarts Ruin.

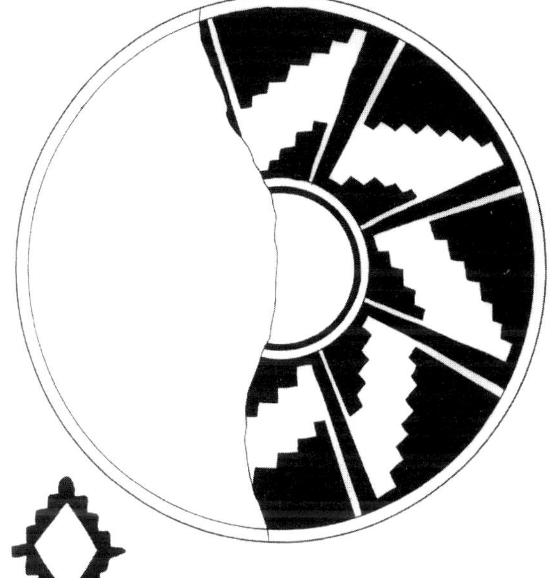

Swarts Ruin.

Swarts Ruin. Flower pot shape.
Three of these on the outside of bowl.

Finds at Swarts Pueblo. 1924.

Swarts Ruin.

Mimbres Classic Black-on-white. San Lorenzo, New Mexico. Contained beads and Medicine Man's outfit.

Fort Bayard, New Mexico.

Ruin at mouth of Little Creek, Gila River.

Hill Top Ruin. Duck Creek, New Mexico.

Hill Top Ruin. Duck Creek, New Mexico.

Golass Ruin (Rock House).

Golass Ruin (Rock House).

Golass Ruin (Rock House).

Nesbitt–Logan Museum Collection.

Nesbitt–Logan Museum Collection.

Villareal Ranch. Gila, New Mexico.

Villareal Ranch. Gila, New Mexico.

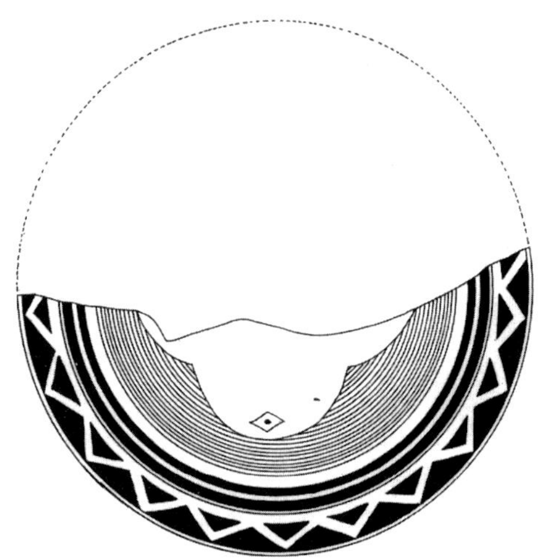

Villareal Ranch. Gila, New Mexico.

Villareal Ranch. Gila, New Mexico.

Villareal Ranch. Gila, New Mexico.

Villareal Ranch. Gila, New Mexico.

Villareal Ranch. Gila, New Mexico.

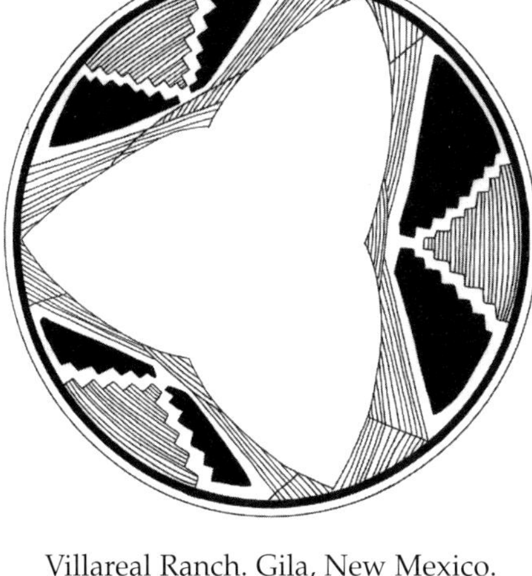

Villareal Ranch. Gila, New Mexico.

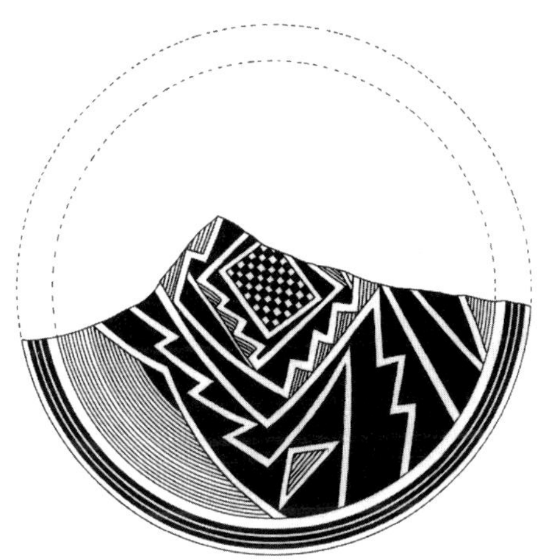

Villareal Ranch. Gila, New Mexico.

Villareal Ranch. Gila, New Mexico.

Villareal Ranch. Gila, New Mexico.

Villareal Ranch. Gila, New Mexico.

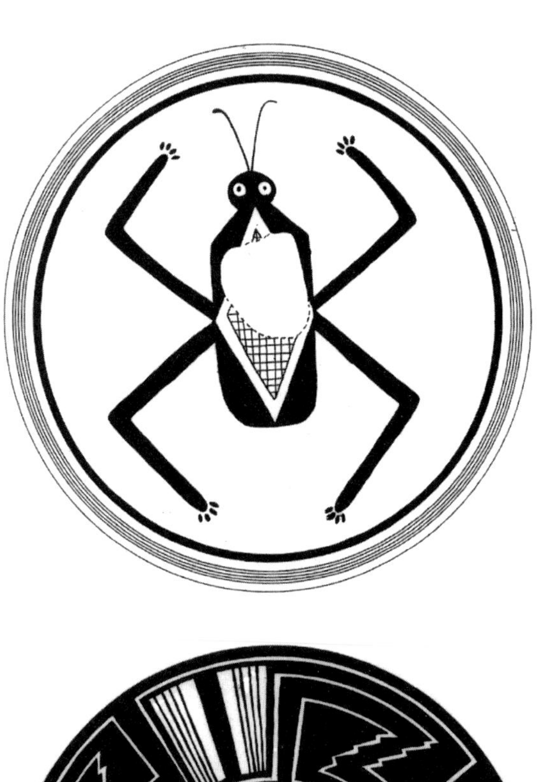

Villareal Ranch. Gila, New Mexico.

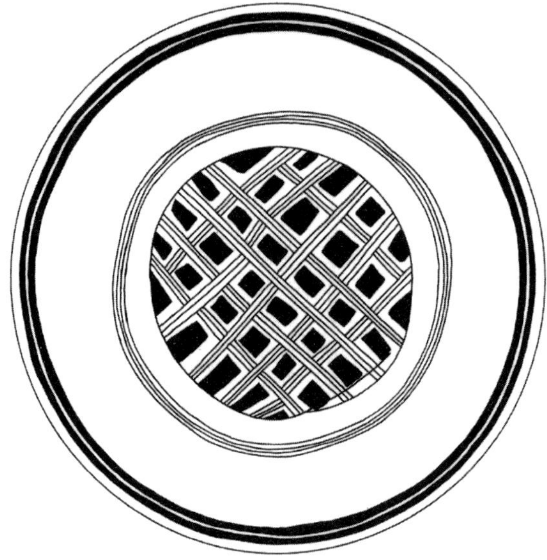

Villareal Ranch. Gila, New Mexico.

Pueblo—Craig Ranch. February 15, 1920.

198

◀END NOTES▶

TREASURE HILL SUNDAYS

1. George Fitzpatrick, "Interview with Billy the Kid," *New Mexico Magazine* (September 1954): 40.

2. Elizabeth McFarland, *Forever Frontier: The Gila Cliff Dwellings* (Albuquerque: The University of New Mexico, 1967), 49.

3. *El Palacio* 3.5 (August 1916): 87.

4. J. J. Brody, *Mimbres Painted Pottery* (Santa Fe: School of American Research, 1977), 7.

5. Barbara A. Babcock and Nancy J. Parezo, *Interview with Watson Smith* (Tucson: Daughters of the Desert Oral History Project, 1985), 3.

6. Burton C. Cosgrove to F. W. Hodge, 30 June 1920, Braun Research Library, Southwest Museum.

7. Richard B. Woodbury, *Alfred V. Kidder* (New York: Columbia University Press, 1973), 31.

8. Douglas R. Givens, *Alfred Vincent Kidder and the Development of Americanist Archaeology* (Albuquerque: University of New Mexico Press, 1992), 38.

9. Woodbury, *Kidder*, 23.

10. H. S. and C. B. Cosgrove, "The Swarts Ruin: A Typical Mimbres Site in Southwestern New Mexico," *Peabody Museum Papers* (Cambridge: Harvard University, 1932), xvii.

11. Wesley Bradfield, "A Day's Work on the Mimbres," *El Palacio* 19.8 (1925): 170–72.

12. Paul H. Nesbitt, *The Ancient Mimbreños* (Beloit, Wis.: The Logan Museum, Beloit College, 1931): 14.

13. *El Palacio* 12.3-5 (1922): 67–68.

14. Barbara Kidder Aldana, "The Kidder Pecos Expedition, 1924–1929: A Personal Memoir," *The Kiva* 48.4 (1983): 243–50.

ON THE MIMBRES

1. Brody, *Painted Pottery*, 9.

2. J. J. Brody, *Mimbres Pottery: Ancient Art of the American Southwest* (New York: Hudson Hill Press, 1983), 26–29. Brody's work has been heavily relied upon for a nontechnical overview of the Mimbres culture.

3. Tamra Andrews, "North American Indian Art and the 1054 Supernova," *Star Date* (Austin, The University of Texas: McDonald Observatory, 1992): May/June 16–19.

4. Brody, *Ancient Art*, 32.

5. Brody, *Ancient Art*, 31.

6. Brody, *Ancient Art*, 20.

7. Alfred V. Kidder, "The Excavations at Swarts Pueblo," Harvard University, Peabody Museum, Accession File 25-11.

8. Cornelius Burton Cosgrove and Harriet S. Cosgrove, "Field Notes of Season 1924 Swarts Ruin, Mimbres Valley, New Mexico," Harvard University, Peabody Museum, Accession File 24-15.

9. Cosgrove and Cosgrove, Harvard University, Peabody Museum, Accession File 26-7H.

10. Kidder, "Progress of the Peabody Museum's Mimbres Expedition," Harvard University, Peabody Museum, Accession File 26-7C.

11. Ibid.

12. Cosgrove, *Teocentli* #2 (December 1926).

13. Kidder, "Season of 1926, Swarts Ranch-Nan Ranch-Doolittle Cave, Mimbres Valley, New Mexico," 5.

14. Woodbury, "*Teocentli*: An Anthropological Newsletter, ever since 1926," *Bulletin of the History of Archaeology*, 4,2: 3–13. Woodbury's *Bulletin of the History of Archaeology* article has supplied much background information in the discussion of the origin of *Teocentli*.

15. Kidder, *Season of 1926*, 9–13.

16. Cornelius Burton Cosgrove, *Caves of the Upper Gila and Hueco Areas in New Mexico and Texas* (Cambridge: Peabody Museum, 1947), 7–9.

17. Kidder, *Season of 1926*, 13.

18. Ibid., 17.

19. Richard B. Woodbury, *Sixty Years of Southwestern Archaeology: A History of the Pecos Conference* (Albuquerque: University of New Mexico Press, 1993), 3.

CLIMBING INTO CAVES

1. Field Notes, 1928. Mimbres Valley Expeditions, New Mexico. Harvard University, Peabody Museum, Accession File 28-3.

2. Ann Axtell Morris, *Digging in the Southwest* (New York: Doubleday, Doran and Co., 1934), 30.

3. Peter Russell, *Gila Cliff Dwellings National Monument: An Administrative History* (Santa Fe: Southwest Cultural Resources Center, 1992), 78.

4. Woodbury, *Sixty Years*, 101.

5. Givens, *Alfred Vincent Kidder*, 100–104.

6. Field Notes, 1929. Mimbres Valley Expeditions, New Mexico, Harvard University, Peabody Museum, Accession File 29-20.

7. C. B. Cosgrove to Neil M. Judd, 2 December 1930. National Anthropological Archives, Smithsonian Institution, Division of Archaeology, Depertment of Anthropology, E.21, Neil Merton Judd Papers,

Miscellaneous Correspondence, 1930–1975.

8. A. V. Kidder to Madeleine Kidder, Boaz W. Long Papers #210, New Mexico State Archives.

9. A. V. Kidder to Donald Scott, 5 May 1931, Harvard University, Peabody Museum, Accession File 26-7D.

10. A. V. Kidder to Benjamin Moore, 19 May 1928, Harvard University, Peabody Museum, Accession File 27-11.

11. Burt Cosgrove to Donald Scott, 18 July 1933, Harvard University, Peabody Museum, Expedition to Cloverdale, Hidalgo County, New Mexico, Accession File 33-102.

12. Alfred Vincent Kidder Diaries, Harvard University Archives, Box 3, 1933. A. V. Kidder's 1933 diary provided much general information about the Hidalgo County Expedition, as did interviews with Burton Cosgrove Jr. and George Pendleton.

13. Expedition to Cloverdale, Hidalgo County, New Mexico, Harvard University, Peabody Museum, Accession File 33-102.

14. A. V. Kidder to Donald Scott, 27 November 1933, Harvard University, Peabody Museum, Expedition to Cloverdale, Hidalgo County, New Mexico, Accession File 33-102.

AWATOVI EXCAVATIONS
(Sherds and Sand-Dune Skiing)

1. C. B. Cosgrove to Emil Haury, 1 June 1936. Arizona State Museum, Emil Haury Papers, LA 86-67, Box 4, Folder 16.

2. J. O. Brew, "The First Two Seasons at Awatovi," *American Antiquity* 3,2 (1937): 122.

3. Jenny L. Adams, *Pinto Beans and Prehistoric Pots: The Legacy of Al and Alice Lancaster* (Tucson: Arizona State Museum Archaeological Series 183, 1994), 33.

4. Adams, *Pinto Beans*, 42.

5. Brew, *The First Two Seasons*, 132–133.

6. Harriet Cosgrove to Jo Brew, 9 November 1936, Peabody Museum, Harvard University, Awatovi Expedition, J. O. Brew Records.

7. Watson Smith, *One Man's Archaeology* (Tucson: 1984), 151.

8. Alfred V. Kidder, Jesse D. Jennings, and Edwin M. Shook, *Excavations at Kaminaljuyu, Guatemala* (Washington, D.C.: Carnegie Institution of Washington, 1946), 7.

9. Jo Brew, Awatovi Diary, Arizona State Museum, University of Arizona, LA 89-7. Much of the information about the social activities, visitors, and daily work at Awatovi comes from the Awatovi Diaries that were dictated by Brew to Evelyn Nimmo Brew. On occasion someone else made entries in the journals, such as Watson Smith's delightful account of the Brew wedding. Other sources of information were interviews with Jenny Adams, Evelyn Nimmo Brew, and Burton Cosgrove Jr.

10. Adams, *Pinto Beans*, 49.

11. Adams, *Pinto Beans*, 46.

12. Emil W. Haury, *Mogollon Culture in the Forestdale Valley* (Tucson: University of Arizona Press, 1985), 10.

13. Givens, *Alfred Vincent Kidder*, 14.

LAST EXPEDITIONS

1. Watson Smith, *Painted Ceramics of the Western Mound at Awatovi* (Cambridge: Peabody Museum of Archaeology and Ethnology, Harvard University, 1971) 8,38: xix.

2. Hattie Cosgrove to Earl Morris, 17 March 1942, University of Colorado at Boulder.

3. Ibid.

4. Earl Morris to Hattie Cosgrove, 16 May 1942, University of Colorado at Boulder.

5. C. B. Cosgrove, *Caves of the Upper Gila and Hueco Areas in New Mexico and Texas* (Cambridge: Peabody Museum of American Archaeology and Ethnology, Harvard University, 1947) 24,2: vii.

6. Ibid., viii.

7. A. V. Kidder, H. S. Cosgrove, and C. B. Cosgrove, "The Pendleton Ruin, Hidalgo County, New Mexico." *Contributions to American Anthropology and History* 50 (1949): 109.

8. Hattie Cosgrove to Emil Haury, 9 June 1948, Arizona State Museum Archives.

9. Woodbury, *Sixty Years*, 183. Richard Woodbury's Pecos history has supplied much general information about the Pecos Conferences.

10. Alfred V. Kidder, *New Mexico Quarterly* 27, 1 and 2, (1957): 52–55.

11. Hattie Cosgrove to Ted Kidder, 3 June 1957, Harvard University, Peabody Museum.

12. Hattie Cosgrove to Inez Cosgrove Ford, 18 May 1958, Silver City Museum.

13. Adams, *Pinto Beans*, 93.

14. Hattie Cosgrove to Emil Haury, 27 May 1964, Arizona State Museum Archives.

15. Steven A. LeBlanc, *The Mimbres People: Ancient Pueblo Painters of the American Southwest* (New York: Thames and Hudson, 1983), 29.

16. David E. Stuart, *Glimpses of the Ancient Southwest* (Santa Fe: Ancient City Press, 1985), 62.

17. Hattie Cosgrove to Emil Haury, 20 March 1967, Arizona State Museum Archives.

18. Elizabeth McFarland, *Forever Frontier*, 49.

19. *The Artifact: Journal of the El Paso Archaeological Society, Inc.* 7,2 (1969): 21.

20. *El Paso Archaeology Newsletter* 3,8 (1970): 7.

21. Richard Woodbury to Carolyn Davis, personal communication, 20 April 1993.

◀BIBLIOGRAPHY▶

Adams, Jenny L.
    1994 *Pinto Beans and Prehistoric Pots: The Legacy of Al and Alice Lancaster*. Arizona State Museum Archaeological Series183. Tucson: Arizona State Museum, University of Arizona.

Aldana, Barbara Kidder
    1983 "The Kidder-Pecos Expedition,1924–1929: A Personal Memoir." *The Kiva* 48 (4): 243–50.

Andrews, Tamra
    1992 "North American Indian Art and the 1054 Supernova." *Stardate* (May/June). The University of Texas at Austin, McDonald Observatory.

Anonymous
    1918 "Called Home by Death of Father." *El Palacio* 5 (12): 204.
    1922 "Gifts." *El Palacio* 12 (3–5): 67–68.
    1927 "The Pecos Conference." *El Palacio* 23 (9–10): 280–81.
    1927 "Southwestern Archaeological Conference." *El Palacio* 23 (22): 554–55.

Anyon, Roger, and Steven A. LeBlanc
    1984 *The Galaz Ruin: A Prehistoric Mimbres Village in Southwestern New Mexico*. Albuquerque: Maxwell Museum of Anthropology and University of New Mexico Press.

Babcock, Barbara A., and Nancy J. Parezo
    1985 Interview with Watson Smith. Tucson: Daughters of the Desert Oral History Project.

Berry, Susan, and Sharman Apt Russell
    1986 *Built to Last: An Architectural History of Silver City, New Mexico*. Santa Fe: New Mexico Historic Preservation Division.

Bradfield, Wesley
    1923 "Summary of Work on Cameron Creek Site, Mimbres Section." *El Palacio* 15 (4): 53–54.
    1923 "Preliminary Report on Excavating at Cameron Creek Site. *El Palacio* 15 (5): 67–73.
    1925 "A Day's Work on the Mimbres." *El Palacio* 19 (8): 170-72.
    1925 "Pit Houses of Cameron Creek." *El Palacio* 19 (8): 173–77.
    1927 "Notes on Mimbres Culture." *El Palacio* 22: 550–57.
    1928 "Mimbres Excavation in 1928." *El Palacio* 25 (8–10): 151–60.
    1931 *Cameron Creek Village: A Site in the Mimbres Area in Grant County, New Mexico*. Santa Fe: School of American Research Monograph no. 1.

Brew, J. O.
    1937 "The First Two Seasons at Awatovi." *American Antiquity* 3 (2): 122–37.
    1963 "James A. Lancaster: Citation for Distinguished Service." *American Antiquity* 29 (2): 230–32.

Brody, J. J.
    1977 *Mimbres Painted Pottery*. Albuquerque: University of New Mexico Press.

Brody, J. J., Catherine J. Scott, and Steven A. LeBlanc
    1983 *Mimbres Pottery: Ancient Art of the American Southwest*. New York: Hudson Hills Press.

Claflin, William H. Jr.
    1931 "The Stalling's Island Mound Columbia County, Georgia." Papers of the Peabody Museum of American Archaeology and Ethnology, Harvard University 14 (1).

Cosgrove, Cornelius Burton
    1923 "Two Kivas at Treasure Hill." *El Palacio* 15 (2): 18–21.
    1929 "The Basket Makers and Their Artifacts." *Harvard Alumni Bulletin* (February): 624–27.
    1929 "A Note on a Trephined Indian Skull from Georgia." *American Journal of Physical Anthropology* 13 (2): 353–57.
    1947 "Caves of the Upper Gila and Hueco Areas in New Mexico and Texas." Papers of the Peabody Museum of American Archaeology and Ethnology 24 (2).
    1948 "Hueco Mt. Caves." *National Speleogical Society* 10: 79–84.

Cosgrove, Cornelius B., and Cosgrove, Harriet S.
    1965 "The Cosgrove Report: A Preliminary Survey of the El Paso Pueblo District." El

Paso Archaeological Society Special Report 3.

Cosgrove, Harriet S., and Cosgrove, Cornelius B.
1932 "The Swarts Ruin: A Typical Mimbres Site in Southwestern New Mexico." Papers of the Peabody Museum of American Archaeology and Ethnology 15 (1).

Cosgrove, Cornelius B. Jr.
1951 "Report on Excavation, Repair and Restoration of Agate House and Other Sites." On file. Western Archaeological Center, Tucson.

Cosgrove, Cornelius B. Jr., and W. E. Felts
1927 "How We Found the Casa Grande Graveyards by Two of the Field Workers." *The Masterkey* 1 (1): 15–19.
1927 "At Work on the Mimbres." *The Masterkey* 1 (3): 21–24.

Dinwiddie, Douglas M.
1982 "History of the Eisele Collection." *Mogollon Archaeology: Proceedings of the 1980 Mogollon Conference*. Ramona: Acoma Books.

Dobie, J. Frank
1990 *The Ben Lilly Legend*. Austin: University of Texas Press.

Fewkes, Jesse Walter
1989 *The Mimbres: Art and Archaeology*. Albuquerque: Avanyu Publishing,Inc.

Fitzpatrick, George
1954 "Interview with Billy the Kid." *New Mexico Magazine* (September).

Gaede, Marc and Marnie Gaede
1980 *Camera, Spade and Pen*. Tucson: The University of Arizona Press.

Giammattei, Victor M., and Nanci Greer Reichert
1993 *Art of a Vanished Race: The Mimbres Classic Black-On-White*. Silver City: High-Lonesome Books.

Gillett, Henry W.
1927 "Contacts Between Archaeological and Dental Research." *American Anthropologist* 29 (2): 291–95.

Gilliford, Andrew
1991 *Museums and the Mimbres People: Interpreting the Mogollon Culture*. Mogollon V. Las Cruces: COAS Publishing and Research.

Givens, Douglas R.
1992 *Alfred Vincent Kidder and the Development of Americanist Archaeology*. Albuquerque: University of New Mexico Press.

Hall, Edward T.
1994 *West of the Thirties: Discoveries among the Navajo and Hopi*. New York: Doubleday.

Haury, Emil W.
1949 "The1948 Southwestern Archaeological Conference." *American Antiquity* 14 (3): 254–56.
1985 *Mogollon Culture in the Forestdale Valley*. Tucson: University of Arizona Press.
1986 *Emil W. Haury's Prehistory of the American Southwest*. Tucson: University of Arizona Press.
1989 "Point of Pines, Arizona: A History of the University of Arizona Archaeological Field School." Anthropological Papers of the University of Arizona, Number 50. Tucson: The University of Arizona Press.

Haury, Emil W., and J. Jefferson Reid
1985 "Harold Sterling Gladwin, 1883–1983." *The Kiva* 50 (4): 271–83.

Herrington, LaVerne
1979 "Settlement Patterns and Water Control Systems of the Mimbres Classic Phase, Grant County, New Mexico." Ph.D. dissertation, Department of Anthropology, University of Texas at Austin. University Microfilms, Ann Arbor.

Herrington, LaVerne, and Darrell Creel
1991 *Treasure Hill: An Agricultural Center and Type Site Revisited*. Mogollon V. Las Cruces: COAS Publishing and Research.

Hibben, Frank C.
1975 *Kiva Art of the Anasazi at Pottery Mound*. Las Vegas: KC Publications.

Hough, Walter
1907 "Antiquities of the Upper Gila and Salt River Valleys in Arizona and New Mexico." *Bureau of American Ethnology Bulletin 35*. Washington, D. C.: Government Printing Office.

Jenks, Albert E.
1928 "The Mimbres Valley Expedition." *Bulletin of the Minneapolis Institute of Arts* 17 (2): 154–59.

Judd, Neil M.
    1968 *Men Met Along the Trail: Adventures in Archaeology*. Norman: University of Oklahoma Press.

Kidder, Alfred V., Jesse D. Jennings, and Edwin M. Shook
    1946 "Excavations at Kaminaljuyu, Guatemala." Carnegie Institution of Washington Publications 561. Washington D.C.: Carnegie Institution.

Kidder, Alfred V., H. S. Cosgrove, and C. B. Cosgrove
    1949 "The Pendleton Ruin, Hidalgo County, New Mexico." *Contributions to American Anthropology and History* 10 (50): 107–52.

Lambert, Marjorie F.
    1956 "Some Clay and Stone Figurines from the Mogollon-Mimbres Area, Luna County, New Mexico." *El Palacio* 63 (9): 259–83.

LeBlanc, Steven A.
    1983 *The Mimbres People*. London: Thames and Hudson.

Lekson, Stephen H.
    1990 "Mimbres Archaeology of the Upper Gila, New Mexico." Anthropological Papers of the University of Arizona 53. Tucson: The University of Arizona Press.

Lister, Florence C. and Robert H. Lister
    1968 *Earl Morris and Southwestern Archaeology*. Albuquerque: University of New Mexico Press.

McFarland, Elizabeth
    1967 *Forever Frontier: The Gila Cliff Dwellings*. Albuquerque: The University of New Mexico.

Montgomery, Ross Gordon, Watson Smith, and John Otis Brew
    1949 "Franciscan Awatovi: The Excavation and Conjectural Reconstruction of a 17th Century Spanish Mission Establishment at a Hopi Town in Northeastern Arizona." Papers of the Peabody Museum 36. Cambridge: Harvard University.

Morris, Ann Axtell
    1933 *Digging in the Southwest*. New York: Doubleday, Doran and Co.

Moulard, Barbara L.
    1984 *Within the Underworld Sky: Mimbres Ceramic Art in Context*. Pasadena, California: Twelvetree Press.

Nesbitt, Paul H.
    1931 "The Ancient Mimbrenos Based on Investigations at the Mattocks Ruin, Mimbres Valley, New Mexico." *Logan Museum Bulletin* 4. Beloit: Logan Museum.

Reynolds, Edward
    1930 "Peabody Museum." *El Palacio* 29 (4–10): 49–150.

Rodeck, Hugo G.
    1976 "Mimbres Painted Pottery." *American Indian Art* 1 (1): 44–53.

Russell, Peter
    1992 "Gila Cliff Dwellings National Monument: An Administrative History." Santa Fe: Southwest Cultural Resources Center, Professional Papers 48.

Smith, Watson
    1971 "Painted Ceramics of the Western Mound at Awatovi. " Papers of the Peabody Museum 38. Cambridge: Harvard University.
    1972 "Prehistoric Kivas of Antelope Mesa, Northeastern Arizona." Papers of the Peabody Museum 39. Cambridge: Harvard University.
    1984 *One Man's Archaeology*. Tucson, Arizona.
    1985 "Victor Rose Stoner, Founding Father." *The Kiva* 50 (4): 183–99.

Stuart, David E.
    1985 *Glimpses of the Ancient Southwest*. Santa Fe: Ancient City Press.

Watson, Editha Latta
    1927 "Some New Mexico Ruins." *El Palacio* 23 (7–8): 174-235.

Woodbury, Richard B.
    1973 *Alfred V. Kidder*. Leaders in Modern Anthropology Series. New York: Columbia University Press.
    1983 "Looking Back at the Pecos Conference." *The Kiva* 48 (4): 251–66.
    1993 *Sixty Years of Southwestern Archaeology: A History of the Pecos Conference*. Albuquerque: University of New Mexico Press.
    1994 "Teocentli: An Anthropological Newsletter, Ever Since 1926." *Bulletin of the History of Archaeology* 4 (2): 3–13.